Qat in Yemen

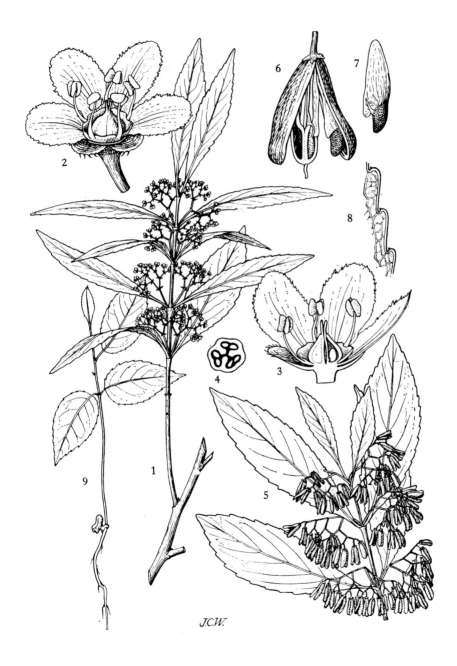

J.C.W.

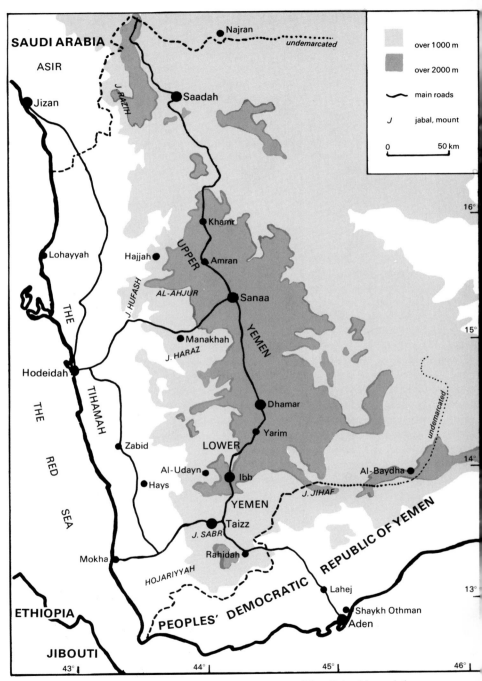

Fig. 1   The Yemen Arab Republic and adjacent areas of Saudi Arabia and the People's Democratic Republic of Yemen showing the principal towns and places mentioned in the text.

Qat in Yemen

Consumption and Social Change

Shelagh Weir

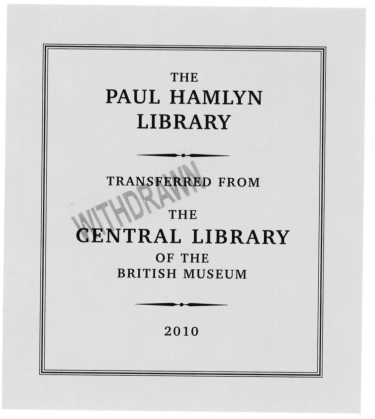

Published for the Trustees of the British Museum
by British Museum Publications Limited

Cover   A qat party in Razih, 1980

Frontispiece   Botanical drawing of *Catha edulis*. 1. Flowering shoot 2. Flower
3. Vertical section of flower 4. Transverse section of ovary 5. Fruiting shoot 6. Fruit
7. Seed 8. Leaf margin 9. Seedling
(From Excell, A.W. *et al, Flora Zambesiaca*, Vol 2, Part 2, 1963–66: Tab. 80, p382 by
kind permission of the editors)

Published by British Museum Publications Limited

British Library Cataloguing in Publication Data

Weir, Shelagh
    Qat in Yemen : consumption and social change.
    1. Qat——Yemen
    I. Title   II. British Museum. *Trustees*
    306'4   HV5822.Q3

    ISBN 0-7141-1568-1

Designed by Arthur Lockwood
Set in Monophoto Times Medium
and printed in England by
Henry Ling Ltd., at the Dorset Press, Dorchester, Dorset

Contents

List of Illustrations

Preface

This book is about the impact of recent economic change on the centuries-old Yemeni custom of chewing qat – the mildly stimulant leaves of the shrub *Catha edulis* Forssk. which is cultivated in the Yemeni Highlands. Until the 1970s regular qat consumption was mainly confined, because of its expense, to a small, rich, mainly urban elite, but during the 1970s it spread among all classes in the towns and among the rural population throughout the length and breadth of Yemen; probably three-quarters of adult Yemenis became regular qat consumers. The social and economic importance of qat in present-day Yemen can hardly be exaggerated. Most qat is chewed communally at social gatherings which take place every afternoon throughout the country, and the consumption and production of qat involve the expenditure and circulation of huge sums of money. In 1979–80, the period on which this book mainly focusses, most consumers were spending between US$30 and $80 a week – between a quarter and a third of their earned incomes – on qat, and national expenditure on qat was around US$2000 million.[1]

This recent dramatic increase in qat consumption is closely related to the unprecedented financial prosperity which Yemenis experienced during the 1970s as a result of large-scale labour migration to Saudi Arabia and the consequent vast influx of cash remittances. As incomes increased, so also did qat consumption – despite inflation in qat prices caused by soaring demand. Obviously the widespread rise in incomes enabled more people to afford qat, but the key question for understanding this consumption phenomenon is why were increasing numbers choosing to spend such a high proportion of their new-found wealth on this particular item? How also did qat consumption survive – and flourish – despite the escalating living costs and rampant Western-style consumerism created by the new economic conditions? Traditional practices often decline or disappear with the urge for modernisation and 'progress' which usually follows the absorption of underdeveloped countries such as Yemen into the world economy. Qat could well have been branded 'old-fashioned' and left to conservative old men. So why did enthusiasm for qat intensify and consumption increase to span both sexes and all generations and classes of Yemeni society?

The recent efflorescence of qat consumption in Yemen is not a puzzle for most observers because they believe qat to be an addictive drug. They therefore assume that Yemenis spend so much money and time chewing qat because they are physically dependent on it, and that overall consumption has increased because more people can now afford qat and are in turn becoming addicted to it. However, there is no evidence that qat causes dependence or that it is anything other than a weak and relatively innocuous stimulant. The usual description of qat as a 'narcotic' is therefore mistaken, and the orthodox addiction theory of qat consumption must be rejected. Of course the social significance of any institutionalised indulgence is independent of its physical effects, but the weaker the substance the greater the weight which can be placed on social explanations for its mass consumption. The significance of qat parties in Yemen can no more be understood in terms of the physical effects of qat than the importance of coffee houses in seventeenth-century London can be explained by the effects of caffeine.

Qat consumption is a complex social and cultural phenomenon which is primarily sustained by social not biological factors. Clearly the economic events of the 1970s invested the custom with unprecedented importance, but to understand how and why we have to examine qat chewing and the institution of the qat party in relation to the values, customs and structures of a society in the process of fundamental change.

I decided to write about qat consumption some time after returning from the second of two periods of extended field research in Yemen in 1980. Like all anthropologists who live for long periods in Yemeni communities, I appreciated qat parties as opportunities for socialising in a relaxed atmosphere and for enquiring about those aspects of local society in which I was chiefly interested. While in the field, however, I did not consider making qat consumption itself a primary object of research. I was more interested in the cultivation and trade of qat since those were major economic activities in the community in which I lived. In the course of preparing my material on these topics for a short publication I realised that an introduction was needed on the little-known consumption practice which stimulates all the agricultural and commercial endeavour I was describing. Once I began to think and read about qat consumption, however, I became increasingly aware of the intrinsic interest of the practice, and of the need for a better understanding of it. The outcome was that the introduction eventually grew into this book.

Initially I felt that something on which a whole nation spends so much time and money demanded greater anthropological attention than it had so far received. I also had an intuitive sense that the institution of qat consumption encapsulated essential features of Yemeni culture and society; that by grasping the significance of qat other aspects of Yemeni life which I wanted to understand would become more intelligible. It seemed that qat consumption could be a window which would offer a clear if partial view of a society reeling under the impact of sudden deep involvement with the world economy and adjusting to a radical transformation in material conditions. What I eventually saw, and hope to demonstrate, is that a 'traditional' social ritual which had formerly helped sustain the high social position of a privileged minority had become a major forum for the negotiation by the majority of a new social order based on achievement and the deployment and display of monetary wealth.

I also became aware that qat consumption is not solely of academic interest, but is of great concern to the Yemen government, international agencies and a wide range of people professionally involved with the welfare and development of Yemen. This concern stems from the widespread belief that qat is retarding the development of Yemen by diverting money, time and valuable agricultural resources to what is generally regarded as a harmful, wasteful, meaningless indulgence.

While writing this book I have therefore had a mixed audience in mind: the general reader who seeks to know more about the countries of the Middle East and the rapid and profound changes they are experiencing; specialists interested in consumption practices and in the culture and society of Yemen; and officials and experts of governments and international organisations who are concerned about what is usually defined as the 'qat problem'. If I cause other researchers to explore the issues I have raised in greater detail and depth than my limited data has allowed, I will have achieved one of my aims. If I cause decision-makers to reappraise certain common assumptions, and become more aware of the social dimensions of the qat phenomenon, I will have achieved another.

Terminology and Transliteration
Qat is the Arabic term for *Catha edulis* and is used throughout Yemen and other Arabic-speaking areas. In Yemen qat is pronounced *gat* (with a hard g) or *kat* (with a soft guttural k). Arabists accept two correct transliterations of the term, *qāt* and *ḳāt*, as either *q* or *ḳ* can represent the initial Arabic letter *qaf* in different systems. Qat is the transliteration used throughout this book except in certain quotations from other authors. There are two other transliterations of the term in the literature, *khat* and *ghat,* which are inaccurate and misleading because *kh* and *gh* are commonly used to represent Arabic letters which are pronounced quite differently from qaf. It is therefore unfortunate that *khat* has been adopted as the official transliteration by international organisations such as the World Health Organization (WHO) and the International Council on Alcohol and Addictions (ICAA).

For ease of reading I have omitted the visually disruptive diacritical signs on words transliterated from Arabic, including those which appear in quotations from other authors.

The guttural Arabic consonant *'ain* is, however, usually represented by ', and the glottal stop (*hamzah*) by ' except in initial position. The exceptions are in place names such as Sanaa, Saadah and Taizz, and in certain personal names. Plurals have been indicated by the addition of 's' to the Arabic singular. More precise transliterations and Arabic plurals are provided in the Glossary and Index.

The nomenclature employed for the two Yemens and their regions must be clarified as confusion frequently arises. This book is about the country known since 1962 as the Yemen Arab Republic (YAR). Before then, and often also today, it was called 'Yemen,' 'The Yemen' or 'North Yemen'. Throughout this book I normally refer to the YAR as 'Yemen' to avoid tiresome repetition of the cumbersome official name. The exception to this is when it is necessary to distinguish the country from its southern neighbour, the People's Democratic Republic of Yemen (PDRY) – the former British Aden Colony and Protectorates. PDRY is often referred to in the literature as 'South Yemen', but I have used neither 'North Yemen' nor 'South Yemen' to avoid confusion when referring to the north or south of the Yemen Arab Republic. When I refer to 'north Yemen' or 'northern Yemen' I therefore mean the north of YAR, not the entire country. I alternatively use the terms 'Upper Yemen' and 'Lower Yemen' (which follow Yemeni usage) to refer to northern and southern YAR respectively.

Currency

The official currency of the Yemen Arab Republic is the Yemeni riyal (YR). However, in some northern parts of the country the main currency of everyday use during the 1970s was the Saudi Arabian riyal (SR). Both these currencies are given in the text as appropriate, with the then current US dollar (US$) equivalents in parentheses. During most of the 1970s the Yemeni riyal stood at about YR4.5 = $1 and the Saudi riyal at about SR3.5 = $1.

Acknowledgements

This book is based on library research, discussions with colleagues, and extended field research in Razih, a province in the north of the Yemen Arab Republic where I spent a total of fourteen months in 1977 and 1979–80. I am grateful to the Trustees of the British Museum for special leave of absence to do this field work.

I am deeply indebted to the people of Razih who accepted me in their midst with such generosity and kindness. Only a few of those who helped me can be mentioned here, but I would particularly like to express my gratitude to Muhsin Ahmed Abu Talib and all the members of Bayt Abu Talib, to Shaykh Awadh Mansur Farah and all the members of Bayt Farah, to Abdurrahman Ali al-Madani and family, to the members of Bayt Mansur Ali and to Ahmed Muhammed Jibran and family. I am also grateful for the help and support I received in Sanaa from the Director of Antiquities, Qadhi Ismail al-Akwa, the officials of the Yemen Centre for Research and Studies, Jon and Jan Mandeville at the American Institute for Yemeni Studies, and Sarah Soulsby.

I would like to thank all the friends and colleagues, too numerous to mention, who gave advice and encouragement during the preparation of this book. I would especially like to express my gratitude to Stace Birks, Ian Dunn, Ernest Gellner, Ianthe Maclagan, Emanuel Marx, Tim Morris, Jonathan Parry and Bob Serjeant for the time and trouble they took to provide detailed comments on various sections and drafts of the book. All are of course absolved from responsibility for the book's remaining inadequacies and for the opinions expressed. I would also like to thank Ian Dunn, Bonnie Glover and Cynthia Myntti for all their help in the field, Bonnie Glover and Owen Wright for help with transliterations, and Aida Kanafani and Sarah Soulsby for help with translations.

The objects illustrated are from the collections of the Museum of Mankind, and the numbers given in the captions are Museum registration numbers. I am grateful to John Kennedy for permission to reproduce the diagram in fig 4, and to Ronald Lewcock (plates 18 and 20) and Cynthia Myntti (plate 16) for allowing me to reproduce their photographs. All the other field photographs are my own. Lastly I would like to express my appreciation to Henry Brewer, who was responsible for studio photography, to Josie Hurst for her patient typing and retyping of the manuscript, to the messengers and security staff at my place of work, the Museum of Mankind, for all their helpfulness, to Nancy Matthews for help with proof-reading and to the staff of British Museum Publications Ltd for their courtesy and care in the production of the book.

1

The Yemen Arab Republic

Until recently Yemen was a relatively isolated country, rarely visited by foreign travellers and of peripheral importance on the world stage. It was a minor and intermittent outpost of the Ottoman Empire and, in contrast to most countries of the Middle East and North Africa, was never colonised by a European power. For these reasons little is known about Yemen outside specialist circles and it is necessary to provide some background information about the country.

For many Westerners 'Arabia' evokes contrasting images of vast hot deserts peopled only by bedouin with their camels and tents, or of bustling modern cities of concrete and glass filled with rich oil shaykhs driving Cadillacs. These clichés reflect partial truths of Saudi Arabia and the Gulf states but must be banished from the mind when picturing Yemen. Yemen is a green and mountainous country with a mainly temperate climate, relatively high rainfall and rich agricultural resources, and until recently about ninety per cent of its population were sedentary farmers. It is not an 'oil state' like its neighbour Saudi Arabia, although it may soon become one. In mid-1984 oil was reported to have been discovered in the east of Yemen, but the commercial potential of the field has not yet been established.

Geography, Climate and Population

Yemen has an area of approximately 135,000 sq km and a population, at the time of the first national census in 1975, of a little over five million (including men temporarily working abroad). It lies in the south-west corner of the Arabian peninsula and is bounded by the Kingdom of Saudi Arabia to the north and east, the People's Democratic Republic of Yemen (PDRY) to the south and the Red Sea to the west. Bordering the Red Sea is a narrow plain called the Tihamah – a tropical area of low rainfall which extends into the Saudi province of Asir to the north. However, most of Yemen is high and mountainous with a temperate or subtropical climate. In the west the Yemeni Highlands rise steeply from the Tihamah to heights of over 2000 metres, then extend eastwards in a series of craggy peaks and ridges, some over 3500 metres high, before descending to a high central plateau. This extends the length of Yemen, varying in altitude from 2000 metres in the north of the country to 1500 metres in the south. In the east this plateau slopes down to meet the deserts of the 'Empty Quarter'.

The climate of Yemen is dominated by the south-west monsoons which blow from the Red Sea during spring and summer and bring the country most of its rain. The variable action of these rain-bearing winds on the rugged topography of Yemen accounts for marked variations in agricultural potential within the country. The warm moisture-laden winds blow across the arid Tihamah and, on hitting the western escarpment of the Highlands, rise and cool, precipitating heavy rain on the exposed western slopes above an altitude of about 1500 metres. These high western areas also benefit from mists and heavy dews throughout the year. As the winds continue east they gradually lose their remaining moisture, and on reaching the central plateau are dried out by the warm east winds which blow off the inner deserts of Arabia. Within the region of the Highland massif, therefore, rainfall and agricultural production decline from west to east.

The main exception to this pattern occurs in the southern Highland region of Ibb, to the west of which the mountains are relatively low and do not present a barrier to the monsoon winds. This region receives the highest rainfall in the country (estimated to average 1000–1500 mm a year) and is the richest agricultural region of Yemen[1]. Other exceptions to the general pattern are areas adjacent to permanent or seasonal streams where a high level of agricultural production can be sustained through artificial irrigation. Such areas exist not only in the Highland regions but also in parts of the otherwise arid and unproductive Tihamah where streams flood into the plain from the Highlands during the rainy season.

The monsoon season normally extends from about March to October but there is considerable annual and regional variation in the timing, incidence and intensity of the rains, and in some years they fail entirely. Yemen's history is punctuated by periods of severe economic hardship or famine caused by inadequate rains or prolonged droughts. The most recent drought began in 1967 and lasted about seven years, and the most recent famine occurred in 1943 after the rains failed the previous year, and affected the whole of south-west Arabia (USAID, 1982: 6; British Admiralty, 1946: 450). About ten per cent of the total land area of Yemen is cultivated with crops (fifteen per cent is potentially cultivable), and about 80 per cent is pasture or forage land (USAID, 1982: 130).

The distribution of population in Yemen largely corresponds to the differing agricultural potential of the various regions, with the highest population densities (about 100/sq km) in the western and southern Highlands. The population is predominantly rural and extremely dispersed. Three quarters of the population live in about 50,000 settlements of less than 500 inhabitants – small villages and tiny hamlets scattered throughout the mountains and the plain. The remainder of the population lives in small rural townships or in the capital Sanaa (population 210,000), the main mercantile town of Taizz (123,000), the main port of Hodeidah (127,000), and in small towns such as Amran and Saadah in the north and Dhamar, Yarim and Ibb in the south.[2] Highland dwellings are imposing multi-storeyed houses of stone or mud, while in the Tihamah the traditional home is a small African-style hut of mud and thatch.

Religion and Politics[3]

Yemen is a Muslim country with a population divided almost equally between those who adhere to Zaydism, a sub-sect of the Shi'ah sect of Islam, and those who hold to the Shafi'i doctrine of orthodox Sunni Islam. In religious law and ritual observance only minor differences exist between Zaydism and Shafi'ism, but there is a major political difference – the Zaydi institution of the Imamate. Zaydis acknowledge as the legitimate religious and temporal leader of the Muslim community an Imam who must be chosen from among the 'noble' descendants (*sayyid*s or *sharif*s) of the Prophet Muhammad through either Hasan or Husayn, the sons of his daughter Fatimah and son-in-law Ali. The first Zaydi state was founded in Yemen in 893-4, and for over a thousand years until 1962 Zaydi Imams ruled parts (though rarely all) of present-day Yemen, including the non-Zaydi Shafi'i areas. Periodically their sovereignty was usurped by various local and foreign rulers (Sulayhids, Ayyubids, Rasulids, Tahirids, Mamluks), and Yemen also suffered two widely separated periods of Ottoman Turkish occupation, the first from the 1540s to 1636, the second from the 1870s until 1918.

The areas of Zaydi and Shafi'i Yemen roughly correspond with important differences in local political organisation. The Zaydi area, which extends from north of Yarim through the northern Highlands (Upper Yemen), is characterised by the existence of tribes (*qabilah*): relatively autonomous political and administrative units of variable size and territorial extent, whose members bear arms and have the organisation to rally and form alliances under traditional leaders (*shaykh*s). The tribes were the crucial force employed by the Imams in imposing their rule in both Zaydi and Shafi'i areas of the country.

The Shafi'i area extends over the southern Highlands (Lower Yemen) and the length of the Tihamah, and is generally characterised by small-scale village organisation and an absence of large tribal groupings led by powerful shaykhs, although there are or were some tribal areas, mainly in the southern Tihamah. The southern Highlands were therefore vulnerable to the depredations of the northern tribes, and were more easily controlled and administered than Upper Yemen, not only by the Imams, but also by the various non-Zaydi rulers including the Turks. As the most productive agricultural region of the country, yielding the highest tax revenues, Lower Yemen was always vital for the maintenance of state power, and it increased in strategic importance with the development of trade with Aden. State control of the Tihamah was also important because of the revenues from customs duties on imports, and to protect the ports, the trade routes from the coast to the Highlands, and the overland trade route along the coast.

The End of Imamic Rule

From 1918 to 1948 Yemen was ruled by Imam Yahya Hamid al-Din who had become Imam in 1904 but whose political authority in the early years had been restricted to the northern Highlands by the Turks. His first major task was to expel the forces of the Idrisi of Asir who had taken control of the Tihamah after the departure of the Turks. Following a prolonged campaign led by his son Ahmed, this was accomplished in 1926. In 1933–34 he conducted an unsuccessful war against the Saudis over sovereignty of Asir, and after this was lost Yemen acquired its present north-western boundary. (The southern boundary with the then British Aden Protectorate had been established by an Anglo–Turkish boundary commission before World War I.)

During the latter part of his reign Yahya strove to strengthen and concentrate power in his own hands and within Bayt (the House of) Hamid al-Din, and was more successful in his centralising endeavours and in establishing the authority of state government throughout Yemen than any previous Imam. This was partly due to the rudimentary administrative framework and telegraphic communications system which he inherited from the Turks, and even more to the embryonic professional army which they had established and which some Turks remained in Yemen to help train and develop after World War I. Another important factor was Yahya's policy of extreme isolationism aimed at keeping out foreign influence and the forces of modernism which might threaten his conservative regime. However, in the 1930s he received military assistance and training from Iraq, and he also established relationships with certain foreign countries in order to obtain supplies of sophisticated arms. Through the efficient collection of agricultural tithes (*zakah*) and customs dues, Yahya and the Princes of Bayt Hamid al-Din amassed enormous personal fortunes which were instrumental in maintaining the political dominance of their dynasty and combatting rivals. However, none of this wealth was deployed in developing the country; economic, technological and social change would have threatened the Imamate and was strenuously resisted.

Resentment at Yahya's monopolisation of power was a major factor leading to his assassination in 1948. He was succeeded by his son Ahmed whose approach to government was closely modelled on his father's. During his reign help in military training was provided by Egypt, and some economic and technological changes took place: projects were begun with foreign economic assistance, and the Chinese built the first surfaced road in the country between Sanaa and Hodeidah, a magnificent engineering feat. Imam Ahmed's reign also brought growing dissatisfaction at Yemen's isolation and 'backwardness', and the privileges of the *sayyid* aristocracy, particularly among the increasing numbers of Yemenis who travelled, worked and studied in Aden, Egypt and other foreign countries. Many of these men acquired secular, liberal values, and felt that Yemen's progress was being retarded by the Imamic mode of government. Several unsuccessful attempts were made to oust Ahmed but he died of natural causes in 1962.

His son Muhammad al-Badr succeeded him as Imam but after only one week a coup was engineered by a coalition of army officers, Shafi'i merchants, intellectuals and dissidents who held a variety of political views but were united in seeking the overthrow of the traditional political system, not merely the particular Imam and his supporters who held power as had been the case in 1948. A republican government was established in Sanaa, but al-Badr escaped and sought refuge among the Zaydi tribes of the north, some of which rallied to his support. The tribes had been less affected by the new ideologies of modernism and change, and their political structures, which they wanted to protect, had always existed in a kind of symbiotic relationship with the Imamate – the Imams granting them substantial autonomy in the management their own affairs in return for tax revenues and military support when required. It is an integral part of the tribal ethic to mobilise militarily on behalf of whoever supplies sufficient material reward (arms and money), though that is not to deny that some tribes were also motivated by ideological commitment to the Imam and the Zaydi state.

There ensued a seven-year civil war in which the royalist forces were supported with arms and finance by Saudi Arabia, and the republicans with arms and troops by Egypt. Nasser withdrew his forces from Yemen after the Arab–Israeli war of 1967, and the civil war came to an end in 1969. Certain royalist areas in the north which had not been conquered by the republicans, including Razih, finally capitulated in 1971. By then even the most remote tribal areas had acquired a firm vision of the modern amenities they desired – and which they expected the republican government to provide. This is evident, for example, from the fact that the fifteen conditions laid down by the Razih tribes for their acceptance of republican sovereignty, which are mainly of a political and legal nature, include demands for a telegraph system, roads, schools and a general hospital.

The Economy[4]

At the time of this political revolution in the 1960s Yemen was one of the least developed countries in the world and in most regions life was much as it had been for centuries.[5] The Chinese-built road between Sanaa and Hodeidah was the only surfaced road in the country, and there were few dirt roads suitable for motor vehicles because of the mountainous terrain. Travel was mainly on foot and most goods were slowly and laboriously transported by donkey or camel. There were virtually no modern amenities outside Sanaa, Taizz and Hodeidah, and even there water and electricity supplies and sewage disposal were inadequate and unreliable. The majority of the population still depended for their subsistence on agriculture and animal production. Despite recent changes these remain vitally important economic activities but they are no longer the main sources of livelihood for many households.

The main crops cultivated in Yemen are drought-resistant cereals – sorghum, millet, wheat and barley, depending on the area. These grains are the basis of the staple foods of bread and porridge, and the stalks and leaves, especially of sorghum, are important as fuel and fodder. Some areas specialise in the production of cash crops, the most important of which are coffee, qat, banana and grapes. In much of the Highlands crops are grown entirely on narrow, stone-walled terraces which clothe all but the steepest and rockiest slopes. In the central and southern Highlands, and in areas of the Tihamah adjacent to wadis (water courses), the land is flat enough for large fields of crops. Most crops in Yemen are rain-fed.

Small numbers of livestock (cattle and sheep) are kept by many households for their meat and, in the case of cattle, for their milk products, for their dung which is used as fertilizer, and for ploughing. Larger herds of sheep and goats are kept in the more arid areas of the Tihamah and the central and eastern Highlands where the land is less fertile and the terrain is more suitable for pasturing. Sheep's wool and goat hair were used until recently for weaving rugs and other articles in the central Highlands, and hides were an important export from the western Highlands to the Red Sea ports. Most agricultural production is for consumption within the household or for sale or exchange in one of the network of weekly markets which span every region in Yemen. In most of the country the farmer-landowners do not market their own surplus produce; this is generally undertaken by people who specialise in small-scale market trading. It is thought that until this century Yemen was self-sufficient in food production – a condition the present government has laudable but perhaps Utopian dreams of recreating.

In most of Yemen landholdings are relatively small and evenly distributed, although in some areas, especially in parts of the southern Highlands and Tihamah, large estates were created in the past by landowners and officials who made cheap purchases during famines or who were given land as a reward for political services or seized it in lieu of taxes or fines for legal misdemeanours. However, the Islamic inheritance system tends to fragment large holdings over several generations.

The basic unit of production and consumption is the household, the members of which work their own land or sharecrop the land of others, and raise their own animals. In the north of Yemen sharecroppers are not necessarily considered socially or economically inferior to landowners, but rather are seen as partners; they often own land of their own. In the large estates of the south and the Tihamah, however, the relations between owner and sharecropper are more often characterised by social inequality and dependence.

For about four centuries Yemen's main export was the famous 'Mocha' coffee, named after the port of Mokha from where many bulk consignments were shipped abroad. Coffee was also exported from Lohayya, Aden and Jiddah. The heyday of the Yemeni coffee trade was in the seventeenth and early eighteenth centuries when 'Mocha' coffee monopolised the world market, but with the later growth of large-scale coffee production in Indonesia, South America and East Africa, the Yemeni coffee trade declined. Coffee remains an important cash crop, however, though most of the coffee produced in Yemen today is for domestic consumption or is exported to Saudi Arabia. Owners of large coffee plantations, coffee agents and coffee merchants were formerly prominent among the rich elite of Yemen.

In the past a minority of the Yemeni population – large landowners, tribal and state officials and big merchants – was able to accumulate wealth from the sale of agricultural produce, and from taxation, extortion and commerce. But until after the civil war the majority of Yemenis led an often precarious existence close to subsistence level. Any surplus that remained after meeting physical needs and social obligations, and paying tribal dues and Islamic state taxes (*zakah*), was saved as a hedge against recurrent periods of hardship caused mainly by the vagaries of climate and intermittent political strife. Living conditions were generally simple and austere, and material aspirations were modest. Until the middle of this century relatively few commodities were imported, chiefly textiles, paraffin, guns, tobacco, sugar and tea.

The main exception to the relative economic self-sufficiency of Yemen before the civil war is the area in the south which was radically affected by the development of British Aden. After their colonisation of Aden in 1839 the British progressively expanded their control over the hinterland and throughout what became the British Aden Protectorate and since 1967 has been the People's Democratic Republic of (South) Yemen (PDRY). Aden was transformed from a small coaling station into a large bustling port and administrative centre with large labour requirements. This labour was mainly supplied from the relatively arid areas of marginal agriculture in the south of present-day Yemen, only a day's travel from Aden. Thousands of men migrated from there to work in Aden, particularly after the end of World War I. The population of Aden rose from 1289 in 1839 to 138,441 in 1955 (Gavin, 1975: 445). (These figures include immigrants from the then British Somaliland and elsewhere as well as British residents.) Many Yemenis took jobs as seamen and eventually settled in the United Kingdom and America where there are large Yemeni communities today. From the mid-nineteenth century, trading links were established between merchants in Sanaa, Hodeidah, Taizz, Ibb and Aden, and there was a great increase in trade between Lower Yemen and Aden. The latter became the main market for much of the agricultural produce (including qat and coffee) of the southern Highlands, and a major source of imported commodities.

Trade with Aden was at its height during and after World War II, but was later severely curtailed – first in 1962 by the revolution in Yemen and then in 1967 by the withdrawal of the British and the establishment of a socialist regime in the PDRY. The commercial expansion of the 1940s and 1950s increased the financial prosperity of Taizz and Ibb and their rural hinterlands, enlarged and enriched the merchant class, and increased Western (especially British) material and ideological influence in Lower Yemen.

Recent Economic Transformations
Since the civil war successive republican governments have grappled with the massive problem of developing the apparatus of a modern centralised state, and in many parts of the country traditional political structures have as yet been little affected by the change of regime. The real revolution in Yemen has been more economic than political, and is only partially related to the policies of the new republican regime, which has reversed the conservative, isolationist policies of the Imamic era. Many development projects have been welcomed from a variety of international aid organisations and foreign governments. A few hospitals and many schools have been built, the principal towns have been electrified, projects for improving agricultural production and water supplies have been initiated, health programmes have

been introduced, and an efficient international cable and telephone system has been installed in Sanaa. However most of these projects are local in their effects and not all have been an unqualified success. The internal development with the most far-reaching consequences for the entire population was the construction during the 1970s of major surfaced roads between Sanaa and Saadah, Sanaa and Taizz, and Taizz and Hodeidah. In the early 1980s a major highway was also completed which runs the length of the Tihamah into Saudi Arabia.

The most important economic event of the 1970s with profound consequences for Yemeni society was the large-scale periodic migration of Yemeni men to work in Saudi Arabia. It began in the early 1970s when the Saudi government lifted restrictions on immigration, but reached massive proportions after the great oil-price rises of 1973–74 and the consequent boom in the Saudi construction industry. The resulting demand for manual labour was largely supplied by Yemen. In 1975 roughly one third of the male workforce was temporarily working abroad, that is about 350,000 men out of a total population of around 5 million. By 1976–7 the number of migrants had risen to about half a million, and continued rising until the end of the decade when it appeared to have levelled off.[6]

The wages earned by these migrant labourers rose substantially during the 1970s, from less than SR5 (US $1) a day at the beginning of the decade to SR50 in the mid-1970s and SR100 by 1980.[7] Skilled labourers could earn two or three times these daily rates. The greater proportion of the migrants' earnings were sent or brought home. It is not known exactly how much wealth flowed into Yemen during the 1970s for the only figures available are based on bank transfers, and a considerable amount of cash and goods brought back went unrecorded.[8] However, the bank figures still give a vivid indication of the enormous sums of money repatriated. According to one reliable source, recorded remittances rose from US$135 million in 1974 to nearly $900 million in 1978.[9] The latter figure is equivalent to nearly US$2000 a year sent home by each short-term migrant worker. It appears that the peak of remittances was reached in around 1978 and that thereafter employment opportunities in Saudi Arabia began to decline, mainly because cheaper labour was increasingly being imported from Eastern Asia.

The sudden, unprecedented increase in financial prosperity immediately transformed the lives of all Yemenis. There was an urgent and widespread desire to acquire modern amenities and improve the quality of life which found one concrete expression in the formation throughout the country of local development cooperatives (known as Local Development Associations, or LDAs) which were eventually coordinated under one national umbrella organisation. Through the LDAs, as well as through individual and community initiative and expense, there was a flurry of self-help improvement schemes. New houses sprang up and old ones were renovated and brightly painted; cisterns were built and wells sunk; generators were bought and thousands of villages and hamlets were electrified; water pumps and flour mills were installed; and bulldozers were bought or hired and hundreds of feeder tracks were constructed to connect the most remote rural areas to the main roads which were rapidly being built. Yemenis were determined to catch up, as they saw it, with the rest of the world.

The great increase in cash incomes brought a leap in material aspirations and a surge of Western-style consumerism – fed and stimulated by a flood of imported commodities. The humble material conditions of Yemeni life were transformed at an astonishing pace. In the early 1970s no rural district was electrified and luxury was a pressure lamp; by 1980 almost every home had electricity, a household without a television was a hardship case and video sets were rapidly becoming *de rigeur*. In the living room goat-hair rugs and palm-leaf mats were replaced by linoleum and imitation Persian rugs. Men sported smart Western jackets over traditional dress, and women were adorned with glittering Far Eastern brocades. Brides disdained the traditional dowry jewellery of hand-crafted silver and insisted on gold. Meat became regular fare for people who had formerly been glad of a daily loaf of bread. Men happy to own a camel or donkey a few years before were joyfully driving Toyota jeeps.

As incomes rose, the price of every commodity and transaction was subject to enormous inflation – wages, food, furnishings, brideprices, litigation, professional services, houses and land as well as the plethora of new consumer durables. People had more money than they had ever known, but with the growth in consumerism and the substantial rise in the cost of living, the demands on their pockets were vastly greater than they had ever been.

Mass out-migration and the influx of remittances caused major economic upheavals. The domestic labour shortage caused inflation in Yemeni wages, and in some rural areas where agriculture requires a high input of labour and rainfall is low, it ceased to be economically viable; terraces were abandoned and men drifted to the towns or remained abroad. Where rainfall is high and reliable, however, grain continued to be widely cultivated, and in relatively flat areas the labour costs of grain production were reduced by mechanisation. The price of cash crops soared, so qat, coffee, banana and grapes continued to be important and profitable crops.

In some areas the rise in cash incomes was accompanied by a decline in livestock production despite the increase in meat consumption. In the new affluent conditions animals and their products were no longer essential as a hedge against hard times. Imported milk products were readily available in every local market and the increased demand for meat was met by the importation of meat on the hoof or frozen.

With the surge of consumerism, trade and commerce became increasingly lucrative and expanded in scale. Thousands of men entered the commercial sector for the first time, and many invested capital saved while working in Saudi Arabia to set themselves up as shopkeepers. Throughout the country the simple weekly market-places where traders laid their wares on the ground became permanent bustling shopping centres filled with lock-up shops of breeze-block or galvanised iron. There was similar expansion in other sectors of the economy. Small old and new artisanal and craft industries flourished, though some but not all traditional craft production declined with the competition from mass-manufactured imports. (This decline had begun in the 1940s, and contributed to the exodus of Yemeni Jews to Israel around 1950, for many Jews were silversmiths and textile producers.) Many men bought vehicles and became transporters or taxi-drivers, and others acquired expertise in the maintenance and installation of mechanical and electrical equipment. Work also greatly increased in the domestic construction industry as remittances were invested in housing.

During the 1970s there was therefore a radical transformation from an economy based primarily on subsistence agriculture and livestock rearing to an economy based to a great extent on wage labour in large-scale capitalist enterprises abroad and on wage labour or self-employment in small-scale capitalist enterprises (including agriculture) at home. Agriculture became more commercialised and a greater proportion of crops, including grain, were sold for cash in the market-place. Foreign grain was imported in large quantities and was sold for less than home-produced grain, the production of which declined though it remained important. Many other foodstuffs were also imported, and Yemen ceased to be relatively self-sufficient in food production.

While some farmers continued to cultivate their land with family labour (if they had it), increasingly labour was hired for a daily wage. At the same time there was a decline in the traditional sharecropping system. In general, there was a substantial shift towards a predominantly cash economy, and most rural people (the majority of the population) no longer depended entirely on agriculture for their living. With the diversification of the local economy and rapid expansion of labour migration, they acquired alternative sources of income and for many agriculture became of secondary importance.

Social and Ideological Change
The political and economic transformations in Yemen must inevitably have profound effects on its society and culture, and already some changes can be discerned.

It was apparent by the late 1970s that there was some erosion of the traditional Yemeni system of social status based on birth into ranked social and occupational categories. In this hierarchy, *sayyid*s are accorded the highest status on account of their noble pedigree as alleged descendants of the Prophet Muhammad, and under the Imamate they formed a powerful religious, legal and political elite. Another social category accorded high rank are the *qadhis* – hereditary legal specialists who, like the *sayyids*, performed important administrative functions under the Imams though they do not share their illustrious ancestry. Within the Zaydi state the *sayyids* and *qadhis* also held a virtual monopoly on religious learning and the application of Islamic (*shari'ah*) law, and this is still largely the case.

*Sayyid*s and *qadhi*s form a small minority of the total population of Yemen. Most Yemenis classify themselves, within this hierarchical system, as either 'arab or ra'aya, in the south of the country or gaba'il (sing. gabili) in the north. These and several other terms connote, in the context of social hierarchy, farmers and landowners of 'good local stock' and 'respectable' family connections. In the north the term *gabili* also has important political connotations for it means a member of a tribe (*gabilah*). At the bottom of this system of social stratification is a minority of the population who are of low status on account of their 'base' or unknown origins and their demeaning or defiling occupations, which are considered as such by their social superiors because they involve the provision of services or contact with polluting substances. These occupations include running cafés and hostels, selling vegetables and other petty market trading, butchery, hair-cutting, blood-letting and tanning. There is some variation in attitudes towards these occupations within Yemen, but the people (*akhdam*) who sweep the streets and dispose of human refuse are everywhere the bottom of the social pile. Those of despised birth and occupation are often referred to collectively as *nuqqas*, which means literally 'deficient'. The social separateness of these status categories was and still is widely maintained in several ways, most effectively by marriage prohibitions which create unequal affinal relations between *sayyids* and *gabilis*, and isolate the *nuqqas* as a virtually endogamous group.

There was and is no precise correspondence between these ranked social categories and economic classes; rich and poor exist in both. But under the Zaydi state wealth was disproportionately distributed between them on account of the privileged access to positions of power and influence of the *sayyid*s and *qadhi*s, and the social disadvantages and relatively unrewarding nature of most of the *nuqqas* occupations. A notable exception is butchery. Affluence correlates with high meat consumption so the wealth of the upper classes was partly redistributed among the butchers, some of whom became rich merchants and landowners.

One of the principal aims of the 1962 revolution had been to banish the power and privileges of the *sayyid* elite, and some politicians even aspired to eradicating all Yemen's basic ideological and social inequalities. Around 1957 Muhsin al-Aini, who was later to become Prime Minister of the Yemen Arab Republic, delivered the following rhetorical blast against the traditional divisions of Yemeni society: 'There should be no Zaydism and Shafi'ism, no Hashimism [*sayyids*] and Qahtanism [non-*sayyid* South Arabian Arabs], no tribes- and towns-men, no turbans and caps, no Tihamah and Mountain folk, no tribes and peasants (*ra'aya*), but only Yemenis!' (Serjeant, 1979). However, there is no sign yet of the republican revolution bringing about the more egalitarian and undifferentiated society which al-Aini hoped for. Indeed many *sayyids* have held important positions in central and local government since the end of the civil war, though this is usually said to be on account of their education and experience, not their religious and social status. The other divisions also remain important either politically, as in the case of the tribesmen/townsmen dichotomy, or as a source of social and cultural identity, as in the case of Zaydism/Shafi'ism, clothing and geographical origins. However, though the traditional social hierarchy still exists, there are signs that its importance may be declining, and that attitudes towards it may be changing.

These changes in attitude differ from area to area, but one that seems to apply throughout Yemen concerns involvement in market trading. Formerly those who worked in the market-place, referred to by the derogatory term *suqi*, were looked down on by farmers and others of higher status. Now market work is not considered as demeaning as before – indeed there are signs that it is even becoming prestigious – and members of all social categories including *sayyid*s now engage in it. This change in attitude may partly be a consequence of sheer weight of numbers, but it must chiefly be attributed to the profits to be made from shopkeeping with the great increase in consumerism. The financial rewards of the retail trade have forced a redefinition of an occupation which growing numbers of men are eager to pursue.

In view of our main focus, it is interesting to note that qat-sellers (*mugawwitin*) were formerly among those of low social and occupational status, and that their standing has also improved with the increase in qat consumption and prices and the consequent rise in profits. It is possible that the evaluation of other low status occupations is also shifting as they become more profitable, although attitudes to butchery seem particularly resistant to change despite the wealth many butchers have acquired. Some low status occupations such as blacksmithing and carpentry may be becoming redefined as a result of their similarity to 'modern' occupations which have high status because they involve Western technology and are highly lucrative. (However in some areas such as Razih and Hufash blacksmithing and carpentry were respected before the recent changes.)

At the same time as the status of certain occupations, most notably shopkeeping, was being upgraded, the economic if not the social prestige of agriculture was diminishing. Farming remained highly respectable but it was no longer the economic backbone of Yemen, the occupation on which everyone directly or indirectly depended. Nor in many areas were large landholdings any longer automatically synonymous with disposable wealth. The landowner might be struggling to recruit and pay for labour to till his lands, especially if they would not support cash crops. The alternative sources of employment readily available to manual workers also shifted the balance of economic power away from the landowner. In some cases those with large holdings had to sell part of their land to maintain the rest of their property and meet the high cost of living.

In general, however, land sales declined as most households developed other sources of income and were no longer forced to sell land to survive (as happened in the past during hard times). Also, inflation in land prices made land an increasingly attractive capital investment. As some larger holdings became something of a burden to maintain and lost some of their social glamour, other lands became suddenly immensely more valuable than ever before. The expansion of qat production invested the smallest mountain terrace in qat-producing areas with unprecedented value, and as men used their cash earnings to build new houses, land around the expanding settlements and towns became extremely valuable as real estate. In short, land ceased to be such a reliable indicator of economic and social position, and the social category 'landowner-farmer' lost some of its former prestige connotations.

In parts of the country, especially in the towns and in Lower Yemen, modernism and the ideology of republicanism have eroded the will or the ability of the *sayyid*s to maintain their social status and exclusivity, and some have started to break the traditional rule prohibiting marriage between their daughters and non-*sayyid* men. However, in the north of the country where *sayyid*s have continued to be revered by those of lower birth and have largely retained their former religious and legal roles and powers, this marriage prohibition is still generally observed, although there are circumstances in which the rules may be bent. For example, a *sayyid* woman from Razih was given in marriage to a man of a lower social category status who was an influential government official in Sanaa. There are probably many instances of the old marriage prohibitions being relaxed with the greater geographical mobility brought about by improved transportation and as rural people seek social anchorage in the towns.

The traditional hierarchy based on birth, occupation and landownership is still of great importance in Yemeni society, but the boundaries between the traditional social categories have been besieged and in some cases breached, and the importance of social category status has been blunted. It may not have become much easier to move up the Yemeni hierarchy, but it has become less vital for the socially ambitious to do so because of the increased importance of wealth as a criterion of social status. Wealth was always a vital ingredient of high social position and power, but its importance relative to birth and occupation has been greatly enhanced by the new economic conditions.

Increased prosperity has created a vast constituency with a vested interest in a generally materialistic and specifically financial ideology of social status. This includes all those unfavourably placed within the traditional ascriptive hierarchy and the generation of younger men whose independence was formerly retarded by the control of property and retention of authority by the paternal generation. Now the sandal was in many cases on the other foot. Sons accumulated cash from working abroad while older men stayed home and managed their lands. A new, relatively poor class was created of those too old or weak to build Saudi towns. In some quarters lip service was paid to egalitarianism, and the co-operative ethic remained important in many areas, especially in the tribal north, but at the same time individualism and competitiveness increased with the perceived potential for upward social mobility through personal effort. The extent to which that potential was realised, however, undoubtedly varied in different communities and different areas of Yemen.

The 1970s therefore brought a shift to a predominantly cash economy, a widespread increase in financial prosperity, and fundamental changes in the sources and distribution of wealth. These economic transformations presented a major challenge to the traditional social hierarchy, which had already been assaulted by the political and ideological revolution of the 1960s. The ranked social categories based on birth and occupation declined in importance, though more in the south than the north, and the importance of disposable wealth as a criterion of status greatly increased. For much of the population there was a heady sense of the potential for improving ones' station in life by personal effort. At the same time great uncertainty was created about social position, which was exacerbated by increased geographical mobility. With the improvements in transport, the growth of employment opportunities at home and abroad, and the expansion of trading networks, people formerly cocooned in relatively closed, isolated communities where everyone knows everyone else were suddenly plunged into new social environments where identity and status had to be established virtually from scratch. This is the economic and social context in which increased qat consumption in Yemen is to be understood.

2

Qat

The Qat Plant

Qat is an evergreen shrub of the family Celastraceae and was first named and described botanically by Per Forsskål, the Swedish botanist who died in Yemen in 1763 during the ill-fated Danish expedition led by Carsten Niebuhr (Hansen, 1964: 275–284). Forsskål Latinised the Arabic name *qat* to *Catha* and added the second term *edulis* because it was 'eaten'. The scientific botanical name of qat is therefore *Catha edulis* Forsskål (Forsskål, 1775: 63–4).[1] The term qat is used throughout south-west Arabia. In Ethiopia the plant is known as *chat* (*tchat*) in Amharic and *jimma* among the Gallas. In Kenya it is called *miraa,* and it has many alternative local names in other areas where it is grown or consumed (see Greenway, 1947 and United Nations, 1956).

Qat can occur as a small leafy bush (sometimes compared to the tea shrub in appearance) or as a tree with a slender, flexible, smooth-barked trunk – depending on its age, the rainfall or irrigation possibilities of the area in which it is cultivated, and the way its leaves and branches have been harvested. In areas with heavy, well-spaced rains or regular irrigation, farmers harvest the new growth of leaves and stalks from the tips of the branches relatively frequently, and the plants remain small. In areas with less rainfall and no irrigation, the harvests are less frequent, the whole branch is harvested with the leaves attached, and the qat grows into a tree (Tutwiler and Carapico, 1981: 53). If the shoots and branches of qat are not harvested during summer, the winter harvest is more plentiful and the plant produces small white flowers.

Rain-fed qat can reach five metres in height and up to ten metres if intensively irrigated (but presumably not harvested regularly) (Schopen, 1978: 71). The plant is easily propagated from cuttings and two to four years after planting produces leaves in quantities sufficient for commercial harvesting.[2] It can continue producing marketable leaves for up to fifty years (Kopp, 1981: 236). Qat leaves are pointed and oval in shape and grow up to ten centimetres long, but the large old leaves are tough and unsuitable for chewing. It is the new succulent shoots and leaves, preferably only days or weeks old, which are picked for human consumption. The leaves range in colour from pale green to dark green and red, and there is considerable variation in their shape, texture and flavour according to their age and such factors as soil types and conditions and the amount of watering the plants have received. Thus, even though it is a single species of plant, qat lends itself to cultural classification into a variety of types based on appearance, place of origin and taste.

The Geographical Distribution of Qat

Qat is a hardy plant which needs little attention and can survive in a wide range of environments, but it thrives best and produces new foliage in greatest abundance in well-watered mountainous districts between altitudes of 1500 and 2500 metres. The intensive commercial cultivation of qat has therefore been restricted historically to highland areas with relatively high rainfall or where regular irrigation is possible from permanent springs or streams.

Significant qat cultivation and consumption are limited to south-west Arabia and north-east and east Africa. Qat is grown commercially in the mountains of the People's Democratic Republic of Yemen, the Yemen Arab Republic, Asir Province in western Saudi Arabia, Ethiopia, Somalia, Madagascar and Kenya, and it is grown on a small scale in Israel for consumption by Jews of Yemeni origin. It also occurs naturally in Turkestan, Afghanistan, Uganda, Rwanda, Burundi, Zaire, Tanzania, Zambia, Mozambique and South Africa (Brooke, 1960; Schopen, 1978: 43–4; Shahandeh et al, 1983). It seems, however, that the widespread institutionalised consumption of qat is confined to the two Yemens, parts of Ethiopia and Somalia, and Kenya.

Qat consumers like the leaves to be as fresh as possible for full efficacy and flavour, and since qat is a highly perishable commodity, it is vital for farmers to market it within one or two days of picking. After that, especially in warm conditions, the leaves wilt and rapidly lose commercial value, for some of the stimulant chemicals in qat are highly volatile and deteriorate quickly once the leaves are picked. The demand for fresh qat meant that until the twentieth century consumption was limited to the highland producing areas and districts nearby. However, the advent of motor and air transportation made it possible to trade larger quantities of qat over much greater distances.

Yemen (YAR) is (and probably always has been) self-sufficient in qat production, and some surplus is exported to the People's Democratic Republic of Yemen (PDRY) and Saudi Arabia. Although qat is grown in the mountains of the PDRY, it has been insufficient for local demand since the great increase in the population of Aden during the period of British rule. For much of this period large consignments of qat were carried in long camel trains from the southern Highlands of Yemen to Aden, and after air transport services were instituted across the Red Sea in 1949, large quantities of qat were also exported from Ethiopia to Aden (Brooke, 1960). During the later period of British rule qat was one of the principal imports of the Aden Colony.[3] In the last few decades there has also been a lively trade in qat by truck from Ethiopia to Somalia, and from Kenya as far afield as Tanzania, Uganda, Zambia, Zaire, Sudan and Somalia (Brooke, 1960; Hjort, 1974). Today Ethiopian qat is even exported by air to London, New York and elsewhere for consumption by emigrant Yemenis and Somalis.

1 Camel caravan transporting qat from Yemen to Aden early this century. (From Moser, 1917).

In Yemen, until the recent advent of motor transport, all qat was traded by donkey and camel. Qat was therefore only sold at markets within the producing areas or at most two days' travel away, which in the rugged mountainous districts meant within a radius of about fifty kilometres. Distribution was revolutionised during the 1970s by the building of motor tracks and the widespread acquisition of motor vehicles, and producers in the most distant rural areas can now market their qat at the large urban markets. Much of the incentive and finance for the construction of the hundreds of feeder tracks built on local initiative came from the qat trade (Kopp, 1981: 237; Weir, 1985).

Improved infrastructures and marketing were not the sole causes of increased qat consumption in Africa or Arabia. Their effect was only to make qat more readily available in areas where it was already consumed or where there was a local cultural potential for qat consumption. The demand that already existed could be more easily met but new demand was not created. That in fact was created, or increased, by changes in economic and social conditions, which *coincided* with improvements in transportation facilities. This needs stressing because the diffusion of qat consumption and analogous consumption practices are often described as though they were diseases which only require carriers in order to spread widely and indiscriminately in any population. But the host culture must be receptive to the adoption of such a complex practice as qat chewing. It is hard to imagine that it would catch on, say, in Edinburgh parlours or Paris salons, however many planeloads of qat leaves were imported.

Qat Cultivation in Yemen

The cultivation of qat in south-west Arabia extends from Jabel Fayfah in Asir Province in western Saudi Arabia in the north to the Hojariyyah District of Yemen in the south west and Jabal Jihaf and al-Baydha in the south and south-east (Schopen, 1978: 65). Within Yemen qat is a major cash crop throughout the length of the well-watered western Highlands, in the southern central Highlands around Taizz and Ibb where rainfall is higher than in the more arid central Highland regions further north and east, and in some Highland valleys where permanent streams allow regular irrigation. Qat cultivation is rarely found below an altitude of about 1500 metres on the western escarpment of the Highlands as the lower mountain slopes and the Tihamah coastal plain are too hot and dry for qat to thrive. Until recently little qat was grown in areas of the Yemeni Highlands situated inland from the western mountains, with the exception of valleys (*wadis*) with permanent streams, because of their relatively low rainfall.[4] The areas where qat thrives receive an annual average of at least 500–1000 mm of rain, and according to some estimates up to 2000 mm, and the western Highland areas are also favoured by frequent mists and cloud cover which deposit heavy dews and reduce evaporation from the soil. The average annual rainfall in most of the central and eastern Highlands, by contrast, is less than 500 mm, and conditions are generally far less humid.[5] However during the late 1970s some farmers in these inland regions were stimulated by the high returns on qat

2 The main settlement of southern Razih surrounded by qat terraces, mid-1977.

3 Qat terraces and terraces sowed with sorghum. Razih, mid-1977.

to try and grow it by means of pump irrigation from wells, and small qat plantations appeared in relatively arid areas where it had never previously been grown.[6]

In the steep, rugged western Highlands qat is grown entirely on narrow terraces; only in certain flatter central Highland areas are relatively large fields of qat to be found. Qat bushes and trees are usually planted a metre to a metre and a half apart which allows the passage of a bullock-drawn plough between the plants.[7] Qat is hardy and provided it is sufficiently well watered, needs relatively little attention to thrive. However, it will produce a greater abundance of new leaves the more often the earth is tilled, and a farmer needs to weed, plough and hoe a qat terrace three or four times a year to obtain optimum harvests. During the late 1970s increased yields were obtained by the use of artificial fertilizers and insecticides.

Most qat is rain-fed or irrigated by run-off water from the steep mountainsides, although in some areas, such as Wadi Dhahr near Sanaa, it is irrigated from permanent streams. The qat producers in areas with constant water supplies have the advantage of being able to stimulate the growth of new qat leaves when they choose, according to the state of the market. (New shoots sprout days after watering in warm weather.) However, in most areas qat farmers are dependent on rainfall. The south-west monsoons occur roughly between March and October, but there is no reliable or regular annual rainfall pattern. In some areas such as Razih rain also often falls in the winter months, which are dry in most of Yemen. In years with reasonable rainfall qat farmers expect to harvest their qat leaves twice or three times, but in years of low rainfall or drought they may harvest only once or not at all. The heaviest rain normally falls in August and September and it is then that qat is most abundant and prices fall. However, because of improved transportation facilities and regional variation in the incidence of rainfall there is usually some qat available in most markets throughout the year, though supplies fluctuate. Qat is not a crop like grain or fruit with a specific harvest time when it must be reaped or be lost. It is an evergreen which is continuously producing new leaves at a rate determined by the temperature and rainfall.

Daily social life can and does revolve around qat chewing, despite the high perishability of the picked leaves, because qat is a dependably available commodity in which a whole system of meaning and cultural practice can safely be invested. The fact that qat is a locally produced crop – cultivated and consumed by members of the same culture – may also help explain why it has remained an important article of consumption for over five hundred years. Because it is as familiar in the fields and on the terraces as in the market and the home, a rich and elaborate body of knowledge surrounds qat in Yemen which would probably not have developed were it imported in amorphous bulk consigments from a distant unknown country.

Marketing Qat in Yemen
The dominant concern of qat traders is to market their crop quickly before it wilts, which has led to an intricate and efficient informal marketing system within Yemen. The perishability of qat and its relatively constant availability

4 Ploughing between the qat trees. Razih, December 1979.

5 Farmers taking a mid-morning coffee break (*buri*) among their qat bushes. Razih, January 1980.

are the main reasons why a class of big merchants has not emerged within the qat 'industry' as happened in the coffee industry. Coffee can be stored indefinitely and the coffee trade therefore favoured those with substantial capital who could buy in and accumulate large quantities of beans, and transport and sell them in bulk consignments. It is also a seasonal crop which requires a heavy labour input for picking. The qat industry has not become dominated and monopolised by such big merchant capitalists because, in contrast to coffee, qat cannot be accumulated after it is picked and is easily harvested in small quantities throughout the year. Also price fluctuations and unreliable rainfall are disincentives to speculation in qat. It is doubtful whether much qat is sold before the leaves are ready for harvesting when landowner and trader are both aware of the current state of the market (Weir, 1985). The present marketing conditions therefore favour small-scale trading units (most of which are family-based) which can buy, pack and transport small qat consignments (a truck-full or less) to market within two or three days of picking. Flexibility in trading tactics and the ability to react quickly to sudden price rises are important factors in successful qat trading.[8]

The way qat is marketed depends on the geographical position of the producing area, especially its proximity to the main towns, and on local transportation facilities and road conditions. Qat may be sold in one of the hundreds of small qat markets scattered throughout the rural areas, where it is bought mainly for local consumption, or it may be taken to the major qat markets of Saadah, Sanaa, Hodeidah or Taizz, especially if urban prices are high. Donkeys are still used in some areas for carrying qat short distances from settlements not directly served by motor tracks.

Various categories of people trade in qat. Some farmer-landowners take their own qat to market, and others sell to local men (who are often farmer-landowners themselves) who specialise in qat trading. There are also town-based qat traders who drive out to the producing areas to buy qat. When rural qat traders arrive in the market they may simply take a spot on the ground and sell their qat themselves. Alternatively, and probably more frequently, they sell their qat through a retailer or through a wholesaler who distributes it to one or more retailers. In either case the trader is not normally paid until his qat has been sold, when the retailer or wholesaler takes an agreed commission – usually about ten per cent of the money taken.

The Expansion of Qat Cultivation in Yemen
The great increase in qat consumption which took place in Yemen during the 1970s caused qat production to double. (It has been estimated that in 1981 qat was being grown on about 40–45,000 ha, or four per cent of the arable land of Yemen (USAID, 1981: 81). The ease and speed with which Yemeni farmers grew more qat to meet escalating demand are important factors in understanding the phenomenon of qat consumption.

Most of the increase in production can be accounted for by the spread of qat cultivation within traditional qat-growing areas. The new qat plantations were not on previously uncultivated land; they were on fields and terraces which were already farmed. The expansion of qat therefore took place at the

6 *above*. Loading sacks of qat packages (*guruf*) onto trucks for market. Razih, January 1980.

7 *left*. A qat traders' market in Razih, January 1980. The donkeys have brought the packaged qat from settlements not served by motor transport. From here the qat is taken by truck to the big urban markets.

expense of other crops. This would obviously not have occurred had the major alternative crops to qat – summer sorghum and coffee – been more profitable, but on neither crop were the returns as high (or reliable) as those on qat. The profit from qat for the farmer was generally estimated to be about five times that of coffee during the 1970s, and up to twenty or more times that of sorghum.[9] Qat is also a hardy plant, is easily propagated, yields harvests two or three years after planting, and requires little attention or labour. There was therefore a great financial incentive to grow qat, and few practical disincentives to doing so. The main reasons for refraining from qat cultivation in Razih were fear of theft (when terraces could not easily be guarded), insecurity of tenure and, in the case of sharecroppers who wanted to buy the land they worked, the desire to avoid increasing the returns on the land to the owner which would make him less likely to sell it.

Many of those concerned with the economic development of Yemen disapprove of qat partly because they assume that it is coffee which has been the main casualty of the increase in qat cultivation. Most economists prefer coffee, which is grown in the same areas as qat, as a cash crop because it might earn Yemen foreign currency. However, it is doubtful whether in practice it could successfully compete in quality and price on today's world market. One of several unsubstantiated claims about qat is that throughout Yemen there has been widespread uprooting of coffee trees to make way for qat,[10] but no nationwide survey of qat- and coffee-producing areas has been carried out to ascertain to what extent and where this uprooting has happened, and where it has, to examine the various local ecological and economic factors involved. In Razih, for example, despite the superior profits to be made on qat, there was no sign of any major decline in coffee production. The expansion of qat was mainly at the expense of grain. Coffee remained a valuable secondary cash crop, sold in local markets and exported to other areas of Yemen and Saudi Arabia, and also important for local consumption.[11] However, the area concerned is ecologically ideal for the successful production of both qat and coffee. This is probably not the case in the areas where coffee trees *are* being replaced by qat, where coffee may therefore be a marginal crop, and harvests too meagre or unreliable to make its continuing cultivation worthwhile – especially as coffee is a labour-intensive crop and labour costs have become high.

Coffee cannot survive frosts as well as qat and may not flower and therefore fruit in cold conditions. For this reason it is rarely found above about 1700 metres, whereas qat can be grown up to an altitude of about 2500 metres. Coffee is also less able to survive without water than qat, and the decline in coffee production may be attributable, as much as anything, to the years of low rainfall and drought which Yemen suffered from the mid-1960s to the early 1970s. Coffee is also less tolerant of prolonged sunshine than qat, and on south-facing slopes requires mist cover or shade trees to thrive (sometimes qat trees provide the necessary shade).[12] It is probable, therefore, that the areas where coffee *is* being uprooted are particularly high and exposed, and have low or unreliable rainfall.

When detailed agricultural surveys of Yemen are available, they will probably reveal that in most areas it is mainly grain production which has declined as qat production has expanded. Grain is a much more labour-intensive crop than qat, which is partly why it is so much less profitable, and the returns to the farmer are often insufficient to finance expensive terrace maintenance.[13] This is particularly the case in the steep western Highlands where the terraces are especially vulnerable to erosion from heavy monsoon rains. It is in just those areas that qat (and coffee) thrive best and the greatest increase in qat production has taken place. In view of the general condemnation of qat cultivation by economists, it needs emphasising that in areas which will not support qat or other lucrative cash crops, many terraces have been neglected or abandoned and irrevocably damaged by the elements (World Bank, 1979: 97). It can therefore be asserted that the profits from qat have in many areas of Yemen helped preserve terraced agriculture for the future (see Weir, 1985).[14]

The widespread expansion of qat onto former grain terraces would presumably not have occurred had grain crops remained essential to survival. But in the economic circumstances of the 1970s grains were no longer important subsistence crops. Foreign wheat was readily available and cheaper than home-produced grain, and people had the cash to buy it. In addition the economic importance of sorghum as a source of fodder and fuel was reduced by the decline in domestic livestock production, the trucking of firewood on new motor tracks and the increased use of paraffin stoves. In short, the economic conditions which stimulated qat consumption were also conducive to an increase in qat production so as to meet rising consumer demand.

3

The Physiological Effects of Qat

In most Western accounts of qat consumption, its physical and mental effects have been greatly exaggerated, presumably because qat is so popular among Yemenis and so pervades their daily lives, and because consumers pay so much for their supplies. The possibility that what they are paying for is more than sensual gratification has rarely been considered. It has been almost universally assumed that qat must either be physiologically addictive or give such intense pleasure that it creates strong psychological dependence. In fact neither is the case as Yemenis themselves realise.

The Yemeni View of the Effects of Qat
Yemenis know that they are not dependent on qat. They have no serious problems when forced to abstain – for example during dry spells when supplies are unobtainable – and many who are regular consumers at home easily forgo it during long periods working abroad. They may miss it and long for it, much as an English person might pine for a cup of tea, but that is very different from true dependence. Qat is also regarded by Yemenis as a rather mild stimulant compared with other substances categorised as 'drugs' by Westerners. Depending on the circumstances in which it is consumed, Yemeni consumers believe that qat increases stamina, concentration and mental alertness and elevates mood. However those who have tried hashish or alcohol, for example, know that the effects of qat are not at all comparable in intensity.

The native experience of qat is reflected in the way it is categorised. It is considered neither a 'drug' (*mukhaddir*) like hashish nor comparable with intoxicating liquor (*khamr*); it is in fact placed in a unique class of its own – 'qat'. The term *mowla'i* is applied to exceptionally enthusiastic and heavy consumers of qat, and is often translated as 'addict' by English-speaking Yemenis, but this is probably because they are unaware of the full implications of our term, or are using it in the vague colloquial sense as in 'film addict'. The term *mowla'i* does not normally carry derogatory connotations: on the contrary it can be prestigious to be called *mowla'i* because it usually implies that you can afford to indulge your taste for large quantities of the most expensive qat. The term *wala'ah*, derived from the same linguistic root, refers to qat of the best quality – for example the choice tips of the qat branch which merchants reserve for their personal consumption (Abd al-Karim al-Maqrami, personal communication). From this evidence it seems that the sense of *mowla'i* is best conveyed by the term 'connoisseur' or 'gourmet'. This interpretation is reinforced by the fact that another term, *mudman*, is used for those who are dependent on alcohol or heroin but is rarely used in connection with qat (Kennedy *et al*, 1980). Occasionally the term *mowla'i* is used to criticise a heavy qat consumer, but this is when he is consuming beyond his means (see Chapter 9). In this specific context the best translation of the term would probably be 'glutton'.

Not all qat consumers experience its mildly stimulant effects but those who do appreciate its beneficial influence on their capacity to function effectively in two principal spheres of daily life: when working (or engaging in any demanding physical exercise) and when 'socialising' – which in Yemen as elsewhere subsumes a variety of serious and important business. Their appreciation of qat in these contexts reflects the importance in Yemeni culture of the work ethic and of sociability (and all it entails).[1] The true picture is therefore the opposite of that painted by the many writers who, as we shall see in the following chapter, have opposed qat on the grounds that it promotes idleness, detracts from productivity and provokes anti-social behaviour.

In the work context qat is consumed to enhance stamina and promote wakefulness. Those engaged in hard manual labour, such as stonemasons and house builders, chew qat to alleviate their fatigue and increase productivity. Before the advent of motor transport men would also chew qat to reduce exhaustion during arduous journeys on foot through the steep mountains, and nowadays many taxi- and truck-drivers chew it to prevent drowsiness during long journeys.

Most qat is consumed at the afternoon qat parties which are the dominant feature of daily social life in Yemen. Here qat is appreciated for the positive contribution it is believed to make to the relaxation, inter-communication and general conviviality of the gatherings. It is felt to stimulate the intellect, facilitate the articulation of ideas, and help generate a pleasant atmosphere of bonhomie. From references to qat use in early historical sources qat appears to have been used in the past by men of religion to stave off sleep during long nights of prayer, and was believed to enhance their communication with God. It is possible that some individuals may still use qat for these purposes, but such religious explanations are not generally offered by Yemenis today. However some qat parties do have a predominantly religious character, as for example when religious experts discuss theological matters, or when recitations take place from the Holy Quran.

The Effect of Qat at Qat Parties
Qat parties last for four or five hours, from two or three in the afternoon until dusk. During this period a definite sequence of mood and behaviour can often be observed which is usually attributed to the effects of qat. This atmosphere has been well described by Kennedy *et al* (1980):

8 A qat party of *sayyids* in Razih, November 1979. The *sayyid* in the left hand corner is reading from the Quran.

At the beginning of a session, conversation usually involves the entire [room]. News and gossip are passed and jokes are told or a well-known speaker or story-teller may set the whole group laughing. . . Frequently, spirited arguments occur, but never have we seen any violence in a qat session.

After chewing for about an hour or sometimes less, many individuals attain a state they call *kayf*, an elevation of mood during which the chewer feels not only optimistic, confident and active, but alert and highly attuned to the subjects of conversation. A few individuals who chew a substantial amount in a short time become so animated that a kind of logorrhea occurs; their tongues cannot keep pace with their thoughts and this creates a disconnected quality to their speech. This sometimes occurs on a group level, but often it is confined to one or two people or does not occur at all.

Many sessions are meetings of special interest groups and in these the topic may be something confidential or secret, such as political action or a business transaction. In others, the group may wrestle through a complex set of intellectual or legal intricacies concerning some local dispute, or perhaps argue some theological question in great depth. A conversational theme emerges which may be developed for as long as an hour or more. . . We do not wish to imply that much trivial conversation does not occur in qat sessions, but only to indicate that a condition of high mental concentration and focus on a single topic is often achieved by all members of a group. The attainment of this high level group communion appears related to the use of the drug, as Yemenis believe.

As the session proceeds beyond two-and-a-half to three hours, the noise level begins to diminish. A mood of reflective quietude settles over the occasion. As shadows lengthen, it becomes 'Solomon's Hour', a time of contemplation and rumination. Many low-voiced, dyadic conversations may be observed, and some individuals sit quietly, their glowing eyes giving evidence of the seething thoughts within. There may be some fatigue from the hours of talk, but the chewer does not feel less stimulated; there is only a turning inward of racing ideas and plans. Thoughts often eventually turn to plans that have failed or to difficult problems, but they may also move in a positive direction. Grandiose ideas for the future frequently are mentally worked out in great detail.

At some point, usually after some three-and-a-half or four hours have elapsed, individuals begin to rise, and, with a barely audible '*Salaam Alaykum*', leave the room, replace their shoes, and go quietly out into the evening.

This description not only conveys how qat parties are often perceived by outside observers, but also how they are experienced by Yemenis themselves. According to Schopen, Yemenis divide the sequence of moods into three distinct phases. In the first they feel awake and alert, their thoughts are clarified, memories flow, loquaciousness increases, and communication and a sense of community are enhanced; the second (*kayf*) is when the peak of communal

41

understanding and well-being is reached, men feel in harmony with themselves and others and may be transported to a more religious or philosophical plane of contemplation where countless projects seem attainable and problems soluble;[2] and the third is characterised by temporary sadness and spiritual unease as the qat is finished, its effects wear off and the party draws to a close (Schopen, 1978: 93–5).

This should be regarded as the idealised sensual structure of a qat party, for mood and atmosphere can vary considerably from one qat party to another. Also the effects of qat are experienced to varying degrees by different individuals, and many claim that qat never has any effect on them at all. In Schopen's opinion (1978: 60) only a small proportion of qat consumers really enjoy it.

The above descriptions clearly demonstrate that qat does not induce anything comparable to alcoholic 'intoxication', although this term has frequently been used to describe the condition of qat party participants during the phases of animated conversation or deep contemplation. It would also be misleading to translate the Arabic term *kayf* as 'high', for there are no sensations comparable to those experienced by cannabis smokers or users of cocaine or heroin. There is no sudden, intense rush of excitement. Nor is there any loss of physical or mental control.[3] This is one of the main reasons that qat has not been banned (in Yemen) on religious grounds; it does not alter consciousness nor cause stupefaction like alcohol and other strong drugs, which are forbidden – *haram* – to Muslims on that account.

The Yemeni View of Qat and Health

In addition to the stimulant effects that qat is believed to have in the contexts of work and socialising, it is also thought to have a number of other immediate and delayed effects, some of which are considered desirable, others less so – although none of the latter is considered serious enough to warrant abstention from qat consumption. Certain prophylactic measures are taken in order to minimise the less desirable side-effects attributed to qat, and other measures are taken to enhance those which are particularly valued. These ideas and the measures associated with them are best understood in relation to Yemeni concepts about the working of the human body.

The Yemeni view of the way the body functions is imbued with concepts which derive from traditional Graeco-Arab medical doctrine.[4] A central feature of this doctrine is the idea that a healthy body is one in which a precarious equilibrium is maintained between its four constituent humours – blood, phlegm, yellow bile and black bile – which are produced by the transformation of food in the stomach. Each humour has two inherent qualities drawn from the categories wet/dry and hot/cold. Thus blood is moist and hot, phlegm is damp and cold, yellow bile is dry and hot and black bile is dry and cold. A wide variety of agents are thought to be capable of affecting the condition of the body: all substances which are consumed internally (including food, qat and medicines), external therapeutic measures, climatic conditions, age, psychological trauma and so on. Any of these may upset the body's ideal balance by causing an under- or over-production of one or more of the four humours, or by causing the body to become too hot, cold, wet or dry on account of their own inherent heating, cooling, drying or moisturising effects. Physical well-being therefore depends on avoiding the agencies or substances which cause an excess or diminution of these qualities in the body, and offsetting those which are unavoidable by an antidote which has the opposite inherent qualities and effects. For example, foods which are considered to have a moistening or heating effect are fed to people whose illness or weakness is attributed to weak or insufficient blood (see Myntti, 1983: 145ff).

All substances which are ingested are classified according to the hot/cold or wet/dry dichotomies. The classification does not necessarily depend on whether the substances are hot or cold in temperature or spiciness, or wet or dry in texture, although they may be, but on the heating, moistening, etc., effect they are thought to have on the body. Within this system qat is defined as 'cooling' and 'drying', and certain beliefs about the effects of qat, and certain cultural practices associated with its consumption, can best be understood in relation to this classification.

In order to achieve the most enjoyable results from an afternoon's qat party, and to offset the 'cooling' effects of qat, a man should make himself as 'hot' as possible by eating beforehand a good lunch composed of 'hot' foods, and avoiding those classified as 'cold'. 'Hot' foods are boiled mutton, mutton broth, fenugreek (*hilbah*) broth, chili pepper, white radish, wheat bread and sorghum porridge (Bornstein, 1974: 35; Schopen, 1978: 121).[5] The cooling effects of qat are also counteracted during the qat party by closing all the windows of the room and generating a warm and stuffy atmosphere.

The 'dry' and 'cool' qualities of qat lead to both desirable and undesirable consequences. The thirst which it engenders is seen as highly desirable for it enhances the pleasure of sipping water (ideally chilled and often scented with rosewater or incense), which is considered one of the major delights associated with qat-chewing. A Yemeni scholar told me that ideally a man should take a vigorous walk before the party to make himself as hot and thirsty as possible, and that slaking the thirst with water beforehand partly or entirely spoils the pleasure of chewing qat. For that reason, he said, a man bargaining for qat in the market might request a drink of water as an indication that the maximum price he is prepared to pay has been reached. The seller then knows that he must settle or lose the sale (Abd al-Malik al-Maqrami, personal communication).

Among the undesirable consequences of the cooling and drying properties of qat are that it is thought to cause or exacerbate various digestive problems, including constipation. The latter is a common complaint in Yemen, and much use is made of purgatives to 'purify' the system. Some qat is also thought to have a temporary effect on sexual functions because of its 'dryness'. However, the claims in this area are confusing and contradictory, for they include on the one hand loss of libido, temporary impotence, premature ejaculation, and involuntary loss of semen (spermatorrhea) at night or when urinating, and on the other hand an increase in potency and aphrodisiac effects. There is also a belief that only certain types of qat reduce potency, while other types do not.[6] It is possible that varying soil conditions and other factors could account for different kinds of qat having different effects,[7] but it is difficult to accept that this could result in a clear-cut division into two distinct types, one of which does have this sexual (or any other) effect, and one which does not. The belief is probably an example of the universal tendency towards binary classification – to group things in two opposed categories.

There may also be some propaganda element involved. I gained the impression from my fieldwork that it was always the qat of one's neighbours which affected one's sexual capacities (or had any other bad effects), never one's own qat. The qat producers in Razih had a short verse on this subject about the qat of the nearby tribe of Birkan. The fact that Birkani qat was the main competitor to their qat in local markets is probably not irrelevant to its content. The speaker of the verse is supposed to be a woman whose husband has just returned home for the night after chewing Birkani qat:

> *khazant qat Birkani!*   You've been chewing the qat of Birkan!
> *ant fi makanak*   You (sleep) in your place.
> *w-anih fi makani!*   And I in mine!

(There is no sign of a decline in the population of Birkan.)

Obviously some people chew qat which others think has undesirable side-effects or it would not continue to be cultivated and sold. One must conclude therefore that they do not believe it has these effects, or that they have faith in the efficacy of their countermeasures. These include eating plenty of 'hot' foods, especially at the lunch before a qat party (Myntti, 1983: 202). All such foods are thought to be generally beneficial to men's potency quite apart from their possible help in staving off any deleterious sexual effects from chewing qat.

Qat is also thought to cause insomnia and loss of appetite. In some parts of Yemen men are increasingly resorting to drinking large quantities of whisky, ostensibly to facilitate sleep after chewing qat. This practice is likely to cause far greater health problems than qat consumption has ever caused – as many Yemenis realise.[8] The temporary reduction in the desire for food is not regarded as a problem; the main daily meal is at mid-day before qat parties commence, and the appetite has returned by breakfast-time the following morning. In the south of the country husk coffee (*qishr*) or tea is served to the guests who remain when the qat party comes to an end, and these drinks are believed to diminish any undesirable after-effects from qat (Kennedy *et al*, 1980). In Yemen it is anyway customary to offer coffee as a way of drawing any social gathering to a close.[9]

Yemenis do not appear to make any significant connections between qat use and any of the large numbers of serious diseases and illnesses which are endemic in the population; it is not considered to cause or exacerbate them, nor to affect any major cures. Many Yemenis do, however, believe that qat can alleviate the unpleasant symptoms of minor ills such as colds, fevers, headaches, body pains, arthritis and depression (Kennedy *et al*, 1980 and 1983).[10] There is also some evidence of the existence of beliefs in qat having talismanic functions. Forsskål (who visited Yemen in 1763) recorded that Yemenis believed land where qat is planted to be secure from the inroads of plague, and that a twig of qat carried on the person protected them against infection (Hunter, 1877: 140). Also al-Maqrami (1982: 254) mentions a story he collected in which various notables surrounded themselves with qat branches for protection against evil forces; and he notes the belief current in Jabal Sabr that qat placed under the pillow protects the sleeper from a terrifying monster which appears in nightmares.

Yemenis do not therefore regard qat consumption as a major contributory factor to the many debilitating ills from which they suffer, and indeed there are many obvious explanations for the generally low level of health in the population, including polluted water supplies, poor hygiene, inadequate medical facilities and the harsh environment. Nevertheless, Western health experts have repeatedly blamed qat for a variety of specific illnesses and diseases and the generally poor physical condition of the Yemeni people. Until recently there was no adequate scientific evidence available to substantiate or refute these allegations, so a recent article on the medical effects of qat in Yemen is a welcome contribution to this highly emotive subject (Kennedy *et al*, 1983). The evidence presented in the article indicates that the deleterious effects of qat have been greatly exaggerated by Westerners, and supports the view of the majority of Yemenis that qat is a relatively harmless substance.[11]

Western Research on the Effects of Qat
The Yemeni view of the mildly stimulant and non-addictive properties of qat has been upheld by scientific research, which has failed to provide any convincing evidence to support the Western view of qat which dominates the literature. This is relevant to our central concern of trying to understand the factors which sustain the practice of qat consumption, and it is therefore necessary to summarise the main results of recent research in this area.

Western-trained scientists have been trying to determine the chemical constituents and pharmacological effects of qat for nearly a century.[12] However, it is only during the last decade, with improvements in preservation methods, in the speed with which leaves can be transported to laboratories, and in biochemical techniques, that the active ingredients in qat have been isolated and identified. These had previously eluded chemical investigation because of their extreme volatility which causes them to deteriorate or disappear soon after the leaves are picked.

The progress which has recently been made in understanding the chemistry and pharmacology of qat is the result of research conducted since the early 1970s mainly at the United Nations Narcotics Laboratory, at the University of Bern and at Nottingham University. The most recent findings were presented at the international conference on qat held in Madagascar in January 1983, the Proceedings of which were published late that year (Shahandeh *et al*, 1983). This publication contains the most up-to-date summary available at the time of writing of investigations into the composition of qat and its effects.

Recent research has established that qat contains a variety of phenylalky-lamines, polyester-type alkaloids and neutral substances, and several of the principal chemical compounds have now been isolated and identified and had their structures described. However, the work on the chemistry and pharmacology of qat is still far from complete, and many of its chemical constituents have not yet been identified.

Until recently the stimulant effects of qat were attributed to (+)-nor-pseudoephedrine, named 'cathin', although there were doubts as to whether this chemical occurred in quantities sufficient to account for the supposed pharmacological action of qat on humans. Then during the 1970s another compound was discovered in large quantities in fresh qat leaves. This was identified as (−)-*alpha*-propriophenone and was named 'cathinone'. Cathinone appears to have a higher stimulant capacity than cathin and is probably the main active component in qat. It seems to be present only in the young leaves and shoots of the qat plant, which could be one reason why consumers prefer them. Qat also contains (−)-norephedrine, and other active compounds will doubtless be identified after further research. Another compound with possible stimulant properties, cinnamoylethylalmine, may also be present but has not yet been isolated or definitely characterised (Szendrai, 1983: 91–109).

In order to discover the pharmacological effects of cathinone, scientists have extracted the compound from qat leaves and administered it to laboratory animals. This research has shown that (−)cathinone affects the central nervous system of animals in a manner analogous to the effects of (+)amphetamine (though it is structurally different) – that is, it increases heart rate, locomotor activity and oxygen consumption. Cathinone also affects isolated brain tissues from animals in a similar way to amphetamine (Kalix, 1983: 140–3), and it appears to have similar analgesic effects on live animals (Abdullahi *et al*, 1983: 144–7).

It is not however possible to draw firm conclusions about the effects of qat chewing on humans on the basis of the effects of cathinone extract on animals. Animal and human reactions to cathinone could be quite different, the quantities of cathinone ingested by chewing qat leaves have not been measured, and the effects of cathinone could be modified or counteracted by the action of the other chemical constituents of qat. Despite these uncertainties, the principal article on the pharmacology of qat in the Proceedings of the 1983 Madagascar conference contains the following introductory remarks: 'The tendency of many khat [qat] users to *obtain their supply by any means is a clear manifestation of psychic dependence*', and 'cathinone appears to be the main active principle of khat leaves and, especially, the constituent that induces *compulsive* khat consumption.' (Kalix, 1983: 140; my emphases). Like many other writers on qat, Kalix does not consider that cultural and social factors could account for the behaviour he describes as 'compulsive' and interprets as evidence of 'dependence'; it is more surprising, however, that such categorical statements about the addictive properties of qat should be made by a laboratory scientist, for they tend to prejudge the very hypothesis he and others are trying to test.

Compared with the numerous rabbits, monkeys and rats whose reactions to qat and cathinone extract have been studied, very little research has been conducted on human beings. However the Proceedings of the Madagascar conference contains reports on two clinical studies recently conducted on the physiological effects of qat on humans (Nencini et al, 1983: 148–52; Elmi, 1983: 153–8), although both are of limited scope and contain certain methodological deficiencies. Nencini et al were particularly concerned to establish whether qat is addictive (or as they put it, 'is the abuse of khat drug addiction or not?'). They therefore tried to discover whether qat induces tolerance or causes withdrawal symptoms – two of the principal criteria generally applied in the classification of drugs as addictive or non-addictive. Both studies found that after their subjects had chewed qat for several hours there was a significant rise in systolic and diastolic blood pressure, pulse rate, respiratory rate and temperature, and the Nencini et al study also states that several neuroendocrine changes took place. Most of the effects recorded (though not all) are similar to those caused by amphetamines, and the authors conclude that qat causes an 'amphetamine-like type' reaction. However it should be noted that because of the chemical similarity between cathinone and amphetamine, they were specifically testing for such similarities and may therefore have overlooked some effects of a non-amphetamine type (though they note some). Also, as Nencini et al point out (p. 151), the effects they measured are the same as those induced by stress – and chewing qat in a laboratory with various scientific apparatus attached to one's person, and under the scrutiny of medical authority figures must surely count as a stressful situation.

This should be borne in mind when assessing the opinion of Nencini et al (p. 149) on the subject of tolerance. They divided their subjects into two categories, habitual consumers and 'naive' consumers (those who had never chewed qat), and found that the physiological and neuroendocrine changes were greater in the latter than in the former. Because the reactions of habitual consumers were weaker, they conclude that tolerance to qat 'seems to develop'. However, they acknowledge that the naive subjects were probably under greater stress than the habitual consumers, and one would certainly expect a stress reaction from people having to chew their way through a large bunch of leaves for the first time in such a setting. A serious defect in this study is that there is no mention of any monitoring of a control group of non-chewers in identical conditions. These findings cannot therefore be taken as evidence of tolerance.

Nencini et al found no evidence of withdrawal symptoms. The effects of chewing qat had disappeared by the morning after the tests were applied. And in 'basal conditions' no differences were found between habitual and naive consumers in the physiological features which were tested when they were chewing qat. In other words all the subjects returned to normal, and habitual chewers exhibited no permanent changes in their cardiovascular functions or neuroendocrine production from long-term usage. This research is therefore more indicative of qat being non-addictive than addictive.

Elmi wanted to evaluate the influence of qat on physical performance and endurance to fatigue, and found that both were enhanced in his subjects after taking qat. However, his sample was very small (thirty-two), and only three individuals were used as controls in only one of his two main experiments.[13] This cannot therefore be taken as conclusive evidence of total 'similarity of action between khat and amphetamines' (p. 157), although it does appear to support the Yemeni view of qat as an energiser. It should be noted that although cathinone seems to share certain properties with amphetamines, toxic psychosis and aggressive behaviour, commonly caused by high doses of the latter, are rarely if ever caused by qat.

In 1974–76 an important major research project on qat consumption was undertaken in Yemen under the direction of John Kennedy. This project was the first to study qat consumption among a large sample population (over eight hundred people) and within its social and cultural context. The possible stimulant and addictive properties of qat were investigated as part of a wider goal: gathering 'data which would enable an assessment of the major effects of this "institutionalised" drug upon the social life, economics, and the health of the Yemeni people' (Kennedy *et al*, 1980). The project included a study of the effects of qat on a sample of sixty-two men whose psychological and physiological responses were monitored while they chewed qat for periods of four hours – the common duration of an afternoon qat party. The detailed findings of this study have not yet been published, but they inform the first article published on the results of the project (Kennedy *et al*, 1980) which directly addresses the question of whether qat is addictive. The impetus for the Kennedy research came from an awareness of the discrepancy between the opinions of Yemenis and foreigners about the effects of qat. In contrast to many laboratory scientists, therefore, the Kennedy team did not embark on the research with preconceptions about qat being an addictive drug.

The central question addressed in the article is: 'Does the widespread devotion of time, money and activity to qat imply mass drug "abuse" or "addiction" in any precise sense?' As we shall see in the following chapter, it is these aspects of the practice, especially the high proportion of income Yemenis spend on qat, which have led many Western writers to accept the addiction theory of qat consumption. Kennedy *et al* define 'addiction' with reference to opiate addiction, which causes uncontrollable craving for a drug, withdrawal symptoms when deprived of it and the development of tolerance to its effects, so that users need, and compulsively seek, increasing amounts of it.

In 1965 experts of the World Health Organization (who) divided drugs into seven categories according to their characteristics, effects and patterns of use: 1) morphine type; 2) barbiturate – alcohol type; 3) cocaine type; 4) cannabis type; 5) amphetamine type; 6) khat [qat] type; and 7) hallucinogen (lsd) type. They also distinguished between 'physical dependence', characterised by the symptoms described above, and 'psychic dependence', which they vaguely defined as weaker than physical dependence because it does not cause withdrawal symptoms or inevitable tolerance. Both qat and amphetamine were regarded as falling into the category of drugs causing psychic dependence, although tolerance was not thought to develop from qat use as it does from amphetamines (Eddy *et al,* 1965, quoted in Kennedy *et al,* 1980).

Kennedy *et al* challenge this categorisation of qat. First they adduce the evidence of Yemeni qat consumers, many of whom are deprived of qat during long sojourns abroad without suffering any withdrawal symptoms. However, they think it possible that 'a mild form of physiological dependence does result *from extremely heavy use'*, since some heavy consumers reported mild withdrawal symptoms (lethargy, slight trembling, bad dreams) for several days after abstaining from qat consumption. However, they add: '. . . since the percentage of people using [qat] at the very high level is small, true physiological dependence appears to be relatively unimportant in the overall Yemeni picture'.

With regard to the question of tolerance, they point out that the way qat is consumed (by chewing leaves) automatically limits the amount of active ingredients which can be ingested during the several hours of a qat party. The volume of leaves chewed by different individuals varies but not widely. There is also a limit to the quantity of leaves a worker can physically consume in a morning. (They do not mention evening consumers, but these are a very small minority.) In other words the escalating dosages associated with the development of tolerance are in their view less likely to occur because of the temporal, physical and social constraints on individual levels of qat consumption. However, one might add that there are ways in which a consumer *could* consume more qat in a given day were they so minded. Prolonged mastication can easily be avoided by pounding the leaves in a mortar or using an electric grinder – as the toothless do. The fact that these methods are uncommon also suggests that tolerance to qat does not develop.

Kennedy *et al* also consider relevant to the question of tolerance the fact that many new qat consumers only perceive any effects after a period of regular consumption. They think this delay may be explained by a combination of two factors: the effects may only be perceived after a certain level of active ingredients have accumulated in the body (the so-called 'latency effect'), and it may take time for the consumer to learn to identify effects and respond to them. In support of the hypothesis that qat may have a 'latency effect', the writers report an experiment they conducted in Yemen on fifty-five subjects subdivided into categories according to the amount of qat they regularly consumed. The heart rates of these subjects were monitored both before and during a three-hour period chewing qat. It was found that the heaviest consumers started the experiment with the highest heartbeats per minute, with non-chewers the lowest, and the other categories ranged in appropriate order in between, and 'all the groups held their relative positions through the pattern of rise and decline during the three-hour chewing period'. They suggest that 'this provides provisional evidence that each group of chewers began the session with a different and category-consistent level of the active ingredients in their systems, which was proportionately augmented by chewing'. (No mention is made of any monitoring of a control group matched for age, physical size, etc.) It should be noted that these findings contrast with those of Nencini *et al*, discussed above, in which no differences were found in 'basal conditions' between habitual and naive consumers.

On the basis of this experiment and other observations, Kennedy *et al* suggest that a particular kind of 'tolerance' may develop with qat – that is, consumers may regulate their personal consumption so as to achieve or maintain the active ingredients in their bodies at levels which 'feel right' to them. In support of the idea that such a self-regulatory mechanism may be operating, they adduce as evidence the way Yemenis discuss and decide about their consumption levels:

> Most people easily classify themselves as to how much and how often they chew. Without hesitation they say that they chew once a week, three times, or seven. They also make decisions based upon a number of factors, such as income as it relates to cost, future plans, allocation of time, etc. The vast majority of chewers seem to easily control their intake according to rational criteria, which again supports the hypothesis that people try, and generally succeed, to hold steady the levels of active ingredients they judge to be optimum. (Kennedy *et al*, 1980).

This hypothesis is based on a different approach to understanding qat consumption from that taken in this book, though it may not be incompatible with it. Although physiological and pyschological factors undoubtedly influence the individual's experience of qat, they do not necessarily determine his level of consumption. It is rather social and economic factors which are of prime importance in determining individual consumption levels, and account for the variation between individuals in the quantity of qat they regularly consume. For this reason the validity of the hypothesis proposed by Kennedy *et al* when they consider ways of investigating whether qat creates 'dependence' is questionable: 'the degree to which individuals are dependent on qat will be shown in a general sense by the degree to which they will make [financial, material] sacrifices to get it.' The economic data they adduce in relation to this hypothesis will be discussed in Chapter 6.

Kennedy *et al* conclude their article with a discussion of what they call the 'analgesic theory' of qat consumption (and other drug use) – the assumption that people chew qat for escapist reasons, to blot out the pain and discomfort of harsh physical or psychological reality. This is an important issue because many writers on qat consumption have explicitly or implicitly accepted one variation or another of this theory as a satisfactory explanation for the whole phenomenon. The data Kennedy *et al* bring to bear on the subject derive from interviews with a wide range of qat consumers on their personal motivations for chewing qat and the effects they thought qat had had on their various ills and problems. As mentioned, there is a Yemeni belief that qat can have a beneficial effect on various minor ailments.

In analysing this interview data Kennedy *et al* formulated three hypotheses which in their opinion should be substantiated were qat to have analgesic properties, and were those properties a major reason for consuming it. The first of these is: 'Heavy chewers will tend to report more pain-relieving benefits than will light qat chewers.' Their data revealed that seventy-two per cent of qat consumers saw qat 'as providing some kind of relief from pain', while the remaining twenty-eight per cent saw '*no* pain-relieving benefits at all'. Of the group reporting no benefits, thirty per cent were heavy consumers of qat. However, more heavy consumers reported pain-relieving benefits than light chewers, and significantly more light consumers reported experiencing no benefits than did heavy consumers. The authors conclude that this data does provide some provisional support for the above hypothesis. However, they point out that all their findings might demonstrate is that the heavier consumers are more likely to *believe* in the pain-relieving properties of qat, and they also note that these trends might 'simply reflect a tendency to rationalise use'.

The second hypothesis is that 'poor chewers will tend to report more pain-relieving benefits than wealthier chewers', and the third that 'chewers who are more ill will tend to report more pain-relieving benefits than chewers who are less ill'. These hypotheses were formulated on the premise that if qat is a drug which alleviates the distress, discomfort and pain of poverty and illness, then the poor and ill will be more likely to chew qat for that reason. This is a reasonable premise, but it does not follow that the poor and ill will *report* more benefits from chewing qat than the rich and healthy. One would expect the reverse to be the case. And indeed this is what the Kennedy team found: 'contrary to the hypothesis, the wealthier a chewer is, the more he or she is likely to report pain-relieving benefits' and 'well people actually tend to report more pain-relieving benefits than do sicker people'. Also, among those Yemenis interviewed who were suffering from painful illnesses, those with the least painful claimed more pain-relieving benefits from qat than those with the most painful illnesses.

Kennedy *et al* conclude that their results do not support the analgesic theory of qat consumption. However, they do not mention that they very possibly illustrate the existence of a Yemeni *belief* in the analgesic efficacy of qat which includes the notion that it is unreliable and variable in its effects. Given such a belief, we would surely expect the rich and healthy to have greater faith in the beneficial effects of qat than the poor and sick, for among the former qat has clearly 'worked', while among the latter it conspicuously has not! Nevertheless, the conclusion of the Kennedy team seems sound: 'The motivation of attempting to escape hard reality, although it may be important in particular cases, is probably not a major reason for the massive chewing of qat.'

Related to the analgesic theory of qat consumption, and as popular in the literature, is what we might call the 'pleasure principle' theory, according to which qat is consumed entirely because of its pleasurable effects. The Kennedy team also looked at whether their data could provide any support for this theory, and hypothesised that if intellectual stimulation and pleasurable sensations are major motivations for consuming qat, then 'heavy chewers will tend to report more pleasurable experience effects than will light chewers'. This they found to be the case. However, as they suggest may be the case with analgesic effects, but which they do not repeat in respect to this finding, it may simply demonstrate that heavy consumers have a stronger belief in the effects of qat (possibly with consequent placebo effects) or a greater tendency to rationalise qat use in terms of its rewards.

The most interesting information to emerge from the Kennedy *et al* (1980) article is that among the sample interviewed *fourteen per cent of consumers reported feeling no stimulant* (kayf) *effects at all*; and furthermore, of those who reported no stimulant effects, ten per cent were heavy qat consumers and ten per cent were moderate consumers. Although the authors dismiss these percentages as 'insignificant in the overall picture', they may be among their most significant findings for they point to an alternative way of understanding why Yemenis chew so much qat at such expense. If nearly one in seven of all qat consumers are paying large sums of money for a substance which they feel has no effect on them, then is it not possible that what they are paying for is something other than pleasurable stimulation? And is it not therefore equally possible that the majority of consumers who claim to find qat stimulating may actually be *paying* for something apart from its stimulant effects?

All that has so far been revealed by the extensive chemical, pharmacological and medico-social research on qat is that it has rather mild stimulant properties and does not appear to be generally addictive in any accepted medical sense of the term.[14] Nor is there any evidence that qat chewing causes any serious medical effects. In fact the view put forward by doctors of the Aden Medical Service in 1958 still holds good despite twenty-five years of research since then that has been mainly based on contrary assumptions:

> There is no evidence that the qat habit is dangerously injurious to health. It does cause constipation, but it has never been suggested that it may seriously damage the body as may tobacco, which is alleged to cause lung cancer, or alcohol, which may cause liver complaints. Qat does not create an addiction, like opium or hashish, in that those who are suddenly deprived of it, do not suffer physical consequences. Deprivation may cause mental distress, but that is all. Confirmed qat eaters who are deprived of the leaf, when they visit foreign countries, quickly adapt themselves to its absence. (Aden Colony, 1958: 10–11 quoted in Serjeant, 1983: 172).

It is clear that the orthodox explanation of qat consumption according to which the pleasurable or addictive properties of qat have Yemenis helplessly in their thrall is inadequate, and that an alternative anthropological explanation of the practice is required. There is of course an anthropology to be written of all 'drug' consumption practices; even heroin consumption takes place in specific social contexts, in specific groups and for cultural and social reasons, as well as for reasons of a psychological or physiological nature. However, if the pleasurable and addictive properties of a drug are known to be powerful, considerable weight can be placed on medical, physical explanations for its consumption. But in the case of a weak substance such as qat, we must lean more heavily on social explanations for its popularity and expense.

Unless we are prepared to believe that Yemenis place a disproportionately high value on a rather low-grade sensual pleasure, comparable perhaps to coffee drinking, the high price paid for qat cannot be entirely or even mainly explained in terms of its stimulant effects. There is an important distinction to be drawn between the reason something is *consumed*, and the reason for a *high monetary value* being placed on it. Obviously Yemenis chew qat socially rather than, say, lettuce or parsley, because of its stimulant effects. And those who experience its effects appreciate and value them. But not surely to the extent of spending a quarter or a third of their incomes for them? An alternative view is that the high expenditure on qat and its increasing popularity are better understood if they are seen less as a reflection of the value Yemenis place on qat's stimulant effects and more of the value they place on the social effects of being a qat consumer.

4

Attitudes and Explanations

The Views of Early Foreign Visitors

Most recent writings on qat consumption by Westerners present the whole practice in a highly unfavourable light. This critical attitude seems to have developed mainly during this century. Early foreign visitors to Yemen were tolerant or indifferent to the practice and contented themselves with factual descriptions of qat parties and of their personal experiences of attending them and sampling the leaf for themselves. Niebuhr, for example, the leader of the famous Danish expedition to Yemen of 1763, provides the following benign description of the first time he tried qat – when received by the Governor of Taizz:

> When we were seated he presented us with qishr [husk coffee] and pipes following the custom of the country. Here and there on the sofa there were several bundles of qat, young shoots of a certain tree which the Arabs chew as a pastime, similar to our custom of taking snuff and of the Indians' custom of chewing betel. But we had not yet had the chance of tasting this Arabian delicacy.

Elsewhere he notes: 'This delicacy was not at all to our taste. Moreover, it seemed that qat prevented sleep and had a dessicating effect. Nevertheless every well-bred Arab ... must love it.' (Niebuhr, 1776, Vol I: 299; and 1774: 51; my translations). Few recent writers have referred to qat by so appreciative a term as 'delicacy' (*friandise*) or compared qat consumption with more familiar and 'acceptable' consumption practices.

The Frenchman Botta, who visited Yemen in 1837, recognised the beneficial effects of qat and clearly found it to his own liking:

> The evening of my arrival in Maamara and constantly thereafter, Shaykh Hasan, in conformity with the custom of his country, sent me a packet of qat branches. These are the branches of a tree ... originally, like coffee, from Abysinnia, which is cultivated with great care. It is the shoots and most tender leaves which are eaten, and they have a stimulating, even slightly intoxicating quality, and relieve fatigue, prevent sleep, and make one enjoy passing most of the night in calm and sociable conversation.

There are no men who sleep as little as Yemenis, yet despite this their health does not appear to suffer for there are many examples of longevity in the country. The stimulant properties of qat are such that messengers carrying urgent missives often walk several consecutive days and nights without taking any other sustenance than the leaves of this plant – a packet of which they carry with them to eat en route. As for myself, I quickly became accustomed to using it, and ended up getting great pleasure from its gentle stimulation and the vivid dreams which followed. (Botta, 1841: 45–6; my translation).

An English traveller, Cruttenden, who visited Yemen in 1836, the year before Botta, alludes to qat consumption as follows:

The Sanaanis are very much addicted to chewing the leaf of a tree which they call 'kat'. It appears by their account to exhilarate and produce appetite; it also causes great thirst, and if taken in large quantities, will bring on spasms. It is the never-failing accompaniment to the breakfast or dinner; and, from long use, appears to be indispensable. (Cruttenden, 1838).

Cruttenden got some of his facts wrong. There is no evidence that qat causes spasms, nor that it was ever taken with meals. However, despite these errors, and his apparent assumption that Yemenis are 'dependent' on qat in the modern medical sense, he was not led to disparage qat consumption as a cultural practice like recent writers.

One of the earliest explicitly critical descriptions of qat consumption is that provided by Wyman Bury, who visited Yemen in the last days of the second Turkish occupation of the country just before World War I. His account mentions most of the health and economic grounds on which later writers condemned qat, and sets the tone for subsequent treatments of the subject.

Unfortunately, all but the poorest classes are addicted to the kat habit, more or less; *the degree of addiction being in proportion to the amount procurable.* . . . The leaves and tender shoots are chewed for their exhilarant properties. At first there is a pleasurable sensation of intellectual ability, and parties of kat-eaters will sit up all night discussing anything and everything. By-and-by the habitué *finds himself incapable of clear and consecutive thought* without the herb, and its deprivation engenders much mental discomfort and nervous irritability. Further addiction induces marked symptoms such as constipation, insomnia and, finally, impotency. The *teeth are much affected, becoming permanently discoloured and loose,* for the gums become flaccid. By this time *the victim of the habit is incapacitated for real thought or efficient work by any accidental deprivation,* which is bound to occur at intervals, for the supply of kat is by no means regular, and it will not keep.

In cases of slight addiction, *the only marked failing is that of memory,* and many who thoroughly enjoy kat, but can only get it in small quantities at long intervals, are very little affected. There is, however, always a certain mental 'fuzziness', even after a short bout; the natural reaction after a strong, nervous stimulant. . . .

I have had several cases of *habitual addiction* through my hands, usually in advanced stages, when suffering the pangs of deprivation or alarmed at their own symptoms. . . . All those who indulge in kat admit its bad effects, but *say they cannot do without it*. It permeates every class that can afford it, and many that cannot, for *sometimes a man will starve himself and his family to get it.*

Women do not often succumb to the vice, and when they do are *worse than the men, for they have less self-restraint*, and it makes them very irritable. Besides this, theirs is a hard enough life even without that handicap. . . .

During all the years I have known the Aden hinterland, I never saw anything like the *general addiction to this vice* as I have met in Yemen, during the last year or two. There, *the habit has become a serious social evil, undermining the mental and physical health of the native population; the foe alike of thrift and industry.* (Bury, 1915: 152–4; my emphases).

This account was presumably one of the main sources for Hess's comments on qat in the authoritative columns of the 1927 *Encyclopaedia of Islam:* 'All accounts agree that the use of kat, as ordinarily taken, which has become regular in all classes of society in Yemen, *undermines the physical and moral health* of the people and also does the *greatest damage from the economic point of view.*' This view is restated in even stronger terms in the revised article in the new edition of the *Encyclopaedia* of 1976 (under the same author's name) where qat consumers are referred to as 'addicts' (a term not used in the first edition). However, a positive effect of the practice is mentioned: 'In this respect [that it is consumed at social gatherings] kat is a factor making for social cohesion and peace, but this is outweighed by its harmful effects . . . all reports state unanimously that the habitual use of kat, despite its supposed prophylactic qualities, *ruins the physical and mental health of people* and, from an economic point of view, causes widespread damage. [my emphases]'. It is interesting to note the switch from 'moral' health being undermined to 'mental' health being ruined, a reflection perhaps of the liberal sixties. Later the article refers to 'the ravages caused by this narcotic', a turn of phrase presumably derived from El-Attar (1964) (see below), whose book is cited in the article.

In 1922 Yemen received a visit from the Arab-American traveller Amin Rihani, who suffered severe culture-shock on first attending a qat party. The addiction theory of qat consumption is reinforced by his purple description of the setting:

But worse than the fear [of being held a prisoner] was the *disgust* I felt when the guard admitted us into the presence of the Ameer [prince]. Imagine yourself in a 12 × 18 room with a very low ceiling, whose small windows, except one, are closed; whose floor is covered with grass and straw; *whose atmosphere is like that of a hasheesh den* of Cairo; and around whose walls are seated a score of bearded, turbaned and robed Zioud [Zaydis], all chewing at something, and some of whom are smoking the *mada'ah* [water-pipe] . . . We had to squeeze ourselves . . . between the two truculent beards and feel, in our boots and breeches, as we tried to squat or sit flat, the most miserable of men. (Rihani, 1930(b): 34).

(Why, one wonders, were they still wearing their boots when it is customary in Yemen, as elsewhere in the Middle East, to remove footwear at the door before entering a room?)

In 1937–38 Hugh Scott travelled in Yemen as a member of the British Museum (Natural History) Expedition to south-west Arabia, and in the account of his visit (Scott, 1942) follows Bury and Hess in assuming qat to have harmful effects on the health and economic welfare of Yemenis, and also refers to qat consumers as 'addicts' (p. 95). He calls the plant 'this baneful little tree' because it occupies land which in his opinion would have otherwise been cultivated with coffee, and asserts: 'When the habit is indulged in more than very little, harmful reactions follow. The poor general health of some people may well be due to this cause' (p. 295). In a discussion of the political roles of *sayyid*s, he associates qat consumption with idleness: 'Noble birth is not a necessary qualification for high office . . . and many of the blue-blooded are unemployed. Such men have little or no occupation save to stroll about the streets or gather together in the *mifrajes* or reception-rooms of friends, where for hours at a time they converse, blow smoke through the water-pipes, and chew *qat*' (p. 131). He also implies a connection between qat consumption and mental instability in his description of a surprise encounter outside Sanaa: 'Returning to the path, to our dismay we found ourselves followed on foot from the city by . . . an unpleasant-looking young man, with *a wild expression in his eyes as though he were slightly mad or intoxicated with qat*' (p. 148; my emphasis).

Scott was responsible for the following florid passage headed 'Addiction to qat' which appeared in the handbook on Western Arabia produced by the British Admiralty during World War II as a guide for Allied Forces, and which became the best reference work on the area after the War when restrictions on its circulation were lifted.[1]

The habit of chewing the young leaves, leaf-buds, and tender shoots [of qat] which has so largely *taken possession* of the people of south-west Arabia, is a *noxious form of drug addiction* . . . As many as from twenty to forty persons may be crowded into an ill-ventilated room. Windows and doors are shut and several hubble-bubble pipes are lit. The participants sit around the walls, each with a bundle of qat and a spittoon in front of him. When a man has chewed for some time, swallowing only the juice of the plant, his cheeks become *uncomfortably distended* with a green paste of chewed leaves (the Yemenis speak of 'storing' rather than chewing or eating qat); this paste is then ejected with the aid of a finger, into the spittoon. The man then *drinks noisily* from a cruse of water, swilling out the mouth and also often swallowing water to assuage thirst; he then begins to chew again. During the afternoon the stale atmosphere becomes even more vitiated, and the participants break into a sweat, without which the party is not thought successful. . . . Qat chewing produces no staggering gait, though some of the addict's symptoms simulate alcoholic intoxication. An addict at the height of his bout is (in Dr Petrie's words) 'a *wild looking, dull-witted gaping automaton*' (British Admiralty, 1946: 462–3; my emphases).

Here again, as in the accounts of Bury and Hess, qat is portrayed as having a harmful effect on the intellect – the exact opposite of the case, as we saw in the previous chapter. Harold Ingrams, who was a Political Officer in the Aden Protectorate in the 1930s, realised that qat was intellectually stimulating and did not cause feeble-mindedness, but he appears to have considered that you had to be feeble-minded to chew it:

It must be a very acquired taste, for I have tried a leaf or two and thought it was filthy, but when you have acquired that taste it makes you feel a devil of a dog so long as the feeling lasts. It is not soporific, but on the contrary wakens you up and sharpens the intellect – at least so addicts tell me. *Most of the addicts, I confess, need a sharpening to their wits, and the pity is that the effects last such a short time*' (Ingrams 1966: 106; my emphasis).

This judgement was presumably based mainly on Ingrams' contact with Yemenis in Aden, although he visited Yemen in 1941 with his wife Doreen Ingrams who later published her own critical comments on qat.

[Yemen] might have been a far more prosperous community than the Hadhramis as they lived in a fertile country, but there was at that time no apparent desire to leave the Middle Ages for the twentieth century and benefit from the know-how of other countries. One reason for the apathy of the average Yemeni was, I am sure, due to their addiction to qat . . . *the most debilitating, time-wasting scourge of Yemen*. The leaves of the shrub are chewed to give the addict a feeling of being on top of the world, of being able to solve all problems, but the after effects are lassitude, apathy and depression. Every Yemeni who could afford it, and most of them *got hold of qat somehow,* spent the afternoons with his friends *chewing, spitting, drinking water and chewing again*. These sessions inspired *a great deal of talk but no action* and I saw no possibility of Yemen developing into a prosperous modern country so long as qat was allowed to *exhaust the people's talents and sap their vitality*' (Ingrams, 1970: 113; my emphases).

The above writers shared an ethnocentric failure to see parallels with Western consumption practices, which led them to devalue the social importance of qat parties. If Yemenis sat in leather armchairs smoking briar pipes and sipping whisky instead of reclining on the floor chewing leaves and smoking water pipes, their conversational gatherings might not have been dismissed as a waste of time. These writers, and others, clearly found the ambiance and behaviour of qat parties aesthetically distasteful, and this fuelled their conviction that qat is an addictive drug – as well as their underlying view of Yemenis as inferior, self-destructive, stupid and even mad. They failed to realise that most of the cultural features of qat parties are customary in any social gathering in Yemen. People always range themselves round the walls of a room and sit on mats or mattresses on the floor which, with pillows, are the standard (and very comfortable) Yemeni furnishings; Yemenis usually sit closely packed together as they require less personal space than Westerners and do not recoil from physical contact but seek it; they also prefer a warm stuffy atmosphere and abhor drafts of cold air as they believe it causes sickness; it is also normal to consume food and drink noisily as a signal of appreciation; and spitting is condoned as a means of purifying the system. By the denigration of these locally acceptable customs and the implication that they are peculiar to qat parties, qat has been portrayed as having a deleterious effect on normal standards of propriety. But if anything there is a more formal observance of good etiquette at qat parties than at other social gatherings. Finally it should be said that the custom of 'storing' qat in the cheek, specific to qat chewing, causes no discomfort to Yemenis though it has discomforted fastidious foreigners.

These cultural practices have figured less in Western criticisms of qat consumption in recent publications of a more scholarly nature, though they continue to be invoked in the popular press – sometimes in an unpleasantly racist manner. A recent newspaper article, for example, creates an offensive animal-like image of Yemenis by the punning title 'Yemenis hooked on chewing the qat' (i.e. the cud), and goes on to repeat the familiar litany of distended cheeks, slurping of water and rooms 'furnished only with a few mattresses' to reinforce the view that Yemenis are uncultured, anti-social drug addicts (Agence France Press, 1982).

The Views of Academics from the 1960s
From the 1960s a number of academic publications have appeared on Yemen, most of which allude to qat and some of which are devoted to some aspect of the subject. In this new generation of writings we find a continuation of the negative attitude towards qat of the travellers and officials of the preceding period, with most writers assuming that qat is an addictive drug with harmful effects on the individual and society. But as a result of increased awareness of development issues, greater emphasis is placed on the supposedly deleterious effects which the consumption and production of qat are having on the economy and welfare of Yemen.

During the 1970s, with the opening up of Yemen to foreign researchers after the civil war, comments on qat consumption also begin to appear by social scientists, mainly anthropologists, whose opinions are based on a deeper understanding and appreciation of Yemeni culture and values. However, most of these writers also accept the drug theory of qat consumption, in one form or another, which leads them to speculate on what psychological or social factors predispose Yemenis to institutionalised drug use. But they display a greater awareness of the complexity of the practice, and although they mostly agree that it is economically undesirable, acknowledge that it also has positive social aspects.

In an influential book on the 'under-development' of Yemen published in 1964, economist El-Attar deduces from the widespread consumption of qat 'in all classes of society' that the practice must be sustained by different factors in different classes. These are, he suggests, that 'the poor want to forget their misery, the idle rich to kill time'. The result is that 'from midday to sunset, *all activity ceases* and Yemenis are plunged into an *ecstatic torpor*' (El-Attar, 1964: 124; my translation and emphases). He denounces qat as an 'addiction' which constitutes a 'veritable national scourge (*fléau*)', and asserts that qat is displacing coffee on the terraces, diverts cash from both the purchase of food and of instruments of production, stimulates corruption, halts production and causes many hours to be 'squandered' unproductively, forms a barrier between men and women encouraging homosexuality, and causes various medical problems with 'disastrous' long-term consequences (El-Attar, 1964: 122–6).

El-Attar's ludicrous idea that sexual segregation and homosexuality can be attributed to qat died the death it deserved, but his implication that qat is some kind of 'opium of the masses' was later taken up by political scientist Halliday:

> Chewers claim that qat, by stimulating, helps the chewer to work and to concentrate, but the social nexus within which the chewing takes place is one of *enforced and routinized lethargy* as groups of men lie around chatting from two to eight. In this way qat, by blocking off the whole of every afternoon with *institutionalised idleness*, i.e. unemployment, greatly contributes to Yemen's problems. But under the Imams, qat produced for domestic consumption also undermined the country, by displacing the growing of coffee and thus undercutting the little export earning Yemen received. For the peasant himself it was a *special bane*, since however meagre his income he would spend a sizeable portion of his earnings on qat rather than on food for himself and his family or on tools for production. While it was obviously in part *a reflection of the misery of life under the Imams*, the prevalence of qat also contributed in its turn to this misery and to the deterioration of the North Yemeni economy. (Halliday, 1974: 89; my emphases).

Most of El-Attar's criticisms of qat were stated earlier by Bury, Scott and others, and they have gained an increasingly respectable pedigree through repetition in numerous books, theses and reports – but not by the production of substantiating evidence (see, for example, Wenner, 1967: 26). Most writers agree that the time Yemenis spend chewing qat would be better spent in gainful employment and regard money spent on qat as completely wasted when it could be usefully invested in financially rewarding ways (see, for example,

Kopp, 1982: 238). They do not realise that Yemenis are investing their money usefully in *socially* productive ways which pay non-material and less immediate or obvious dividends.

The first anthropologist to write on qat in Yemen was Joseph Chelhod, who visited the country in 1969 (Chelhod, 1972). Chelhod agrees that qat consumption is a 'serious drug problem' because it has assumed such 'alarming proportions' and is consumed 'to excess'. Following El-Attar, he thinks that the scale of qat consumption has rendered it a 'veritable social scourge' with 'catastrophic' consequences for the national economy, but he also recognises that qat consumption has positive aspects.

Chelhod emphasises the great importance of qat parties in daily life and in connection with major events of the life cycle, calling them the 'pivot on which the essence of social life turns'. In contrast to many other writers, Chelhod describes the aesthetic aspects of the *mafraj* and the manners of the participants with appreciation and respect. In his opinion, qat parties, unlike alcohol parties, combine gaiety with decorum, and he contrasts their 'warmth and spontaneity' with 'ordinary' (presumably urban or Western) parties, which he sees as 'cold and superficial' occasions where guests are 'aloof and ill-at-ease'.

This benign view of qat as a social lubricant leads Chelhod to suggest an explanation for qat consumption in Yemen, and to conclusions about the social effects of the custom. In a variation of the 'opium of the masses' view of qat consumption of El-Attar and Halliday, in which qat allays the misery of poverty and oppression, he sees qat as assuaging the hunger for entertainment of a rural population plagued with boredom. (This is the opposite of Halliday's and Ingrams' (1970) contention that qat forces idleness and lethargy upon its consumers):

> In an essentially rural society which has long been closed-off, for which
> the thousands of recreations in the world are meaningless words, which
> only knew rudimentary music and the artistic and cultural development
> of which had ceased over a thousand years ago, in which there was much
> leisure time yet few amusements, where alcohol is forbidden and mixed
> parties prohibited, in this tedious society qat is a real balm, consoling and
> pacifying. (Chelhod, 1972; my translation).

This social-psychological explanation of qat consumption rests on several untenable assumptions. Rural life is not one of unmitigated dullness, any more than it was, as other versions had it, unrelievedly miserable or oppressive. But in any case qat consumption has always been heaviest in the towns – where, incidentally, sophisticated lute music was until recently a common accompaniment to qat parties (not that 'rudimentary' music is not equally popular and entertaining). And if high levels of qat consumption are symptomatic of a shortage of 'amusements', why has it greatly increased during the recent inundation of Yemen by radios, television sets, motor cars, books and newspapers?

Chelhod's view that qat consumption fulfils certain human needs is the basis for a functionalist interpretation of its social effects. At parties qat ensures that 'good humour is the rule, everyone is attentive, in a friendly mood, responding spontaneously to whatever his neighbour says'. Qat thus 'creates a truly fraternal feeling among the consumers. Barriers fall and constraints disappear, giving way to understanding and harmony.' Because of all these effects qat favours 'the development of intimate relations between [qat party] participants' and 'contributes to the maintenance of social cohesion' (Chelhod, 1972; my translations).

Chelhod is correct in emphasising the importance of qat parties for strengthening human relationships, but in common with most later writers he exaggerates the part played in this process by qat. Such convivial gatherings are possible, as elsewhere, without the consumption of qat; and Yemeni society did not fall apart when all that most people consumed socially was husk coffee or tea. Indeed in many rural districts, such as Razih, the latter are the main refreshments consumed at women's parties, which are no less lacking in warmth and bonhomie than those held by men.

In 1972 another anthropologist, Gerald Obermeyer, visited Yemen as part of a World Health Organization mission with the aim of studying sociocultural and economic aspects of qat and evaluating the need for more research on the subject. (The research conducted under John Kennedy, discussed in the previous chapter, grew out of this short preliminary study.) Like Chelhod and most anthropologists who worked in Yemen subsequently, Obermeyer (1973) emphasised the importance of qat parties as 'a central feature of the culture and economy of the Yemen' which 'is functionally and intricately related to other realms of society: the economy, the family, and the individual himself'. He correctly categorises qat parties as 'commensal rituals' which like 'the primitive feast, Holy Communion and the modern dinner invitation', bring people together and augment social solidarity.

Because his informants said that they could do without qat, he challenged the prevailing doctrine that qat is addictive and considered alternative explanations for the custom, suggesting that the economic aspect of qat consumption was of central significance. He noted that individual expenditure on qat increased according to wealth, that there were differences in the quality of qat consumed by rich and poor, and that '[the quality of] the qat branch itself is an indicator of class and social mobility in the Yemen!' – all vital perceptions for understanding the practice. Obermeyer also questioned certain criticisms of qat, suggesting that the health hazards had been exaggerated (which has been borne out by the research of the Kennedy team), and challenging the common view that qat is the cause of the decline in coffee production. He also pointed out some of the beneficial economic effects of qat cultivation in comparison with coffee (see Chapter 2).

In 1977 historian Maxime Rodinson published an essay on qat originally intended to update the Hess article in the second edition of the *Encyclopaedia of Islam*. Rodinson acknowledges that the stimulant effects of qat are mild, non-addictive and relatively harmless, but from this he concludes that qat consumption is the more harmful economically:

Paradoxically, it is the relatively benign nature of the noxious effects of qat in conjuction with its cost which makes it a real social scourge . . . the consumption of any other drug costing the same money would quickly lead the consumer to madness or death. But with qat the poison (*intoxication*) can be continued for many years with noxious effects on health which are relatively slow and benign. It is above all the social effects which are catastrophic. (Rodinson, 1977; my translation)

In support of this argument he repeats the allegation that expenditure on qat leads to malnutrition at home, and that this in turn leads to prostitution, theft, delinquency and corruption. However, there is no evidence to support this Dickensian view of stricken familes driven to the gutter by the self-indulgent vices of their providers. And his suggestion that the desire for qat leads to a 'disinterest in bettering the conditions of life' is equally wide of the mark. A striking feature of Yemeni society is the widespread impatience for technological development, and the enthusiasm and vigour with which people are struggling to improve their material conditions.

An illuminating perspective on qat consumption as a sociological phenomenon was provided by Gerholm in the first anthropological mono-graph to be published on a Yemeni community (Gerholm, 1977). Gerholm's main aim is to show how status inequality was maintained in the Highland town of Manakha in 1974–75 when he did his field research. He argues that the social hierarchy based on birth and occupation was constantly reaffirmed because it was 'massively present in a host of daily events', rendering the expression and emergence of any alternative model of society difficult or impossible (p. 160). What is relevant to our subject is Gerholm's description of the qat party as one of the main daily events at which the inequalities in the social order were expressed and consolidated (pp. 176–185). Although it was beyond the scope of Gerholm's study to focus specifically on qat consumption, he advanced the understanding of the phenomenon by his sensitive analysis of the structure, symbolism and behavioural dynamics of the qat party (see Chapter 8).

In 1978 the first monograph devoted entirely to the subject of qat in Yemen was published by Schopen. It provides information collected by Schopen in Yemen in 1974–75, and draws from a scattered and often inac-cessible literature covering a wide range of topics, including the history of qat, qat types, Yemeni dialogues on the permissibility of qat, and qat poetry. Schopen's approach is primarily ethnographical and descriptive, and he does not offer an explanation of qat consumption, although in a section entitled 'The significance and function of the qat session' (Schopen, 1978: 142–4) he suggests a number of its psychological and social effects. Presumably on the basis of idealised descriptions of the effects of qat by Yemenis (see Chapter 3), he asserts that qat stimulates psychological regression, releases inhibitions and replaces perceptions of reality with dreams and desires. As a result people feel in harmony with each other, feelings of omnipotence are generated by 'psychic group processes', and disputes are settled (a remarkably realistic activity for people up in the clouds).

A recent anthropological article on qat by Varisco (forthcoming) addresses the centrally important question of why qat consumption in Yemen has greatly increased. Varisco notes that increased consumption is clearly related to the rise in household incomes, but realises that it is still necessary to explain why so much of the new money is being spent on qat. The explanation, he suggests, lies in the social and ideological changes being brought about by the new economic and political conditions. He cites specifically the erosion of the old symbols of descent status, and the greater social and economic mobility upward and downward of those formerly at the top and bottom of the traditional social hierarchy. 'Members of the lowest status groups have raised their incomes and shifted to new employment opportunities. Members of the former elites no longer have automatic prestige.'

Varisco argues that these changes have led to a kind of cultural or national identity crisis which is 'heightened in the Yemeni context because of the rapid and condensed pace of development and the exposure to new lifestyles through male migration and the media. It is no longer sufficient to be from a certain tribe, town or region in Yemen; there is now a need to define oneself as Yemeni vis-à-vis other Arab cultures and other nationalities.' This need he sees as being fulfilled by qat chewing, 'an act which is distinctively Yemeni and shared with no other Arab culture'. Qat consumption has, he thinks, 'taken on a new meaning as a cultural identity marker rather than simply a pastime for the idle rich or the pious saint . . . Yemenis of all social categories can focus on qat chewing as a symbolic marker at a time when it has become important to have a collective identity as a Yemeni confronting a context of rapid and potentially hostile change.'

Varisco asks the right questions about qat consumption and seeks the answers in the right context – that of a society undergoing fundamental changes which have created uncertainties about social identity – but his social-psychological theory is unconvincing. The image he evokes of Yemenis defiantly chewing qat leaves to maintain their national self-confidence and cultural identity in the face of encroachments and influences from the outside world is difficult to recognise. Although all Yemenis have become aware of the relative material simplicity of their traditional culture through television, mass imports, development programmes, travel abroad and contacts with foreigners, most realise that there are sound historical reasons for their technological backwardness. Insofar as it is legitimate to speak of 'national character', Yemenis are a confident people who are adapting to the demands of their revolutionary new economic conditions with great ingenuity and resilience. It is hard to believe that they would be spending so much money to remind themselves and others that they and their culture are distinctive and valuable when there is no evidence that they seriously doubt it. Varisco's approach to qat consumption is nevertheless an advance on previous theories in that he perceives the act of consuming qat to be a symbolic statement about identity, and that the new social conditions have increased the 'need' for such statements.

International Concern

All the main qat countries of Arabia and Africa have at one time or another tried to control or prevent the consumption and cultivation of qat. The various measures attempted include taxation on qat, registration of qat users, restriction of consumption to certain days of the week (in PDRY), making qat use illegal (in Saudi Arabia and Somalia), and encouraging alternative crops. However, there is no evidence that any of these measures have ever been completely successful, even in Saudi Arabia where penalties for chewing qat are more severe than for drinking alcohol.[2]

Concern about the 'qat problem' has also generated considerable activity at the international level. Since the 1930s many reports have been written and conferences held under the respective auspices of the League of Nations, the Commission on Narcotic Drugs of the United Nations, the United Nations Commission and Division of Narcotics, the Pan-Arab Organisation for Social Defence, the World Health Organization (WHO), and the Food and Agriculture Organisation (FAO). Most recently, in January 1983, an international conference on qat use was organised in Madagascar by the International Council on Alcohol and Addictions (ICAA). Substantial resources have also been poured into research on the chemistry and pharmacology of qat by certain of these organisations. It is therefore of more than academic importance to try to achieve a better understanding of qat consumption, in Yemen and elsewhere, for national and international effort and expenditure might be better directed or even unnecessary.

The anti-qat measures of governments are not of course necessarily motivated by philanthropic concern for the welfare of their people or by the conviction that qat is entirely harmful. However, in the prevailing climate of opinion any Third World government wanting aid from international development and welfare agencies must voice anti-qat sentiments and demonstrate the intent to control or eradicate qat. Governments may also in reality be for or against qat for politico-economic reasons which rarely surface in dialogues couched in the dominant idioms of 'welfare' and 'development'.

Official opposition to qat may actually stem from the fear that the qat-based affluence of producing areas might undermine the centralising endeavours of the state. On the other hand governments may favour qat if they can levy taxes on production or sales. They may also be subject to internal pressures to allow production and consumption from powerful landowners, or from local political leaders who represent the interests of qat traders or qat-growers in the producing areas, not to mention consumers. It is also worth noting that the widespread international laboratory activity, compilation of agency reports and organisation of conferences constitute a lively subsidiary qat industry with its own vested interests and inflationary momentum.

Yemeni Views

Qat has never been prohibited in Yemen on religious grounds (apart from a brief period in the sixteenth century), though religious specialists have debated the permissibility of its consumption for centuries. Qat is not mentioned in the Quran, presumably because it was unknown in Arabia in the seventh century. A constant feature of religious opposition to qat has been disquiet at the ritually polluting aspects of spermatorrhea (as previously mentioned, qat is believed to cause involuntary loss of semen). This complaint is of concern to Muslims because of the religious necessity for ritual cleanliness before prayer. Some critics also voiced opposition to qat on the grounds that it had bad effects on the mind, and even asserted that it was intoxicating and therefore automatically forbidden (*haram*) to Muslims. However this claim was never upheld. Other religious specialists advocated qat on the grounds that it heightened the contemplative powers and staved off sleep, enabling the pious to engage in long nights of prayer. Sufi mystics of the Shafi'i doctrine believed that qat facilitated the ecstasy and clarity of perception which bring about intense union with God, and therefore regarded it as a divine gift.[3]

The ambivalent or conflicting attitudes to qat among the religious elite, and also to an extent among the general population, are reflected in a number of adages and sayings. For example: 'Qat is the food of the upright/pious'; 'God has troubled the Jews with '*araqi* [an alcoholic beverage made from grapes] and the Muslims with qat!'; 'Qat is nice, but there is nothing worse than it!'; and 'Qat in the morning, not girls in the morning' (presumably an allusion to the effect some qat is believed to have on sexual performance) (Serjeant, 1983: 172–3). There are many Yemenis who say they dislike the custom of chewing qat, usually because of the expense, yet feel pressured to do so. Many migrants who have spent a long period abroad without chewing qat announce that they will not be taking up the habit again when they return home. Whether or not they really mean it, they invariably submit to social pressure and soon become regular participants at qat parties (see Chapter 8).

During this century Yemeni doubts about the desirability of qat consumption have been increasingly couched in political and economic terms. Some officials and intellectuals have expressed concern about the effects on the family of high expenditure on qat, while others have pointed out the economic advantages to traders and landowners (Schopen, 1978: 181–2). During the three decades preceding the revolution of 1962, qat became a symbol of the hated Imamate to intellectuals who opposed the royalist regime. Presumably this was partly because Imam Yahya had publicised his approval of qat in a poetic eulogy which was widely disseminated in Yemen (Rihani, 1930b: 211), and perhaps also because approval of qat could easily be portrayed as equivalent to political conservatism and resistance to modernisation. The famous republican polemicist, Muhammad Mahmud al-Zubayri, wrote that 'the devil takes the shape of the qat tree', and explicitly associated the alleged evils of qat with the evils, as he saw it, of the Imamate (al-Maqrami, 1982: 235). Key republican activists had been influenced in their political views by sojourns in Egypt, British Aden and elsewhere, and it can be assumed that they were affected by Western attitudes towards qat so as to despise one of their own most important cultural practices.

Since the civil war international opinion has weighed ever more heavily on Yemeni officialdom. The Yemen government is dependent on foreign aid and officially dedicated to improving national health care, achieving greater agricultural self-sufficiency and promoting rapid economic development. Whatever the private views of its officials, it can hardly condone a crop and a practice which are almost universally believed to be ruining the health of its people and to be retarding Yemen's economic progress by diverting cash from 'productive investment' and monopolising the best agricultural terraces. It is not therefore surprising that the policy of the successive republican administrations of the post civil war period – promulgated in the first two Five Year Plans of 1976–77 and 1981–82 – has been to reduce qat production and consumption. However only a few ineffective attempts have been made to implement this policy.

An attempt to reduce qat cultivation was made soon after the civil war by Prime Minister Muhsin al-Aini, but his measures were vigorously opposed by political leaders in the producing areas, which contributed to his fall from power in 1972 (Schopen, 1978; 174ff; al-Aini, personal communication). Al-Aini was unusual among government officials in not being a qat consumer, possibly because he had lived outside Yemen for many years. This abstention from the central social activity of Yemeni life was considered so unusual that at the time he was trying to implement his anti-qat policy, a Yemeni doctor facetiously remarked to Obermeyer: 'Everyone in the Yemen chews qat and those who do not are known by name – the Prime Minister and myself' (Obermeyer 1973). In the late 1970s the government also moved the thriving qat market of Sanaa into the nearby countryside, ostensibly to exert control on consumption, but this was so obviously a futile measure (the qat market soon returned to Sanaa) that it was possibly window-dressing for foreign observers. The government also extracts taxes on qat by setting up road-blocks on the main roads into the cities, but a great deal of qat is sold in small towns or in the countryside where taxation is difficult to enforce.

The Yemen government has been embarrassed by what authoritative outside experts have defined as their 'qat problem',[4] and at their inability to stem the recent increase in the consumption and production of qat (though other governments with more developed administrative infrastructures have not had conspicuously greater success). This embarrassment has been manifested in an ambivalent public stance. On the one hand qat is publicly denounced and on the other the extent of 'the problem' has been systematically played down. Anti-qat campaigns have been intermittently waged in the press and on television, yet a popular weekly television programme ('Surah Min Biladi') depicting daily life in different parts of the country is unable to mention qat. During much of the programme on Razih the screen was unavoidably filled with qat trees, but qat was never mentioned. As the camera panned across the verdant terraces the commentator delivered a eulogy on the virtues of Yemeni coffee. And when the programme visited Jabal Hufash, where virtually the sole crop is qat, the usual section on the means of livelihood was completely omitted (Tim Morris, personal communication).

International aid organisations which have conducted economic and agricultural studies in different parts of Yemen have also been unable to give qat the attention it deserves as a major item of consumption and production because of the sensitivities of the Yemen government. For example, in the World Bank Country Study of the Yemen economy (World Bank, 1979), which numbers three hundred pages, there are only two short paragraphs on qat. And a large British government Overseas Development (ODA) project of agricultural research in the south of the country had no brief to examine qat production, even though qat is a major crop in the area concerned. Officials of both these organisations admit privately that it is misleading to discuss the development of the Yemen economy as though qat did not exist, but they were unable to investigate or report on qat without the approval of the Yemen government, which was not forthcoming.

A sign that the Yemen government has now decided to give the delicate subject of qat more public airing is the recent publication of a book (Centre for Yemeni Studies, 1981) which grew out of a seminar on qat held in Sanaa in March 1979. The book contains contributions by a number of Yemeni scholars on the following subjects: the history of qat in Yemen; historical dialogues among the learned elite; the permissibility of qat; attempts to legislate against qat; the treatment of qat in Yemeni literature; and the social, economic and health effects of qat. However, in much of the book, qat is made a scapegoat for many of Yemen's problems. Yahya al-Iriani (p. 84) calls qat a 'nightmare' which has weakened the Yemeni people and kept them prisoners of underdevelopment; Abdullah al-Alafi (p. 91) says qat is the source of Yemen's misery and makes people stupid; Hamud al-Audi (p. 104) attributes the 'rottenness' of political and social life in Yemen to qat; and Abd al-Salam al-Muqbil (pp. 115–17) thinks that qat is the reason why Yemenis are not more creative – because it kills individual ambition and scientific thought, makes men lazy, and encourages irresponsibility. Al-Muqbil also claims that qat causes economic decay – it is an 'octopus' which grips agricultural areas in its tentacles. Zayd Hajar (p. 58) does however refute the Yemeni version of the 'opium of the masses' theory of qat consumption which gained currency after the civil war. According to this theory, Imams Yahya and Ahmed are said to have encouraged qat consumption to prevent revolution against their regime, but Hajar points out that the revolution was hatched in the very context of qat parties and that qat consumption did not hinder the Yemeni rebellion against the Turks early this century.

More positive remarks about qat are made by the moderator of the seminar, Abd al-Aziz al-Muqalih (pp. 304–71). Al-Muqalih says that qat consumption should be regarded as a 'custom' not as 'drug-taking'. He also notes that because of its high price, qat has become a sign of social status and urges a sociological approach towards qat consumption, emphasising that the most important aspects of the custom are the sociability and intercommunication it engenders.

An indication that Yemeni officials are now prepared to discuss and even defend their national custom publicly is provided by the Yemeni contribution to the proceedings of the recent international conference on qat in Madagascar (Shahandeh et al, 1983). The joint authors, Morghem and Rufat of the Yemeni Ministry of the Interior, stake a national claim to the qat issue, repudiate the drug theory of qat consumption and the associated denigration of their people, and assert some of the positive social and economic effects of qat.

> Khat is a national question and not a problem concerning the whole Arab community as some people may imagine and as some countries do when they classify it with hashish, opium and other drugs. The consumption of khat is a habit but not an addiction. This does not mean that khat is not harmful. But it disproves the assumption that the people of the Yemen Arab Republic are drug addicts.

They point out that peasants chew qat 'without their physical or mental health being affected by it. On the contrary, this relieves fatigue, increases energy and helps them accomplish their work. The same applies to the craftsmen who chew it while working.' They emphasise the social significance of qat parties for strengthening relationships and the fact that they are the forum for important and serious discussions. They also mention the economic benefits of qat to the producing areas, where qat revenues are used to buy agricultural equipment, build roads and make home improvements. They do however consider qat to be a problem and urge that any solutions proposed should take into account the particular conditions prevailing in each country (Morghem and Rufat, 1983: 215–18; my translations).

Most of the assertions which have been made about the deleterious effects of qat on health, nutrition, agriculture and household and national economies have not been based on hard evidence but on a shaky foundation of ill-informed anecdote, ethnocentric misunderstanding and racial prejudice. The denigration of the leisure activities of members of other cultures or classes by those who consider themselves their social superiors is of course a common phenomenon, and is associated with an inability to appreciate their important underlying social functions. A British example is the game of Bingo, played mainly by middle-aged, working-class women, which middle-class officialdom has long regarded as a waste of time and money and has accused of luring women away from their family responsibilities. However, the recent report of a two-year study of the game stressed its enormous social benefits to the participants. The report is prefaced by a quote from Jane Austen which is equally relevant to qat consumption: 'Half the world does not understand the pleasures of the other' (Dixey and Talbot, 1982).

Apart from the work of the Kennedy team in the mid-1970s, no systematic field research has been conducted on the physical, social and economic effects of qat within Yemeni society. Qat may prove to be a factor exacerbating certain problems in Yemen (and elsewhere), but the wide-ranging detailed data which would be needed to substantiate this possibility does not yet exist. Nevertheless, qat has been seized on as a simple and simplistic explanation for unpalatable realities which have been shaped by a complex variety of political, economic and environmental factors.

The general atmosphere of condemnation has not been conducive to an open-minded examination of qat consumption as a sociological phenomenon. In particular, the deeply entrenched assumption that Yemenis chew qat only or primarily because they are dependent on it has obstructed the search for a more comprehensive explanation of qat consumption. Such an explanation must not only take into account the stimulant properties of qat, but also its institutionalised consumption at qat parties, the cultural beliefs and practices associated with it, the recent great increase in consumption and the high individual expenditure on qat.

Fig. 2 Yemeni newspapers frequently have cartoons about qat which demonstrate the admirable ability of Yemenis to criticise and poke fun at themselves. In this cartoon the small boy is saying 'Look Mummy, he's got a baby in his mouth!'.

This cartoon reflects the urban view of qat traders as wealthy country bumpkins. The man on the right, dressed traditionally, is saying 'Book me and my family on a plane to London', and the man on the left, dressed in Western-style clothes, is saying 'He's a qat merchant for sure!'.

5

Historical Aspects of Qat Consumption

The Origins of Qat Consumption

The historical evidence[1] for the beginnings of qat consumption is meagre and inconclusive, but it suggests that the practice originated in the southern Red Sea region (Yemen or Ethiopia) prior to the mid-fourteenth century. The earliest written reference to the practice of consuming qat which has so far been discovered occurs in an Ethiopian chronicle (in Amharic) believed to be a contemporary account of a military campaign of about 1330 (Hess, 1976). The campaign was undertaken by the Christian king Amda Seyon against the tributary Muslim king Sabr al-Din of Ifat (Awfat) who revolted in 1329. The Christian chronicler puts the following challenging words into the mouth of Sabr al-Din at the time of his revolt and before his defeat:

> I will rule in Seyon [Christian Ethiopia] . . . I will make the Christian churches into mosques for the Muslims, and I will convert to my religion the king of the Christians together with his people, and I will nominate him Governor of one (province), and if he refuses to be converted to my religion I will deliver him to the herdsmen . . . that they make him a herder of animals. As for the queen . . . the wife of the king, I will make her work at the mill. And I will make Mar'ade[2] his capital city my capital also. And I will plant there plants of cat [qat], because the Muslims love that plant . . . [3] (Huntingford, 1965: 55–6).

This reference demonstrates that qat consumption was already well-established in Ethiopia by the early fourteenth century, and that the practice was confined to the Muslim population of the country. It is interesting that the above political and religious threats culminate in the statement of an intent to plant qat. This may be taken as a condensed threat to appropriate the land of the Christians, transform their agriculture and impose on them the Muslim way of life – all of which are represented here by qat. (In Ethiopia qat consumption appears to have always been confined to the Muslim population and never became a Christian practice.)[4]

Another fourteenth-century source (written, in Arabic, between 1342 and 1349) refers to the popular consumption of qat in Ethiopia at that time and describes its physiological effects in terms quite familiar today. The writer of this work, Ibn Fadl Allah al-Umari, quotes the account given to him by an Ethiopian scholar of the introduction of qat from Ethiopia to Yemen:

> A Muslim of Abyssinia, he tells me, went to Yemen and was presented to the king [al-Mu'ayyad Da'ud], who accepted him as a friend. The Abyssinian entreated him to ask a favour, and the king requested some leaves of the qat tree[5]; he forthwith sent someone to Abyssinia who brought back a stalk. This was planted in Yemen and flourished. When the time came to harvest the leaves, the king asked the Abyssinian how the plant was used and he explained to him the effects it produced. On learning that it banished the desire to eat, to drink or to have sexual relations, the king al-Mu'ayyad said: 'And what other pleasures are there in this life except these? I will never eat it! Those three things are all I spend my wealth on; how could I use something which deprived me of just those pleasures I enjoy?' (Gaudefroy-Demombynes, 1927: 12; my translation)

This amusing anecdote cannot of course be taken as firm evidence that qat was introduced to Yemen from Ethiopia at the time of the Rasulid king al-Mu'ayyad Da'ud (who reigned from 1296 to 1321), but it does seem to demonstrate that Ethiopians of the mid-fourteenth century assumed that the practice of qat consumption already existed in Yemen. There is, however, negative evidence which casts some doubt on the existence of qat in Yemen – or at least its widespread cultivation and consumption – by the time of the reign of al-Mu'ayyad Da'ud. Qat received no mention in a Yemeni dictionary of medicinal plants of 1295–96,[6] nor in the 'Travels of Ibn Batutah' who passed through Yemen in 1330 – although he did notice and describe betel usage in various countries he visited (Rodinson, 1977). More significantly, there is no reference to qat in an apparently comprehensive Rasulid treatise on Yemeni agriculture compiled by the grandson of al-Mu'ayyad Da'ud in about 1370, and based in part on the writings of his father and grandfather.[7] Neither is qat mentioned in Rasulid lists of all the commodities on which they levied taxes, dated 1411/12.[8]

Slight evidence that qat consumption was established in Yemen by the early fifteenth century is contained in a legal ruling (*fatwa*) on the acceptability of qat from the religious, moral point of view, which was written in 1553 by the Meccan scholar Ibn Hajar al-Haytami. In this al-Haytami quotes the views of an Adeni, Ibn Kabban, who lived from 1374 to 1438 (Hess, 1976; Schopen, 1978: 50 and 174–6). The original Ibn Kabban manuscript to which al-Haytami was referring is lost, but as its author lived in Aden, his knowledge is most likely to have derived from the use of qat in Arabia, and this seems to indicate that the custom of consuming qat must have been reasonably well-established in that region by the early fifteenth century for a contemporary scholar to have been in a position to pronounce an opinion on it.[9]

Other evidence for the early history of qat consumption in Yemen consists of references in poetry attributed by recent Yemeni writers to poets of the thirteenth and fourteenth centuries (Schopen, 1978: 50). However, the poetry was initially handed down in oral not written form and is therefore unreliable evidence for dating the inception of qat consumption. References to qat could have been inserted later, or later poems could have been attributed to earlier poets. It should be noted that both the early poets cited by Schopen (Ibn Alwan and Miswari) are regarded as men of great piety and religious knowledge, and are both believed to have used qat to enhance their religious studies and observances.[10] The association of these venerated men with qat usage may therefore have helped legitimate its consumption and make it 'respectable' at a later date. Ibn Alwan (who died in 1267) is a particularly interesting illustration of this possibility for he originated in Jabal Sabr, near the big town of Taizz, which has long been one of the principal qat-growing areas in Yemen. He is said to have considered qat an alternative to wine, which he rejected. He was a famous sufi 'saint' (*wali*) and his tomb in Yifrus, south-west of Taizz, is an important pilgrimage centre in Lower Shafi'i Yemen.[11]

There are also a number of legends current in both Yemen and Ethiopia about the discovery of qat. According to Ethiopian and Yemeni legends the properties of qat were discovered by a Yemeni goatherd who observed the effects of the leaves on his goats and, upon trying it himself, found his strength increased and that he was able to stay awake all night to pray and meditate. Another, Ethiopian, tradition has it that qat was brought to Harar (the main centre of qat production in the country) by a mission of local merchants who had been sent to Yemen to collect qat. The mountain air was making the inhabitants of the newly established town of Harar tired and lazy, and it was hoped that qat would counteract these effects (Getahun and Krikorian, 1973; Rihani, 1930b; 37ff). There is also a legend in both countries that qat was introduced to Yemen by a holy man or 'saint' named Shaykh Ibrahim Abu Zaharbui (or Zerbin), one of forty-four Muslim missionaries who came to Harar from the Hadhramaut in about 1430; he became fond of qat and took some back with him when he returned to south Arabia.[12] The Muslims of Harar are also reported to believe that two saints who customarily spent their nights in prayer asked God for something to keep them awake and an angel revealed the qat plant to them (Trimingham, 1951: 228). The interest of these legends lies not so much in the possibility of their authenticity, which is slight, as in their common themes: that the consumption of qat was first adopted because it increased the capacity for work and prayer – both impeccable justifications for the practice in cultures where hard work and religious piety are highly regarded.

The documentary and legendary evidence of the early history of qat consumption obviously needs to be interpreted with account taken of possible bias or ignorance on the part of writers, and of motives other than the desire for historical accuracy on the part of those who propagate legends. Also, the absence of any mention of qat in early chronicles is not necessarily proof that it was definitely not being consumed at the time; it may have been consumed among a section of the population with whom the author had no contact because those people were geographically remote, socially distant or were consuming it rarely or secretly. Or it might have been dismissed as too unimportant to be mentioned, perhaps because it was at that stage of no commercial significance, or was only consumed by members of the lower classes whose customs are often disregarded by their social superiors (who write the histories) unless they impinge in some way on their own lives and interests. I would argue therefore that once references to qat consumption begin to appear in early local sources, the practice must have started to assume some degree of socio-economic importance and institutionalisation. But it could have been consumed on a small scale and sporadically by the illiterate masses long before its recognition and adoption by the members of the literate elite who first put it on record. It is therefore possible, as Schopen suggests (1978: 52), that qat consumption existed in a minor way in Yemen as early as the first half of the thirteenth century, although I would question his assumption that it necessarily began among the upper classes.

What is more open to question is the assumption by Schopen and most other writers on qat that it originated in Ethiopia and was brought to Yemen by Muslim missionaries after the Muslim penetration and conquest of the Ethiopian Highlands between the tenth and twelfth centuries (Trimingham, 1952)[13]. It is mistaken to imagine that it is possible to identify the particular person or category of persons who first brought the plant or the custom of consuming it from A to B, though it is characteristic of myths of origin to portray complex historical processes in this neat simplistic way. Qat grows wild over a wide region of the Middle East and Africa,[14] and it is reasonable to suppose that people could have been casually picking and chewing qat leaves from scattered trees, some of which may have been cultivated, for some time before qat consumption became fully institutionalised. There had been constant communication and contact across the Red Sea from even before the earliest days of Islam, and qat leaves and cuttings could have been transported back and forth by any number of traders, pilgrims, refugees or settlers. It is not like tobacco or moon rock, for which one can state a precise place of origin and subsequent mode of diffusion.

The First Yemeni References to Qat
The first references to qat in Yemeni writings appear in the mid-sixteenth century, by which time qat consumption was clearly a well-established and widespread practice. In the middle of the sixteenth century scholars from Sanaa and Zabid (famed centres of Islamic learning) visited Mecca to request the judgement of the renowned Shafi'i religious expert (mentioned above) Ibn Hajar al-Haytami (1504–67 or 1587) on the religious-legal status of qat. Al-Haytami consulted other scholars' writings and solicited views from consumers, and found that opinions conflicted. Those against qat claimed it brought confusion, intoxication and sleeplessness, reduced the desire for cohabitation and food, and caused dehydration and spermatorrhea – the latter complaint being said to interfere with the efficacy of ritual ablutions before prayers. Those in favour of qat argued that it had stimulating and pleasurable effects, and that by its use they achieved closer communion with God. Al-Haytami's subsequent legal ruling (*fatwa*) dated 1553

is a masterpiece of diplomatic compromise. He took the surprisingly modern approach that the variety of opposing opinions must derive from the intrinsic differences in people's natures which cause them to experience qat in diverse ways. He concluded that qat should be considered a 'doubtful substance' which should if possible be avoided, but he did not rule that it should be made illegal (*haram*) (Rodinson, 1977; Schopen, 1978: 174–9; Serjeant, 1983; 173–4, provides a translation of al-Haytami's treatise).

The dialogue about the permissibility of qat has continued among Yemeni scholars up to the present day, with health and economic considerations becoming of increasing concern. However, in historical documents the justi-fication for its consumption on the grounds of its alleged enhancement of religious observance has dominated the discourse, and the religious-based ruling class has most of the time approved the practice. An interesting excep-tion is the Zaydi Imam Yahya Sharaf al-Din, who reigned from 1507 to 1557. According to Yemeni accounts, he disapproved of qat and ordered trees to be uprooted (Rodinson, 1977; Serjeant, 1983; 173), but he was later persuaded that qat did not cause intoxication as he had supposed and was won over to qat consumption, composing the first known poem in its praise. This includes the following lines, which clearly express the status connotations of qat consumption at that time:

Oh crowd of noble *sadah* [*sayyids*], upright friends
If you desire the way to be opened for intimate socialising
Qat protects the soul against sensual desire . . .
(Schopen, 1978: 188; my translation from German).

His son Abdullah also eulogised qat, saying God himself had inscribed his name on the leaves, and that it was a ladder on which to climb to God's high dwelling place. According to Schopen these sentiments were regarded as blasphemous in certain orthodox Muslim quarters (1978: 179).

The early association of qat with the religious elite is also evident in a seventeenth-century poem by the Yemeni Jewish poet Shalom Shabazi who was born in 1619/20. The poem personifies qat and coffee as rivals engaged in a competitive dialogue in which each extols its superiority to the other. Coffee bases its case on its association with al-Shadhili, the revered 'saint' and founder of Mokha who according to legend is supposed to have intro-duced coffee to Yemen; on the fact that people drink coffee to start their day; on the widespread trade in coffee outside Yemen; on the absence of either stimulation or depression from drinking it; and on its legal-religious per-missibility. Qat, on the other hand, emphasises its own aesthetic qualities and its prestige value. It evokes the beauty of Jabal Sabr, its 'home', and its superior greenery which adorns both gardens and people; and it alludes to the high social status of those who consume it: 'The learned and nobles (*ashraf*) honour me . . . I am the pride of the area . . . The towns from Taizz to Ibb talk of me . . . Everybody knows me in the land of Yemen . . . *Sayyids* gather on my account . . . My place is among nobles and kings.' Coffee con-cludes in conciliatory vein that although they are enemies, they are found together in the fields and at social gatherings (Schopen, 1978: 201; my translation from German).[15]

Serjeant (1983: 172) points out that qat was both approved of and consumed by the ruling religious elite in the eighteenth century, 'at least to judge by the biography of a grandson of the Imam al-Mutawakkil Isma'il who liked well-being and literature . . . retreat into seclusion, worship, prayer, and who had a fondness for eating qat'. He also quotes a Yemeni saying, 'Qat is the food of the upright/pious', and notes that 'this could be because it enables the man of religion to spend his night in study or religious exercises'.

Qat and Coffee

An intriguing feature of the historical data on qat consumption is the apparently close connection between the early history of qat and that of coffee. The early history of coffee in Yemen is also hazy, but it appears that it began to be consumed during the fourteenth century (at the latest), and that its cultivation and consumption became well-established, as qat almost certainly was, during the fifteenth century (Van Arendonk, 1974). Coffee is generally thought by scholars to have been brought to Yemen from Ethiopia – though this assumption should be treated with the same reservations as the purported Ethiopian origins of qat. In local legends coffee, like qat, is said to have been first consumed by noted men of religion because its stimulant effects brought them closer to God and enhanced their capacity for prayer and meditation (ibid). The two substances also share two Yemeni legends of origin. In one, coffee and qat are supposed to have been planted at a place in the south of Yemen called al-Udayn, meaning literally 'the two branches'. In the other Abu Zaharbui or Zerbin, the missionary from the Hadhramaut mentioned above, is transformed into Abu Zahrayn, 'the father of the two flowers' (both qat and coffee bear flowers), and is attributed with the introduction of both coffee and qat to Yemen (British Admiralty, 1946: 492; Rodinson, 1977). According to one Arab author[16] (writing in 1587), when coffee was introduced to Yemen by al-Shadhili, the patron saint of Mokha (who died in 1418), it took the place of qat leaves (Hess, 1976).[17]

The fact that coffee and qat both appear to have emerged as important items of consumption at the same period of history, and their close association in legendary accounts, suggest the possibility of some causal connection. This historical coincidence may be related to the growth in the commercial importance of coffee. We can surmise that initially both coffee and qat were cultivated and consumed on a small scale, perhaps for medicinal reasons, and also to reinforce conviviality and express hospitality at occasional social and ceremonial gatherings. There must also have been some prestige attached to both crops, since they were grown on prime terraces and were both luxury substances which were pleasurable but not physically nourishing. At this early stage the production of both plants would have been mainly for consumption within the household or the immediate community, for gift exchanges between friends and relatives, and for barter in small regional markets.

What must have had a radical effect on the scale and significance of both coffee and qat consumption within Yemen was the development of a market for coffee outside the country. We know this occurred well before 1500 for there are records of coffee husks being consumed (by chewing) in Mecca in the early fifteenth century, and coffee was well-established as a beverage among devotees at the Great Mosque in Mecca and the al-Azhar mosque in Cairo by the beginning of the sixteenth century (Van Arendonk, 1974). The subsequent spread of coffee drinking was rapid and is well-documented. Coffee began to be traded to the Levant and Turkey during the sixteenth century, and trade with Europe was thriving by the mid-seventeenth century when the great proliferation of coffee houses took place (Chaudhari, 1974; Ukers, 1935).

Coffee therefore became well-established as a valuable export commodity mainly during the first half of the sixteenth century, which is precisely the period when the first references to qat appear in Yemeni sources. This is not, I suggest, because both crops had recently been suddenly and simultaneously introduced to Yemen, but because during that period both acquired commercial importance – initially coffee and secondarily, and as a consequence, qat.

The transformation of coffee into a commercially valuable export commodity would have had several important effects on qat consumption. The coffee trade greatly increased the monetarisation of the Yemeni economy. Money had existed in Yemen for centuries but the volume of foreign currency which flowed into Yemen from coffee sales was unprecedented. Money became more widely used as a medium of exchange and wealth was increasingly accumulated in silver and gold coinage, especially by those who were directly profiting from the coffee trade as agents, merchants, land-owners, tax-collectors and customs officials. Also, as Becker *et al* (1979) have noted, the influx of foreign currency enabled Yemeni merchants to import more foreign goods, causing an expansion in trade and commerce. In short, coffee lined the pockets and swelled the ranks of the rich upper classes.

As the monetary value of coffee increased and cultivation expanded to meet growing international demand, one might have expected qat cultivation to decline since the two crops thrive in the same areas and no international trade in qat developed parallel to that in coffee because of the high perishability of qat – otherwise we might all be chewing it today. Nevertheless, there is little doubt that qat production also increased. There is no means of knowing the precise extent of qat (or coffee) cultivation at different periods of history, but we do know from Yemeni documents that qat was already well-established as an important and expensive consumption item in Sanaa by the early eighteenth century (Serjeant, 1983: 171–5).

So qat not only survived on the terraces in competition with coffee but flourished, and I suggest that this is precisely because the commercialisation of coffee increased the cultural importance of qat and invested it with high monetary value. It acquired this value through the interaction of several factors. Coffee monetarised agriculture in the regions where it (and qat) thrived by endowing prime, well-watered Highland terraces with the capacity to yield a cash return. Any alternative luxury (i.e. non-subsistence) crop grown in a plot where coffee could be planted would automatically be invested with a theoretical cash value. Had no-one been prepared to pay this price then the crop would surely not have been grown instead of coffee. (This argument assumes that the demand for coffee, in the sixteenth to eighteenth centuries at least, easily absorbed the expanding supply, which does seem to have been the case.) But if, as must have happened with qat, its monetary value increased its prestigiousness, then a new demand could have been created in certain quarters by a) the fact that it had a *money* value, and b) the fact that it was expensive. The key fact is that the rich are always looking for flamboyant expenditures with which to demonstrate their superior wealth and acquire prestige. And if their wealth is measured in terms of money, there will be a tendency for their luxury consumption to be measured financially too.

Hence at the same time as the future of qat was in the balance because of competition from coffee, the demand for articles of conspicuous consumption of high monetary value, including qat, increased among that sector of the population whose wealth was being directly or indirectly augmented by coffee revenues. It was not simply that profits from coffee enabled the rich elite to purchase qat, as Schopen has noted (1978: 55), although that is true, but that they sustained and increased the demand for it. And the particular nature of the demand made the price qat had to fetch to survive as a crop in competition with coffee not merely acceptable to the consumer but positively desirable. For the whole point was to be a regular consumer of something for which one was known to be paying substantial sums of money.

The transformation of coffee into a lucrative cash crop therefore also resulted in a similar transformation of qat, and provided farmers with the incentive to continue growing it. Even after qat was well-established as a prestige consumption item, its survival continued to depend directly or indirectly mainly on the coffee trade as long as the latter remained Yemen's most important export commodity and principal source of currency.

Qat, Prestige and Class

Qat did not therefore in reality emerge on the stage of Yemeni history as a fully-fledged prestige commodity associated with the wealthy elite. That is simply the impression conveyed by the earliest chronicles, legends and poems because it is only after it had achieved high status and been adopted by the upper classes that it became socially, politically and economically important enough to be mentioned in local historical sources and to provoke the legends and dialogues concerning its pedigree and permissibility. Then the prestige of qat and the high social status of its principal, regular consumers would have been mutually reinforcing.

As we have seen, consumers are depicted in the early sources as '*sufi*' mystics,[18] or as *sayyid*s, or as specific Imams of Yemen. This association does not however mean that qat was exclusively consumed by religious specialists or only for religious reasons. Certainly once it had become commercialised only the richer classes could have afforded to consume it frequently, but these would have included many individuals of predominantly secular interests and no religious pedigree or special expertise. The religious aura which surrounds qat in the early literature should be interpreted rather as a justification and legitimation of the practice in the acceptable and powerful idiom of piety. Then, as now, there must have been many social and economic factors which were also sustaining the practice. What the mainly positive religious references demonstrate is that from its early days as a widely consumed commodity, qat had the stamp of approval of the ruling class. The legendary story of the Imam Yahya Sharaf al-Din and the poem attributed to his pen demonstrate the approval of the establishment and give it all the more force by depicting the Imam as a convert to the practice. It can be assumed, however, that in addition to genuine religious reasons, there were probably other vested interests being served by the good publicity qat received – remembering that the chronicles and poems were written by and for a religious elite who had a virtual monopoly on literacy, and who customarily expressed and imposed their interests through the medium of religion. In the case of qat these interests would have included revenues from the sale and taxation of produce, and also, to anticipate my later argument, the maintenance of social exclusivity and elevated position by the mode of its consumption and bestowal on others. The intermittent opposition to qat, also couched in a religious idiom, may therefore be a manifestation of such interests in collision.

The Historical Cost and Scale of Qat Consumption
The hypothesis that qat must have had a high monetary value from the time coffee became an important export commodity can only be confirmed once more historical evidence becomes available. However, firm evidence of the high price of qat in relation to wages in the early and mid-eighteenth century is provided by a fascinating collection of documents known as the Statute of Sanaa (*Qanun* Sanaa). An annotated English translation of these has recently been published by Serjeant (1983: 179–192; 225–240). The documents comprise regulations for the market of Sanaa promulgated by the Imams of the time, and are mainly concerned with laying down fees payable by wholesalers, profit margins, service fees and carrying charges, wages and nightwatchmen's expenses. The documents which have survived, which probably have antecedents stretching back centuries, are a 1748 copy of a Statute written between 1716 and 1727, and supplementary regulations added to the 1748 version in 1819.

In the 1748 documents (Serjeant, 1983: 189) the price of a bunch (*rubtah*) of 'good quality' qat is quoted as one eighth of a *qirsh*. The *qirsh* was a silver coin subdivided into forty *buqshas*. Thus the price of a *rubtah* was five *buqshas*. A *rubtah* is nowadays the minimum amount of qat most men chew in a day or at one qat party, and as it appears to have been the principal retail unit on sale in the market, it probably also was then (see following chapter). In another section of the document (ibid, p. 227), it is stated that the wages for an unskilled building labourer (*shaqi*) are one eighth of a *qirsh* (a day), in other words the same as the price of a bunch of good qat. The documents also mention the existence of cheaper qualities of qat, though without stating their prices. At the other end of the earnings scale the daily wage of a master builder is given as a quarter of a qirsh and two and a half buqshas, that is twelve and a half buqshas.

We can assume that then, as now, the daily wage earned by an unskilled labourer represented the maximum earning capacity of the majority of the male population, although we cannot know what proportion of the work-force was selling their labour. It was certainly far less than today, since until recently most men in the rural areas were still farming their own lands or working as sharecroppers for other landowners, and only a minority was working as wage labourers in agriculture or other occupations. Nevertheless, this data indicates that qat was as expensive in relation to wages in the early eighteenth century as it has been during the past decade when the average price of the *rubtah* has also approximated to the daily wage for an unskilled labourer. However, qat cannot have been as accessible to most Yemenis as it is today, since the monetarisation of the economy had not approached today's levels and few farmers produced a surplus which they could have exchanged for qat.

In the supplementary regulations of 1819 the price of a *rubtah* of 'best qat' is given as 'half of an eighth of a qirsh', from which it would appear that the price of qat has been reduced by half in the intervening seventy years. On this assumption, Schopen (1978: 55) deduces that the price was lowered by Imamic decree in order to encourage the consumption of qat and compensate landowners for a decline in coffee exports which he suggests had been caused by a combination of increased competition in international markets from Indonesia and various political factors. The problem with this theory is the assumption that the Imams of the time could have effectively imposed price restraints in the Sanaa market with an unsophisticated policing machinery and with the competition from numerous rural markets.

This also leads me to query Serjeant's statement that a major concern of the Statutes was price-fixing (1983: 180), which does not appear to be the case from the internal evidence of the text.[19] It is probably safer to assume that the price of qat (and other commodities) was determined as it is today by free market forces and that the prices mentioned in the Statute are notional averages on the basis of which calculations could be made about fair profit margins, taxes, etc. Also, even if the price had been successfully lowered by the Imams, it would not have helped the farmers unless consumption levels had more than doubled; production is stimulated by high not low market prices.

If the price of qat did in fact fall in real terms between the mid-eighteenth century and 1819, this could have been brought about by a slump in Yemeni coffee sales during the same period caused by international competition, for such a slump would have substantially reduced the cash circulating within the economy and the wealth of regular qat consumers. However, we do not know for certain that the Yemeni coffee trade and the economy were as hard hit by the expansion of coffee production in other countries as Schopen, Chelhod (1972) and others have assumed. This theory is based on various export figures for the chief coffee port of Mokha, but these are extremely unreliable, and also exclude the quantities of Yemeni coffee which were exported from other ports (Lohayya, Jizan and Jiddah) or overland through Arabia to the Levant. It is just as likely that the increase in international coffee production was absorbed by a parallel increase in international consumption.

Krikorian (1983: 23) quotes evidence of the high cost of qat in relation to incomes in the late nineteenth century, provided in a French translation of a Turkish account of the 1870 Turkish campaign in Yemen: 'There is no inhabitant, even if he is poor, who cannot find some money for his supply of khat. A workman who barely makes 5 piastres a day (1 franc 15 centimes) spends 4 for his purchase'.[20]

A number of other foreign visitors to Yemen have commented on the high price of qat and the high expenditure of consumers, but unfortunately without making illuminating correlations with incomes or wages.[21] For example, a vivid glimpse of the high cost of qat in the early nineteenth century is provided by the Frenchman Botta who visited Yemen in 1837. After commenting on the fame of the qat of Jabal Sabr, where he says it was the most important crop, he adds that 'the branches of this tree are of greater commercial importance within the interior of Yemen than coffee and much more lucrative for the owners'. He also comments that the use of qat had become 'a necessity' for everyone and was very dear, 'it being easy to spend four or five francs a day on it because of the liberality with which visitors are treated to it' (Botta, 1841: 99; my translations). Elsewhere he says that his host (Shaykh Hasan) bought qat to the value of a hundred francs each day of his stay (1880: 126–7). This information is not of course an indication of the expenditure of ordinary individuals but of the hospitality expenses of a presumably rich political figure. He may also have been exaggerating his expenditure to impress Botta.

Another nineteenth-century traveller, Harris, was entertained by a local notable and remarked on the expense of qat:

> ... salutations over, [the Sultan of Lahej in present-day PDRY] proffered me the amber mouth piece of his pipe and a bunch of kat, a shrub to which the Yemenis are much addicted ... The leaves are eaten green, growing on the stalk, and are said to cause a delightful state of wakefulness ... In Yemen it is considered a necessary luxury; and as it only grows in certain parts of the country, where it is carefully cultivated, and has to be transported often a long distance, it fetches a high price. (Harris, 1893: 170–1).

Some visitors also remark on the popularity and extent of qat consumption, occasionally giving the certainly erroneous impression that people of all classes consumed qat on the same scale, and that qat consumption was almost universal within the Yemeni population. For example, Niebuhr, who visited Yemen in 1763, mentions that qat was already enjoyed by labourers and artisans, but this does not mean they consumed as much or as frequently as the richer classes. It may be significant, though, that he mentions men who probably earned money as being consumers. Elsewhere, however, he mentions encountering qat use among 'the distinguished people in the Yemeni mountains' (1774: 51; my translation).[22]

Bury, who visited Yemen before the First World War, commented:

> Unfortunately, all but the poorest classes are addicted to the qat habit, more or less; the degree of addiction being in proportion to the amount procurable . . . It penetrates every class that can afford it, and many that cannot, for sometimes a man will starve himself and his family to get it. (Bury, 1915: 152–4).

All such statements have to be evaluated with caution. It is possible that the perceptions of this writer, and others, were coloured by their obvious disapproval of the custom, and by their conviction that consumers were addicted to qat and that consumption was determined by a cultural (or human) predilection for stimulation and was unrestrained. They were therefore unaware that consumption levels were controlled by social and economic factors. Generalisations by visitors were also inevitably based on limited experience and biased samples of the population. As Chelhod (1972) has pointed out, foreigners mixed mainly with members of the upper echelons of society – important officials and big merchants. Such people being wealthier than others were more likely to have been regular consumers, and would also have invited visitors to qat parties to be hospitable. Most foreigners also travelled in limited areas of the country, and almost always between Taizz and Sanaa where we can assume consumption has always been higher than elsewhere in the country because of the greater prosperity of urban populations. Qat was particularly obvious in the Taizz region because the town is situated adjacent to the famous qat-growing mountain of Jabal Sabr. Impressions gained during a short stay in any community can also be misleading because those who chew qat are highly conspicuous (although a short visit cannot reveal how often they do so), whereas those who do not are socially invisible. All this could have led visitors to gain a socially and geographically distorted view of the scale of the practice.

6

The Economics of Qat Consumption

Consumption Levels Prior to the 1970s

Until the 1970s qat was only consumed regularly and frequently by a wealthy minority of the Yemeni population. Over the centuries there had probably been an overall increase in consumption levels, with, as Rodinson (1977) has put it, 'advances and retreats' according to economic conditions, but for most of its history qat consumption was an expensive luxury which only those with substantial surplus income could afford to indulge. The less affluent majority of the population, living close to subsistence and survival level, only chewed qat on special social and ceremonial occasions. As the towns contained a relatively higher proportion of financially prosperous people than the rural areas, qat consumption in the past was also a predominantly urban phenomenon. The national scale of qat consumption before the recent period can be roughly gauged from the fact that even in the mid-1970s only ten per cent of the total population of Yemen lived in the towns; and in the past, as today, by no means all town-dwellers were wealthy. In the rural districts inhabited by the great majority of the population, only a small rich elite of large landowners, merchants and local political leaders were regular qat consumers.

This appears to be the general picture of consumption levels until the 1970s, though there was probably some increase in urban qat consumption during the relatively stable and prosperous regimes of Imam Yahya and Imam Ahmed (1918–62). Older Yemenis perceive a dramatic contrast between the widespread consumption of qat during the 1970s and pre-civil war consumption levels. According to one of Stevenson's informants in the small town of Amran, north of Sanaa, before the civil war most people chewed qat only at weddings, and only the rich could afford to chew qat every day (Stevenson 1981: 76). Similar statements were made by people in the qat-growing area of Razih where before the civil war most of the local qat production was exported to the northern town of Saadah for the consumption of notables and officials. Only a few local men are said to have consumed qat regularly. Adra (1982: 155) has also noted that qat consumption is a recent phenomenon in the rural Highland district of al-Ahjur.

The only available statistics on qat consumption levels in the pre-civil war and civil war period derive from the Taizz region. These figures are not representative of national or rural consumption levels because the town of

Taizz and its rural hinterland comprised then, as they do now, the most prosperous agricultural and mercantile region in Yemen. Also qat was, and is, grown in abundance on Jabal Sabr – the mountain overlooking Taizz – so was readily and probably more cheaply available to the people of Taizz than to those of other major towns, none of which are situated so close to a qat-growing area. The figures can therefore be taken as some indication of probably the highest consumption level in any area of Yemen at the period. The data should however be treated with some caution because it is based on consumers' personal accounts of their past and present consumption patterns. As it is prestigious to be a heavy qat consumer, it is possible that some exaggeration of consumption levels may have occurred, especially if interviews were conducted in the presence of other Yemenis (a situation difficult to avoid in a Yemeni hospital where the information was gathered).

The consumption figures concerned derive from medical records for the years 1955–67 kept by Italian physicians Mancioli and Parrinello while they were working at the Taizz hospital. Of the 15,000 males from the local catchment area who attended the hospital during that period, sixty per cent claimed to chew qat daily and to have done so for long periods of their lives; and thirty-five per cent of the 12,000 women seen from the same area also claimed to be daily users. In addition, a further thirty per cent of males and twenty-three per cent of females said they chewed qat occasionally at special events or when engaged in tiring work (Kennedy *et al,* 1980).

It is possible that qat consumption in the other main Yemeni towns of Sanaa and Hodeidah approached these levels but it was certainly far less among most of the population of Yemen at that period. Qat consumption may have increased during the civil war of the 1960s, when large financial subsidies and valuable arms were sent to both the royalist and republican sides by outside supporters, but the war coincided with a period of low rainfall and drought, so qat supplies may have been insufficient to meet any increase in demand. The consumption of qat nevertheless attained some national, political or economic significance by the end of the civil war for it aroused the concern of Prime Minister Muhsin al-Aini and provoked his attempts to limit qat production in 1971–72.

A small survey conducted by Yacoub and Akil in 1970 indicates consumption patterns at that time among a sample of 125 male household heads in the rural district of the Hojariyyah. Seventy-two per cent of the men were full-time farmers and the rest were part-time farmers. Seventy-four per cent were over thirty-five years old. Of this sample 108 (eighty-six per cent) were qat consumers, and from the expenditure figures provided it is apparent that about half the consumers were attending qat parties several times a week or daily (Yacoub and Akil, 1971: 11, 31). The survey pre-selected the older, wealthier generation by choosing heads of households for interview so the data is not representative of local male consumption generally at that time. A broader survey of men of all ages and occupations conducted in non-qat-growing as well as qat-growing areas would have probably revealed lower consumption levels.

The Increase in Qat Consumption During the 1970s

Despite no systematic qat-consumer survey ever having been conducted among a representative sample of the Yemeni population, the fact that qat consumption did greatly increase during the 1970s is clear. An obvious indication is the proliferation of men's qat parties in every kind of community. In Razih, for example, where few people had chewed qat before the civil war, qat parties were being held in many homes almost daily by the late 1970s, and there were only a few where none was ever held. Qat parties also increased among women – both in the towns where qat consumption had been a long-standing custom among women, and in many rural districts where it was adopted only during the 1970s (see Mundy, 1981: 61). In Razih qat chewing had not yet been generally adopted by women by 1980 but there were signs· that it might be in the near future. A handful of women who had lived for a time in Sanaa chewed qat – with a marked degree of flamboyance – at women's tea parties, and it was clearly regarded as a desirable sign of urban sophistication, like the Sanaani costume which was rapidly becoming fashionable.

The use of the term 'party' is not meant to imply that all the gatherings at which qat is consumed are of a formal nature, for they vary greatly in formality as well as size. The main point is that by the late 1970s the majority of men and a large minority of women were spending their afternoons chewing qat with other people, mostly in private homes. In townships there was also an increase in informal qat parties, which took place in small shops in the rapidly expanding markets. Many more Yemeni men were also chewing qat while they worked. By the late 1970s it was common to see builders, taxi-drivers, labourers and shopkeepers chewing qat at all times of day, whereas in the early 1970s this was a much rarer sight.

Other marked evidence of the increase in qat consumption during the 1970s is the expansion of qat markets in size and number. Especially during the second half of the 1970s new qat markets appeared almost overnight throughout the rural areas and others were enlarged as more people entered the qat trade.[1] In 1980 an enterprising local man set up a filling station on a newly constructed motor track in Razih, and a bustling qat market soon sprang up next to it. Each day donkey-loads of qat were carried there from the surrounding mountains, and truck-loads were transported to Saadah and as far as Sanaa. Soon butchers set up their slaughtering tripods so that qat traders could return home with meat bought with the proceeds of their sales, and a small café and grocery shop opened.

Increased qat consumption has been clearly reflected in production: many new plantations of young qat can be seen throughout the Highlands. Several anthropologists have estimated the extent of qat cultivation in the areas where they worked in the 1970s, and some have also estimated the amount by which it increased during the qat consumer boom. Referring to a fertile qat-growing wadi near Sanaa, Mundy (1981: 54) states that 'large-scale commercial plantings date from the reign of Imam Yahya [1918–48] and since then the amount of land under qat has gradually increased. Its spread accelerated after the 1962 revolution, limited only by the plant's sensitivity to frost in winter. By the middle 1970s people felt that it had been planted in any plot where it would prosper'. She estimates that qat was planted on about eight per cent of rain-fed land and on over twenty-five per cent of irrigated land in the wadi in the mid-1970s (1981: 55).

Gerholm (1977: 53) estimates that in Jabal Haraz in the mid-1970s, qat and coffee together occupied about twenty per cent of the cultivable land, and states that qat was more widely planted than coffee. Varisco (1984) says that about fifteen per cent of the irrigated land in the valley of al-Ahjur was planted with qat in 1978–79. Tutwiler and Carapico (1981: 49–52) say that qat was variously credited with between seven and twenty per cent of the agricultural land of the Governorate of Ibb in the late 1970s. They also found that the area planted with summer sorghum, which had formerly comprised about seventy per cent of the cultivated land in the area, had been reduced by half mainly by the planting of qat.

About fifteen per cent of the cultivated part of the main qat-growing mountain in Razih was planted with qat in 1977, and the area had roughly doubled by 1980 (Weir, 1985). In Jabal Hufash, where qat had been grown on about a third of the cultivated upper slopes before the civil war, it was grown on about ninety per cent of the still cultivated terraces lying above 1800 metres by 1981–83, and qat was also being grown at lower altitudes than ever before (below 1500 metres) with the help of irrigation by Toyota truck. There was also a parallel increase in banana cultivation – banana stems and leaves being used, as in Razih, for packing and preserving qat for transportation to market (Tim Morris, personal communication). The expansion in qat production in Jabal Hufash was at the expense of both coffee and grain, but coffee was in any case almost certainly a marginal crop at 1800 metres and above.

On the basis of the reports from different qat-growing areas, it is safe to assume that qat production in Yemen must have at least doubled during the 1970s – much if not most of this increase having taken place during the boom in qat consumption of the second half of the decade.[2] The precise extent of qat cultivation in Yemen is unknown, but Kopp estimates that qat was being grown on two to three per cent of all arable land in the mid-1970s (1981: 237), and the Yemen Ministry of Agriculture and Fisheries estimated that 40–45,000 ha of land was devoted to qat cultivation in 1981. This is equivalent to about three per cent of the total estimated arable land of Yemen (USAID, 1982: 81). No assessment had been made of what proportion of arable land in the country has the potential to support qat as a commercial crop.[3]

The expansion in qat cultivation during the 1970s was a response by farmers to increased demand and high prices. The return on qat was greater than for any other cash crop, including coffee, so farmers were planting it wherever they could. The expansion was also facilitated by great improvements in transport and technological innovations in farming. These factors would not, of course, have led to increased qat production had the price of qat been falling, or if profits from qat had been lower than from alternative crops.

During the 1970s surfaced roads were completed between the major Yemeni towns, and during the second half of the decade a vast network of unsurfaced feeder tracks was built throughout the country. By 1980 most rural settlements were served by motor transport for the first time. This had a profound effect on the qat trade as farmers and traders in even the most remote Highland areas could now send their qat to the biggest qat markets in the main towns. Improved transportation did not in itself create a greater demand for qat; people do not consume qat just because it is available (though it has to be available for them to consume it), but because they want it and can afford it. In fact it is truer to say that the demand for qat was a major factor in the development of motor transport, since much of the impetus to build feeder tracks came from qat farmers and traders keen to improve the efficiency of their marketing. Furthermore it is revenues from qat which in many areas actually helped finance motor tracks and the purchase of motor vehicles. However, improved transportation did mean that qat traders had no problem in meeting the rising national demand for qat, which would have been the case had motor tracks not existed.

The high profits available from qat and the increase in qat farmers' incomes provided the incentive for many growers to sink new wells and install pumped ground-water irrigation. As a result, qat cultivation not only expanded within the fertile western Highland areas with high rainfall, where qat is a long-established major cash crop, but also in the more arid plateau regions of the central Highlands where it had either not previously been grown or only on a much smaller scale because of low rainfall.

A number of writers have mentioned the relation between this technological innovation and qat production. Swanson (1979: 75) mentions the use of pumps for irrigating qat on the central plateau near Sanaa, and Dresch (1982: 13) remarks that in some areas north of Sanaa water for irrigating qat is carried by truck, at great expense, from as far as twenty kilometres away from the fields. It is estimated that eighty to ninety per cent of the new wells being drilled in the southern Highlands of Yemen are used partially for qat production 'which provides the cash flow to underwrite the investment costs of well installation. . . . Qat is obviously financing most of Yemen's ground-water development' (USAID, 1982: 191). In 1980 the qat farmers of western Razih began exporting qat cuttings to the Highland regions further east for sale (at SR30–70 a sack) to farmers who had begun cultivating qat for the first time with the help of pump irrigation from newly dug wells. Mundy (1981: 58) points out that the installation of motorised pumps in a qat-growing valley near Sanaa meant that 'those who have easy access to pumped water can also reap the greatest profits in the market by tailoring their irrigation schedules to produce qat for the market when there is no rain-fed qat available'.

Considering the increase in qat parties, the expansion in markets, and particularly the increase in land under qat production, it is safe to assume that the quantity of qat consumed in Yemen at least doubled during the 1970s – though this may be a considerable underestimate. What is certain is that by the late 1970s regular qat consumption was common for the first time among both sexes and in all sections and classes of the urban and rural population throughout the country. By then perhaps seventy-five per cent of the adult population were frequent qat consumers.[4]

The Economic Context of Increased Qat Consumption

The recent increase in qat consumption is essentially related to the dramatic rise in financial prosperity and greater circulation of cash in Yemen during the 1970s. At the start of the decade a smaller proportion of the male workforce were employed as wage labourers, and a higher proportion were working their own land or were sharecropping.[5] There were fewer opportunities to earn money, still less to accumulate it. However, with the mass out-migration to work in Saudi Arabia, and the expansion of commerce and the transportation and services sectors at home, agriculture ceased to be the only – or even the primary – means of livelihood for many households. As local economies diversified, men eagerly grasped new opportunities, often without abandoning their other work.

By the middle of the decade it had therefore become common for households to have several lucrative sources of cash income. These included agriculture, for with the major shift from subsistence farming and production for exchange to the production of cash crops during the 1970s, agriculture had become increasingly monetarised. Also, many farmers saw higher cash profits on their produce, especially if they could draw on family labour. The result of these fundamental changes was a substantial rise in household incomes and disposable cash across the full spectrum of society, whether the immediate source was wage labour abroad or at home, agriculture, shop-keeping, truck- or taxi-driving, house-building or any other occupation. The primary source of raised income levels was, however, the cash remittances which flooded into Yemen from migrants working in Saudi Arabia.[6]

A measure of the transformation of the Yemeni economy is the rise in daily wages which took place during the 1970s. The earning capacity, in real terms, of every able-bodied Yemeni man greatly increased whether he migrated to work in Saudi Arabia or remained at home. The massive out-migration of workers caused a severe depletion of the Yemeni workforce and acute domestic labour shortages. As opportunities and wages in Saudi Arabia increased, and more Yemenis migrated to take advantage of them, the domestic wage level also increased. Wages rose throughout the 1970s, but the most substantial increase took place around 1975 as a direct result of the great oil-price rises of 1973–74 which had caused a boom in the Saudi construction industry, generating a sharp increase in the demand for manual labour. In 1970 the daily wage for an unskilled labourer working in Saudi Arabia was about SR5 (US$1.4), by 1975 it had risen to about SR50 ($14), and by 1980 to SR100 ($28).[7] Skilled workers could earn several times these amounts. During the same period the daily wage for an unskilled labourer working in Yemen (mainly in agriculture or construction) rose from about YR2 (US$0.4) in 1972 to YR5 ($1.1) in 1975 and YR60–70 ($13–15.5) in 1980, and skilled workers in Yemen's own rapidly expanding construction sector could earn far more. By 1982 masons were earning YR300–350 ($66–77) and carpenters and electricians YR200–250 ($44–55) per day; diesel mechanics and tractor drivers could command YR40–70 ($9–15) per hour (USAID, 1982: 221).[8]

Although Yemeni wages appear lower than Saudi wages from the above figures, it became increasingly common during the 1970s for Yemeni labourers to be given a bunch of qat in addition to their payment in cash. This must have raised the total value of their wages close to Saudi levels, and is a further indication of how popular and pervasive qat consumption had become, for such widespread payments in kind would not have been acceptable unless the majority of the population were qat consumers. If the worker did not consume the qat himself, he must have been able to sell it, or give it to someone else.

The 1970s were also characterised by general inflation in prices including the price of qat.[9] As incomes rose, so did the demand for qat and prices soared. In 1972–73 the average price of a bunch (*rubtah*) of qat (the minimum quantity most consumers chew in a single day) was about YR3 (US$0.6). By the mid-1970s it had risen to about YR19 ($4), and by 1980 to about YR45 ($10).[10] (There were, of course, considerable fluctuations and differences in prices according to season, availability and region.) To assess the economic significance of these approximate figures it is necessary to relate them to wage levels, to employment conditions and to the availability of cash at the beginning and end of the decade.

In the early 1970s the price of a *rubtah* of qat was roughly equivalent to, or a little more than, the daily wage of an unskilled labourer working in Yemen. By 1980 when the average price of a *rubtah* was about YR45, the average daily wage of an unskilled labourer had risen to YR60–70. If account is taken of the customary additional payment in kind of a bunch of qat, the average price of a *rubtah* can be estimated to have dropped to about half the daily wage of an unskilled labourer by 1980. It can therefore be said that though the price of qat rose substantially in riyal terms, it fell in real terms. This must also have helped stimulate higher levels of qat consumption.

The increase in qat consumption was also related to a shift in the distribution of wealth between generations and to changes in male and female work patterns and conditions. Wage labour at home and abroad provided younger men with an unprecedented degree of economic independence from the paternal generation, and many were able to establish their own households at an earlier stage in life than had been possible before. Formerly it was common for a man (with his wife and children) to continue living in his father's house until the latter died, and often for a period after his death until the division of his property. But now increasing numbers of young men are using their savings to build their own houses, with reception rooms which can be used for qat parties. Out-migration also gave many young men increased incentive to consume qat when they returned home, for, as we shall see, the qat party was an important medium for re-establishing relationships weakened by long separation.

The new economic conditions also caused changes in work patterns and expectations which affected qat consumption. The parties at which most qat is consumed last from early afternoon until dusk. In order to be able to attend parties regularly a person must not only have a substantial supply of disposable income but also be able to release himself or herself from work for entire afternoons. A regular qat consumer must also have a certain confidence that his work opportunities, and therefore his income, are relatively secure. These conditions have also been created by the new economic situation.

The greatly improved employment opportunities of the 1970s meant that most men were spending more time than before in gainful and formally structured employment. Before the civil war work in agriculture, which was then the major economic activity, was required only intermittently for relatively short periods of intensive activity – at planting, ploughing and harvest times, and when terraces needed repairing. In contrast, in the 1970s wage employment became available throughout the year and most men were employed on their own behalf, or for others, the majority of the time. Before the civil war the normal working day for agricultural labourers and others extended from dawn until mid or late afternoon, but during the 1970s it shrank in most areas to the hours between 7 am and 1 pm as a direct result of the shortage of labour. Employees were in a position to dictate their terms of employment to their employers, who complained that they could no longer find men who would work after the lunchtime break, as in the old days, without a substantial supplement to the daily wage. So despite the increase in work, most men's afternoons remained free for qat parties. Looked at another way, most men could earn a living as well as support their qat consumption by working a six-hour day.[11]

Another effect of the new conditions and patterns of work was a greater sense of economic security. Men could control and anticipate their work pattern to a greater extent than before, and were able to predict that their incomes would be sufficient for basic necessities, to support the new standard of living – and to purchase qat. As a result there was a greater inclination and ability to become a qat consumer and to establish a regular pattern of attendance at qat parties than when life was more precarious and employment less formalised.

Increased qat consumption among women is also related to fundamental changes in their work caused by the new economic conditions. During the 1970s the domestic chores of both urban and rural women were substantially reduced by technological innovations – especially by the introduction of motorised flour mills throughout the country and by piped water supplies in the towns. The work of rural women was also greatly alleviated by the spread of motor transportation; previously their most arduous and time-consuming tasks were carrying water, fodder and firewood to their settlements, often over great distances. Women's agricultural work also decreased with the reduction in grain cultivation and the expansion of cash cropping (with which women have traditionally had minimal involvement). The customary female task of caring for domestic livestock was also reduced as fewer households kept animals. It also reflected prestige on a household if its women's productive physical labour outside the home was curtailed. As is the case throughout the Middle East, upward social and economic mobility was associated with the conspicuous leisure and seclusion of women. Women's work, which had formerly filled most of the day, was therefore greatly reduced and the time for attending social gatherings was correspondingly increased.[12] And at a growing proportion of these gatherings qat was the principal substance consumed.

The remainder of this chapter will examine the economic dimensions of qat consumption from the perspective of the preferences, choices and expenditures of individual consumers. At this point it is vital to stress that *each consumer normally provides the qat for his personal consumption.* Usually each man makes his purchase in the qat market before or after lunch, and arrives at the qat party of his choice with his personal supply of qat for the afternoon. It is not necessary to be invited; each participant just turns up with his (or her) qat. This is the pattern at the daily qat parties which account for most qat consumption in Yemen. There are also occasions when qat is provided by a host for specially invited guests – mainly gatherings held to celebrate major life events such as weddings or to entertain important officials. But such qat parties are relatively infrequent and account for only a small proportion of individual and national expenditure on qat.

The Marketing of Qat

Because of the individualistic character of most qat purchasing, a useful perspective on consumption patterns can be gained by examining how qat is marketed, for in the market-place there is a direct interaction between the full range of qat consumers and those who are responding to their requirements. Qat leaves are sold in the market-place in bunches called in Arabic *rubtah*.[13] These bunches are carefully prepared by the landowners or specialised qat traders in the producing areas before being transported to market. The qat traders carry the financial risk involved in selling the qat in the market-place, not the retailers who sell the qat for the highest price it will fetch on the day in return for a percentage of the takings – usually about ten per cent. Normally the trader only gets his money after the qat has been sold.[14]

The overwhelming concern of the qat trader is that his qat will sell quickly, preferably on the day he takes it to market or at the latest the following day. Otherwise the leaves will wilt and the price will plummet – for few consumers will buy leaves which are not of optimum freshness. The trader would then lose the considerable investment he has made in buying the qat on the tree (if he was not the landowner) and having it picked, packed and transported to market. It follows that traders prepare their qat to ensure a quick sale and must be acutely sensitive to consumer requirements. The way they prepare their qat is therefore a good indication of what the majority of customers want, which is a particular quantity of fresh, attractive-looking qat at a price to suit their financial means. It is important that the qat looks and sounds fresh (fresh leaves rustle pleasantly while old ones do not), and qat sells more

9 A qat transaction on the terrace. Razih, January 1980. From left to right are a witness to the deal (who was ready to buy the qat himself if it fell through), the qat trader who has bought the qat, and the terrace owner who is counting the money.

easily if it is nicely arranged in bunches.[15] The following description reveals the importance of consumer requirements in the packing process in Razih.

The Preparation of Qat for Market in Razih[16]
The way qat is picked and packed varies from area to area depending on the distance from the market and the transportation facilities available. The preparation of qat for market was the most labour-intensive aspect of the qat trade in Razih in 1980 because of the care taken to prevent damage in transit. The nearest major qat market (Saadah) was then a day's rough travel away by donkey and truck, and the next nearest (Hodeidah) was even further and harder to reach. Less care is necessary in areas close to markets.

Qat is picked (*yugtuf*) in the morning. Those branches with a good growth of new leaves at their tips are broken off about half a metre down from the tip (*ras*) and carefully laid in cowhide bags (*ijaw*) or large plastic sheets (*baghah*) to prevent damage and dehydration. A number of branches with no new leaf growth (*hadhawi*), may also be picked for packing purposes, but most such branches are left on the tree. If it rains soon after harvesting, about two weeks later new shoots sprout from the stumps of the harvested branches. If it does not rain these new shoots take a month or more to appear. The farmer may pick some of these tasty young leaves to chew himself but they are not usually sent to market. Most are left to grow into new branches to be picked at subsequent harvests.

At mid-day the qat is carried back to the house or special packing hut and during the afternoon and evening of the same day the qat is packed for market. This is always done indoors to keep the qat as fresh and cool as possible. Each task in the preparation and packing of the qat is usually performed by a different individual (or individuals) sitting in the same room. Each passes the qat on to the next as he completes his stage of the process. The first stage is stripping off (*yibarrih*) the older inedible leaves from around the young shoots at the tip of the branch so as to expose them to view. The older leaves at the base of the branch are left on for aesthetic reasons and to help keep the tips separate when the branches are tied together. As each branch is stripped it is carefully laid on a pile with its tip towards the centre of the pile to prevent dehydration.

The next stage is the bunching together (*yizarrib*) of two to four of these prepared branches. The number of branches in each bunch (*zurbah*) depends on the leafiness of the branch. Ideally each *zurbah* should contain roughly the same amount of edible foliage. Waste branches (*jafar*) are added at this stage to space the tips, both to protect them from damage and to set them off to best effect. Aesthetic considerations are an important factor in the packaging process, and the care taken in the selection and arrangement of the branches is comparable to that of a Western florist arranging a bouquet. These small bunches are now tied (*yigayyid*) in threes to make a larger bunch called a *tagyud*, and two of these are tied together to make the final bundle, the *guruf*, which is the unit of trade in Razih.

Meanwhile the banana stem (*izzah*) in which the qat is to be packed is prepared. Banana stems consist of multiple layers of stiff leaf sheaths, and these

10   Picking qat. Razih, December 1979. It is often necessary for pickers to climb qat trees.

are separated and cut into lengths of about one and a half metres. The half-metre-long bundle (*guruf*) of qat is laid inside one of these stem sections with the stumps of the branches at one end and the tips towards the centre, and smaller sections cut from the centre of the banana stem are laid over the bundle. The main outer section of banana stem is then folded in two over the qat and tied in two places with ties split from the tough brown outer skin of the banana stem. The qat is thus completely encased in layers of banana stem with the precious leafy tips at the fold. The verbs *yigarrif* and *yibarkis* are applied to this packaging process.

The following is a summary of the different units of qat in Razih:

2–5 tips (*ras*)	= 1 small bunch (*zurbah*)
3 *zurbah*	= 1 large bunch (*tagyud*)
2 *tagyud*	= 1 bundle (*guruf*)
2 *guruf*	= 1 double-sized bundle (*marduf*)

The *guruf* (the main unit of trade) therefore normally contains six small bunches (*zurbah*) or twelve to thirty tips (*ras*) of qat. One *guruf* is equivalent in quantity to approximately two *rubtah*s of qat. The term *rubtah*, used in most of Yemen for the typical consumption unit of qat, is not used locally in Razih though it is of course known.

The following are the important quantities with regard to the preparation and marketing of qat in Razih:

1 bag (*ijaw*) of qat (as picked) gives approx. 20 *guruf*
1 large or 2 small banana stems (*izzah*) are needed to pack approx. 20 *guruf*
1 donkey carries approx. 20 *guruf*
1 Toyota truck carries approx. 300 *guruf*

As in Razih, qat yields, prices, packaging and transportation are all discussed in terms of the *guruf*, it is of interest to examine what determines its size, its subdivision into smaller bunches, and the way it is packed. The primary concern is the protection of the qat from damage or deterioration during transportation to market. Banana stems are ideal packing material for these purposes. They are stiff and tough, so protect the qat from physical damage, and their high water content keeps the qat moist and cool. The size of the *guruf* is therefore partly determined by the size and shape of the sections of banana stem. The way the qat is bunched is also intended to protect the leaves at the tips.

However, the size of the *guruf* and the bunching of the qat are also influenced by the requirements of the retailer and the individual customer. The subdivision of the *guruf* into two halves (*tagyud*) each containing three smaller bunches (*zurbah*) facilitates sales negotiations at different stages along the marketing chain. Buyers can assess the qat more easily if they can see how many tips the packer has tied together in one *zurbah*, and the fact that each *guruf* contains six small bunches of equal size enables the retailer to cater for a variety of needs and pockets in the market-place. At the top of the

11 *right*. Man carrying newly picked qat from the terraces in a cowhide bag (*ijaw*). Razih, January 1980. (There is a similar bag in the Museum of Mankind).

12 *below*. Banana stems on sale in the market. Razih, December 1979. Banana is grown locally and makes ideal packing material for qat.

scale the *guruf* represents the largest quantity of qat that most individual customers would want to buy at one time, as it contains enough qat for one or two qat parties (depending on the person's consumption habits), and men with access to a daily qat market would not want to keep their qat longer than two days.

The rubtah

The basic retail or consumption unit of qat, the *rubtah,* is tailored to consumer requirements, but whereas the demand for qat which looks pleasant and is fresh is constant and universal, there is some variation among consumers in what they can afford and therefore the quantity of qat they want to buy. They all, however, share a preference for buying qat on the day they are going to consume it, or on the previous day, and in conditions of sufficiency the *rubtah* therefore represents roughly the minimum quantity of qat which the majority of consumers require for a single day's consumption. In packing a particular quantity of qat in a *rubtah*, the trader is employing the sensible marketing strategy of catering to the lowest common denominator of demand and thus satisfying the needs of the full range of consumers – for a heavy consumer can always buy more than one *rubtah*.

There is no national standardisation in the size of the *rubtah*. The different producing areas prepare and pack their qat in different ways; some is marketed in short *rubtah*s of leaves and stalks, while other *rubtah*s are up to half a metre long because the leaves are packed attached to their branches. But apart from periods of qat shortage, *rubtah*s usually appear to contain about the same quantity of chewable leaves wherever they come from. This fact has been noted by Schopen (1978: 74) who says that the number of branches packed in a rubtah depends on their length and therefore the number of leaf-bearing twigs they carry, implying that traders pack a specific quantity of leaves in a rubtah. A few writers have estimated the weight of leaves consumed during a single qat party (that is, in roughly four hours of steady chewing). Chelhod (1972) says consumers can chew over 500 grams in one session, and al-Maqrami (1982) says the average daily consumption is half a pound of leaves (i.e. something over 200 grams). Kennedy *et al* (1980) provide a more reliable estimate, based on large surveys of the quantities of qat consumed daily, taking account of differences between individuals. They say that (in the mid-1970s when their study was conducted) the majority of consumers chewed one *rubtah* in a single afternoon session, and that this averaged about 100 grams of picked leaves, i.e. those actually chewed. A minority chewed over 200 grams and some 'as few as' 50 grams.[17]

Kennedy *et al* point out that the normal-sized *rubtah* is 'well-calibrated' for the customary three- to four-hour chewing period of most qat parties. 'When the time of the normal session has elapsed, most chewers are just finishing or have just finished their qat.' This social aspect is in fact the important factor determining how much qat is consumed at a qat party, not physiological 'needs' or dependence. Pharmacologists may eventually establish that there is a minimum quantity of qat which will induce and maintain its stimulant effects – but these certainly vary between individuals and

13 *above*. Placing small bunches (*zurbah*) of qat on a pile. Razih, January 1980.

14 *right*. The boy on the left is stripping the qat branches to make bunches (*zurbah*). The man on the right is tying a package (*guruf*) of qat in banana stem. Razih, January 1979.

many people never experience any. I suggest that it is of equal and possibly greater importance to the consumer that he has enough qat to last him for the duration of the qat party – for to participate adequately it is necessary for appearances' sake to continue chewing your qat for the same length of time as everyone else. The quantity of leaves in a *rubtah* is therefore roughly the minimum quantity one man can spin out for about four hours chewing at a respectable pace. It is social not physical pressures which determine the size of the *rubtah*.

It is instructive to note what can happen to the size of the *rubtah* during qat shortages. Although qat is an evergreen which is continuously producing new foliage, supplies fluctuate during the year according to season, local climatic conditions and agricultural inputs, and this leads to corresponding fluctuations in market prices. It is significant that when there is a national shortage of qat after a dry period, traders in areas which have been exceptionally favoured with rain may market their qat in smaller *rubtah*s than usual. This happened in Razih in December 1979. Razih was blessed with heavy showers while the rest of Yemen remained dry, and the local qat traders decided to pack the qat leaves which sprouted a few days later in *rubtah*s[18] of only five or six branches instead of the ten or so which was the norm for the area. These were subsequently sold in the Hodeidah qat market for roughly the same price that their normal larger *rubtah*s had fetched in the preceding period when qat was more plentiful.

What this marketing strategy reveals is the traders' awareness that *in extremis*, so to speak, the majority of consumers (for whom the trader is catering because of the exigencies of marketing a highly perishable commodity) are constrained or influenced by price to a greater extent than they are motivated by the desire or 'need' for a fixed quantity of qat. It was therefore more sensible for the traders who wanted to profit from the national dearth of qat to reduce the size of their *rubtah*s, and aim to sell them at the usual price, than to maintain the size of the *rubtah* and hope to get a higher price. It is also relevant that at times of qat shortage many consumers' incomes are reduced because they are involved in the qat trade as landowners, pickers, packers, transporters or retailers.

Price and Variety

At all major qat markets there is usually a variety of qat on sale at a range of prices. It is important to realise that neither the high price of qat nor the variations in price bear direct relation to production and transportation costs (though the price fetched should of course cover them and yield a profit). In some cases qat from areas close to the market is more expensive than that from more distant areas. What ultimately determines both the high price of qat and the range of prices at which it is sold is customers' preferences and what they are able and prepared to pay. The crux of the matter is that *people do not pay as little as they can, but as much as they can afford*. Forces rooted in the context and meaning of qat consumption push the expenditure of each consumer to a personal ceiling determined by his income. This dynamic is what makes qat so expensive. However, because people's incomes and

15 A customer examining qat in a Razih market. November 1979.

financial commitments vary, the amount they spend on qat also varies. This is why there is a range of qat at different prices in any market – it both reflects and caters to the variable incomes of the customers.

Where the price of a bunch of qat falls within the price range at times when the qat in the market is sufficient to satisfy demand, depends partly on the condition of the qat (whether it is fresh and undamaged) and partly on the region it comes from. Qat from certain regions of the Highlands or from particular mountains is credited with a better flavour and effects than that from other areas and is more expensive because people are prepared to pay more for it. Schopen (1978: 66) lists thirty-six regional varieties of qat which were on sale in the main towns of Yemen in 1974–75, and this number must have increased since it became possible to transport qat from the most remote rural areas to the main urban markets in a day. In rural markets local qat may even be distinguished and evaluated according to the particular mountain slope or field where it was grown.[19]

Prices, Expenditure and Income

To illustrate the relationship between spending patterns and income, we will focus on the two-year period 1979-80 which was historically a period of peak national expenditure on qat.

Individual expenditure on qat depends on the price per *rubtah*, the number of *rubtah*s consumed per day, and the number of times per week qat is consumed. In 1979–80 the price of a *rubtah* of qat ranged from about YR20 to YR80 (US$4.4–17.7) depending on seasonal and quality criteria. The median price of a *rubtah* during that two-year period was about YR45 ($10). A minority of people chew during the morning (for example, while working) and/or carry on doing so during the evening after a party, and such people might get through up to six *rubtah*s a day. But a more normal day's consumption is either one or two *rubtah*s. The majority of people chew one *rubtah* of qat in any single day, but a large minority chew two.[20] This level suggests a typical man's expenditure to be $10–20 per day. Rates of consumption vary among regular consumers between one day a week at one end of the scale to seven days a week at the other. Yemenis consider two to five days a week to be average, and six or seven days a week to be heavy consumption. (Such evaluations also depend to some extent on the quantity and value of qat consumed.) Average consumption in the late 1970s can be taken to be three or four times a week.

The range of individual expenditure on qat in 1979–80 can be estimated by taking YR45 ($10) as the mean price per *rubtah* during that period. A low-level consumer chewing only one *rubtah* once a week obviously spent $10 a week. However, few who chewed qat regularly spent so little. A 'typical' heavy consumer chewing two *rubtah*s seven days a week spent about $140 a week on qat, and some regularly spent more than this amount – $200 or more a week – by buying the most expensive qat.[21] Most qat consumers, chewing one or two *rubtah*s a day and attending qat parties three or four times a week, spent between $30–80 (YR135–360) a week on qat in 1979–80.

16 A man with his newly-purchased bunch (*rubtah*) of qat under his arm in the Sanaa qat market. March 1985.

During that period qat was expensive relative to the daily unskilled wage, which was then between YR60–70 (US$13–15.5), or YR360–420 ($78–93) for a six-day week.[22] This represents the earning capacity of most of the domestic workforce (excluding possible payments in qat). A little more was earned by Yemenis working abroad. Skilled workers could earn YR1000 ($220) or more a week, but they comprise only a relatively small proportion of the work-force. Therefore it can be seen that even medium-level qat consumers were spending a substantial proportion of their earned income on qat. One *rubtah* of qat at YR45 ($10) amounted to about three-quarters of the minimum daily wage for an unskilled worker, and only two *rubtah*s a week (a low level of consumption) represented about a quarter of his earned income. A skilled worker consuming eight *rubtah*s a week (an average level) was spending about a third of his earned income on qat.[23] A heavy qat consumer must clearly have had more lucrative sources of income than those dependent solely on wage labour.

Unfortunately, only limited survey data is available on qat consumption patterns and expenditure in the 1970s. The earliest survey was conducted in the Hojariyyah district of Yemen by Yacoub and Akil in 1970. The following chart indicates the cash value of the qat consumed per week by the 108 regular qat consumers in the total interview sample of 125.

Value of qat consumed per week (1970)	Number of consumers	Per cent of total sample
YR1–14 ($0.2–3.1)	24	22
YR15–30 ($3.3–6.6)	51	48
YR31–70 ($6.8–15.5)	33	30
	108	100

(Based on Yacoub and Akil, 1971: 11, 31).

The interviewees in this survey were all full- or part-time farmers and of the senior, wealthier generation. The above expenditures cannot be related to income as we do not know how much disposable cash these farmers earned from their produce nor what proportion was spent on qat. Also, about half were qat growers so they presumably did not have to purchase their qat supplies. (We are unfortunately not informed whether the heaviest consumers in the sample were the qat growers.) Nevertheless, it is of interest to compare the above values with the average wage for an unskilled labourer in 1970 of about YR1–2 ($0.2–0.4) per day or YR6–12 ($1.2–2.4) for a six-day week. Thus half the sample were spending more on qat than an unskilled labourer was earning.

In January–March 1973 a small survey of household expenditure was conducted in Sanaa which gives an indication of average expenditure on qat, though not how it related to income. The survey sampled 144 families with an average membership of 5.8 persons, and was conducted in the dry season

17 Buying qat in a Razih market. November 1979.

when qat prices are at their highest. The survey revealed that an average of YR3.5 ($0.7) a day and YR107 ($23.7) a month was spent on qat and tobacco (which were not distinguished in the results), and that this represented nearly 13 per cent of total household budgets. This expenditure compared with 11.5 per cent on meat, fish and eggs, and over 15 per cent on cereals. Wages at this time ranged from YR3–7 ($0.6–1.5) per day (Bornstein, 1974: 30–2). As Bornstein notes, these averages do not reveal the different expenditures there must have been in different income groups; the spending pattern must have been very uneven, with a rich minority spending much more than the majority and inflating the resulting averages.

Schopen (1978: 82–84) was the first writer on qat to illustrate the crucially important correlation between income and expenditure on qat. He observed that in 1974–75, the qat in Sanaa fell into four major price categories: (1) YR10–25 (2) YR7–15 (3) YR6–10 and (4) YR4–6 per *rubtah,* and notes that each category of qat was bought by customers of a different social and economic class. Shaykhs (tribal leaders), the wealthy middle class, high civil servants, academics, small businessmen, (presumably rich) *sayyids* and upper-class farmers (*ra'aya*) with a monthly income of YR650 (US$144) upwards bought qat of categories (1) and (2) (YR7–25 or $1.5–5.5 per *rubtah*). Medium-level civil servants, traders and craftsmen (who were also farmers) with an income of YR350–550 a month bought category (3) qat (YR6–10 or $1.3–2.2 per *rubtah*). Labourers and members of the lowest social category (*naqis*) with a monthly income of YR125–300 bought category (4) qat (YR4–6 or $0.8–1.3 per *rubtah*). One could quarrel with the division of Yemeni society into the above socio-economic groups, but the important point is that those of higher income buy more expensive, better quality qat.

The only detailed and systematic survey which has ever been conducted on qat consumption among a large sample of the Yemeni population is the work done under the direction of John Kennedy in 1974–76. The first article on this research (Kennedy *et al,* 1980) presents statistical data which illustrate the high proportion of income being spent on qat at the time the survey was conducted, and relates household expenditure on qat to expenditure on food and to income.[24]

The sample consisted of 439 men and 364 women drawn from the cities and environs of Sanaa, Taizz and Hodeidah, and selected to cover a range of qat consumption habits. As the sample was mainly urban it was not intended to be representative of Yemen as a whole. Nor is the sampled sex ratio indicative of the relative proportions of men and women who chew qat. The sampled population was classified as non qat chewers and 'light', 'moderate' and 'heavy' qat chewers. Those who consume qat about twice a week are referred to as 'moderate' chewers, and those who chew one or two *rubtahs* daily as 'heavy' chewers. This is similar to my definition of consumption patterns for 1979–80. The members of the sample are defined as belonging to 'low', 'middle' and 'upper' income groups respectively, though the incomes of each group are not specified.

In order to illustrate the great value and importance of qat to Yemenis, the authors of the article compared expenditure on qat with expenditure on meat and other foodstuffs among households in each of their economic categories. This data is presented in graph form and is reproduced in fig. 3.

The survey revealed that:

a   A very high proportion of family income was spent on qat in all households where qat was consumed, whatever their economic status;

b   In the households of moderate or heavy consumers, expenditure on qat amounted to thirty to forty per cent of income in the lower and middle income groups, and twenty to thirty per cent of income in the upper income groups;

c   Although the upper income groups spent a smaller *proportion* of income on qat, that proportion represented a greater *amount* of money than that spent by households of moderate or low income. In other words, the higher the household income, the more money was spent on qat. Conversely, although lower income households spent a greater proportion of income on qat, they spent less money on it than higher income households; and

d   Higher expenditure on qat correlated with lower expenditure on meat in particular and food in general.

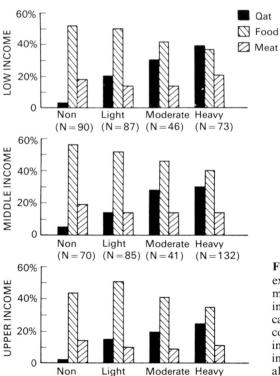

Fig. 3   Chart showing expenditures on qat, food and meat as percentages of total income in three income categories. The data was collected from men and women in Sanaa, Hodeidah and Taizz in 1974–6. (From Kennedy et al, 1980 by kind permission of the authors.)

This data provides statistical confirmation of the opinions of Yemenis and foreigners alike that it is common for people to spend up to a third or more of their incomes on qat.[25] However, its essential importance for the present analysis is that it strongly suggests that individual rates and levels of consumption are determined above all by income. Evidence of the fundamental importance of the economic aspect of qat consumption is the fact that when Yemenis are asked about their own level of qat consumption or that of others, there is a strong tendency to phrase the reply in terms of expenditure rather than quantity. This applies even when the question is explicitly phrased in quantitative terms. If one asks 'How much qat (or how many *rubtah*s) do you chew in a day (or a week)?' the answer is most likely to be something like 'Normally one (six), but it depends on the price of the *rubtah*'. A similar emphasis is evident when people discuss the consumption patterns of others. A very heavy consumer is more likely to be defined as a 'YR150 a day man' than as someone who chews three *rubtah*s. There is also a spontaneous tendency to relate expenditures to income levels. When I asked one Yemeni how much people spent on qat, he said, 'It depends what they earn. People spend between a quarter and a half of their wages on qat. For example a man who earns YR100 a day spends YR20–50 on qat and so on.' When I asked another how much qat he consumed, he replied, 'I spend YR150 a week on qat.'

This monetary emphasis may be contrasted with Western attitudes to drinking and smoking which focus primarily on the quantity of cigarettes or drinks a person regularly consumes and secondarily on the money they cost. The preoccupation is more with the consumer's physical or psychological susceptibility to these substances (which are known to be harmful in excess) and less on how his consumption habits affect or reflect his economic circumstances. With qat the emphasis is reversed. This is because Yemenis know that each person's level of qat consumption depends on, and is determined by, his financial status and not by his bodily or emotional needs. And we shall see that it is precisely because people's patterns of qat consumption are such a clear indication of their financial status that Yemenis exhibit, as they do, such a keen interest in them.

Here a word should be said about expenditure on qat in relation to expenditure on food, for one of the most highly charged criticisms made of qat consumption is that essential foods are sacrificed to support the practice, and that in some cases this may be causing malnutrition. This Western view of the deleterious effects of qat consumption is admittedly fuelled in part by remarks made by Yemenis. One sometimes hears men boasting that they spend more than they earn on qat, or criticising others for 'starving their families' to support their qat consumption. Such statements should not however be taken at face value, but as different expressions of the prestige associated with high expenditure on qat. In the former case the speaker may be broadcasting the fact that he is not solely dependent on wages for his livelihood but has other lucrative sources of income; in the latter case he may be motivated by the desire to enhance his own standing as a regular consumer who is so wealthy that he has *not* been made destitute by high expenditure on qat.

However, financial choices and sacrifices do have to be made in order to consume qat regularly, especially among the lower income groups. The important question is whether the diversion of money to qat consumption causes actual physical hardship or harm. More research is needed on this, but it is unlikely that men deprive their families of food or clothing essential to their well-being in order to buy qat. The picture is confused by the fact that many Yemenis see the sacrifices they make for qat as deprivation, for material aspirations have risen greatly and many foodstuffs and other articles formerly classified as 'luxuries' have, as a result of increased affluence, been reclassified as 'necessities'. It must also be realised that a household which eats on a low budget may be as well nourished as one where large sums are spent on food, because the price of food bears no relation to its nutritional value. One would like to know whether Kennedy's upper income households were buying expensive local meat, butter or honey, for example, or the imported varieties which are many times cheaper.

This leads to another important point. Certain local (*baladi*) foods such as those mentioned have become more prestigious with the influx of cheaper foreign equivalents. So high expenditure on food is not only a misleading indicator of family nutrition; it might also be a bad guide to the motives of whoever holds the purse strings. As with high expenditure on qat, the household head may be choosing to buy expensive foods to gain esteem – by dispensing lavish hospitality or simply having it known (as it always is) that only the best (dearest) will do for his family. He is not necessarily doing so because he thinks the foods are nutritionally superior, though he may think so.

The general point to emphasise is that food choices cannot be entirely explained in terms of physical survival, any more than the decision to chew qat can be entirely explained in terms of its stimulant effects. Both food and qat have significance beyond physical needs and should not be opposed as alternative targets of expenditure as though one were sensible and practical and the other irresponsibly self-indulgent. A man who spends modestly on food and a lot on qat is not necessarily juggling his priorities between family sustenance on the one hand and selfish pleasure on the other, as critics often imply. He may be opting for one prestige system rather than another – possibly because he cannot afford to compete in both. And in the context of Yemeni society, choosing either can be a responsible and sensible decision because social and economic advancement may depend on it.

7

The Social Importance of Qat Parties

Qat consumption is primarily a sociable activity and most qat is consumed communally. Although many people consume qat while working, even then the practice has its sociable aspects since most work in the company of others or encounter others while they work. It is unusual for people to consume qat alone and in private, and those who do are liable to be criticised as anti-social loners. Qat consumption implies gregariousness, a quality which is highly valued, almost prescribed, in Yemeni culture; solitariness is suspect and held in scant regard. In order to appreciate the status of qat consumption in Yemeni culture, we therefore need to jettison the Western stereotyped view of drug-taking as an illegal, secluded, surreptitious activity of an anti-social minority flouting majority norms of acceptable behaviour. Qat consumption in Yemen is legally and socially sanctioned, public and ostentatious, and is not merely respectable but prestigious. It is highly institutionalised through the qat party, and to understand the phenomenon we need to examine the status and significance of the qat party in Yemeni culture and the various functions it performs.

Here it needs stressing once more that qat parties fall into two main categories. The first comprises parties held on important social occasions. These are generally 'hosted' in the sense that many or all of the participants are present at the invitation of a host who is celebrating a special event, such as a wedding, a circumcision or an important visitation, and who supplies the guests of honour and other invitees with qat. In the past qat parties were hosted on special occasions in every type of community throughout Yemen; this was also the main type of party most Yemenis ever held or attended and provided their main opportunity to chew qat. The 'hosted' qat party has not significantly increased in frequency.

The second category comprises 'everyday' qat parties. These do not usually mark any special event. They take place relatively spontaneously at the initiative of those who want to 'chew qat together' and with the co-operation of the owner of the room or house in which they are held. The latter may suggest his home as a venue, or it may become a regular, customary meeting place; and he (like any other participant) may ask friends along. But he does not issue invitations in any formal sense. The essential features of 'everyday' qat parties are that anyone is free to attend without invitation, and that each participant supplies his (or her) own qat. As already mentioned, formerly only the wealthy attended 'everyday' qat parties regularly and frequently, as only they could afford the expense of buying an afternoon's supply of qat for every attendance. Before the civil war 'everyday' qat parties were therefore a predominantly upper class, urban phenomenon. This was noted by a number of foreign observers, including the writer of the following passage (probably Hugh Scott) who was referring to the 1930s and 1940s:

> In Sanaa and other cities every house has at least one qat-chewing room, and in many cases a second for the women. In the better houses a beautiful pavilion or *mifraj,* on the roof or in the garden, is used for this purpose. Seiyids and other wealthy people hold large chewing-parties, often repeated day after day among the same persons.

The same writer also associated regular attendance at qat parties with being a member of the rich leisured classes. Afternoon sessions lasting from 2 pm until 8 pm were 'for those who only work in the morning or do not work at all' (British Admiralty, 1946: 462).

It is this second category – the 'everyday' qat party – which has greatly proliferated and which largely accounts for the recent massive increase in qat consumption. The regular, frequent consumption of qat is no longer confined to the rich, mainly urban upper classes, but has spread throughout all classes of society and into the most remote rural communities, and the majority of Yemeni men and a large minority of Yemeni women are now attending qat parties several times a week. It is therefore 'everyday' qat parties which must be studied in order to understand the recent increase in qat consumption. What is it about the event which has attracted increasing numbers of participants at considerable personal expense? Or, to look at the problem another way, why has the consumption of qat penetrated Yemeni social life to such an extent that it has become virtually impossible for men, and in many areas women, to function adequately as social beings without being qat consumers?

Like all communal human activities, however pragmatic or functional, qat parties have both social and ritual aspects. At one level there is overt and obvious social interaction; at another level more subtle symbolic communications are taking place. Qat parties are therefore simultaneously 'society' actually functioning and rituals of social relations. For analytical purposes, however, it is necessary to discuss the ritual and social aspects of qat parties as if they were distinct and separate, though in reality they co-exist and each is a component of the other. This chapter will focus on the social aspects of qat parties, and the following chapter on their ritual, symbolic aspects, which will provide us with the necessary context for the discussion of the role of qat in the final chapter.

At this point it is necessary to give a more concrete impression of the qat party, of the physical, material context in which most qat is consumed.

The Qat Party
Most qat parties are held in private houses. In some parts of southern Yemen

there are or were public rooms specially for qat parties but they are not common. There were formerly such rooms, called *mabraz*, in Aden. But in most of Yemen institutionalised qat consumption has evolved so as to preclude the necessity for such places, for though qat parties are held in people's homes, they are 'public' in the sense of being open to anyone. This has also avoided the organisational and financial problems which would arise were qat parties held in a public, common place – when it would be necessary to allocate responsibility for arranging the furnishings, cleaning, and supplying the various utensils needed for any qat party. The way qat parties are held means that the preparations (which are not onerous) devolve on the house-owner and his family. It is interesting to note that Yemen has no coffee-house tradition like the Levant. Cafés are places to snatch refreshment when travelling or working away from home, not places for prolonged socialising.

Any room large enough to seat the participants in the customary fashion is suitable for a qat party. Most often a general-purpose living room (*diwan*) is used, which at other times reverts to use as a family sitting, eating and sleeping room. In other words the same space is alternately 'private' and 'public'. In most multi-storeyed Highland houses, the living quarters are above the ground floor – the latter being used for domestic animals and for storing agricultural implements, fuel and grain. In the villages of the Tihamah, where most homes are small mud huts, men chew qat in the open and sit on the Indian-style beds with wooden frames and rope lattice-work popular along the coast and also imported by the rich into the Highlands. Many Highlanders now own a metal bedstead, which is placed at one end of the room. In the old houses of Hodeidah, men's reception rooms have wooden platforms round the walls which also raise guests above the floor. In most of Yemen, however, the customary place to sit is on the floor.

Among the wealthy city dwellers, the room in which qat parties were held became differentiated in name, purpose and decoration from the rest of the rooms in the house. This room is called a *mafraj*. According to Serjeant and Lewcock (1983: 457, 578), the word derives from the verb *faraja* meaning 'to dispell grief or anxiety' and is related to a noun from the same root (*furjah*) meaning 'a joyous occasion'; hence in this etymology *mafraj* means 'a place for joyful gatherings'. As qat consumption became more widespread, *mafraj*s were built throughout the country. In some areas, mainly in the south, the *mafraj* is usually on the ground floor of the house, and in Sanaa it can also be at ground level on the edge of a garden (Kennedy *et al*, 1980; Lewcock, 1983: 461). But most *mafraj*s are at the top of the multi-storeyed houses typical of the Yemen Highlands. This is partly to provide a better view over the surrounding countryside and partly because such rooms are often a final addition to a house which has been constructed in stages. The fourth, fifth or sixth floors are often added only after a family expands, or when the owner can afford to build them. According to Messick (1978: 34–5), in Ibb men hold everyday qat parties in their *diwan*s and reserve the use of the *mafraj* for special occasions.

The most elegant and beautiful *mafraj*s in Yemen are those of Sanaa.[1] The Sanaani *mafraj* may stand alone on the roof of the house or it may be one of

18 House in Sanaa showing the ornate windows of the upper stories where the *mafraj* and other reception rooms are situated. Mid-1970s.

19 House in Razih showing the later addition of a *mafraj* with large windows to the original building. 1977.

several rooms occupying the topmost storey. It is a spacious lofty room usually about six metres long and four metres wide, and entered through folding doors from a lobby about four metres square. One long wall of the *mafraj* and the short wall opposite the lobby have low-set windows, flanked by shutters, which give the seated guests spectacular views over the house-tops and towards the mountains which surround Sanaa. Ideally, the long wall should face south for maximum warmth – for Sanaa lies at over 2000 metres and is often cold. High on all four walls are ornamental fanlights of creamy alabaster or of delicate plaster tracery set with coloured glass which throws a spectrum of beams onto the whitewashed walls. The walls are decorated with plaster mouldings in curvilinear designs, and ornamental shelves hold the various utensils used for qat parties. There are small cupboards in the walls with richly decorated doors; a rich man's window shutters may also be decorated with lacquerwork and paintings.

The Sanaani *mafraj* was imitated by the wealthy throughout the central and southern parts of the country. However, only the rich could afford to adorn their rooms in a similar way, or indeed to build a *mafraj* at all. In most of the country the *mafraj,* where there is one, is architecturally plain and undecorated, and is only differentiated from other rooms in size, in its position at the top of the house and in its larger, low-set windows. In the northern areas, such as Razih, the latter are a recent innovation dating from the first importation of glass window panes in the middle of this century.

In most of Yemen *mafraj*s, like other rooms, are usually entered through a small doorway at the end of one long wall, and have windows in two other walls and sometimes in a third. There are generally small glazed skylights above the windows, and small cubbyholes in the walls for books or clothing. As in all domestic rooms, pegs project from the walls for hanging lamps, clothing, weapons and pictures. Nowadays the *mafraj* and other rooms are usually whitewashed, but this was not the case in the recent past. In less affluent times mud walls were often unpainted, and it was a sign of wealth to have a whitewashed *mafraj* or *diwan*. This may be why it is customary when painting a room to publicise the fact by splashing a blaze of whitewash around the windows on the outside walls.

The *mafraj* or *diwan* is furnished with mattresses and cushions in typical Yemeni style, though usually the furnishings are of a higher standard than in the rest of the house – the quality depending on the owner's wealth. The four walls of the room are lined with mattresses laid on the floor, and along the back are put long, heavy bolsters which serve as back-rests. Smaller bolsters topped with cushions are placed at intervals along the mattresses to divide them into individual seating places. Nowadays these cushions and bolsters are often covered with gaudy brocades imported from the Far East. Traditionally the floor was covered with locally made palm-leaf matting or goat-hair rugs, but these have now been replaced throughout Yemen by imported linoleum and Persian rugs.

The wealth of the owner of the house is also evident in the paraphernalia he generally provides for a qat party. A large brass or aluminium tray (*ma'sharah*) is placed in the middle of the room, and on this stand several

20 A highly decorated reception room (*mafraj*) used for qat parties in Sanaa. Mid-1970s.

21 A room used for qat parties in Razih, and typical of most rural districts of Yemen. October 1979.

hubble-bubble tobacco pipes (*mada'ah*) and perhaps pottery or brass incense burners (*mabkharah*) and wooden tobacco boxes inlaid with mother-of-pearl. Placed at intervals around the room are pottery jugs or vacuum flasks of cold water, brass or aluminium spittoons (*madfal*) and ashtrays. The trays, tobacco pipes and spittoons of the rich are often intricately decorated with incised geometric and floral designs or Quranic inscriptions.

No fundamental change took place in the way rooms were furnished for qat parties (or general living and entertaining purposes) during the 1970s except that the majority of people could afford to furnish their rooms in some degree of style. In addition to the traditional furnishings, the walls are now often covered with pictures and rugs brought back as souvenirs from Saudi Arabia, and in the richer communities television and video sets had become commonplace at qat parties by 1980. As in the past, the owner of the room hopes to impress the participants with the splendour of his furnishings. But in the case of 'everyday' qat parties, he does not incur any onerous expenses. His responsibility is limited to providing the drinking water for the flasks and the tobacco leaves for the pipes, and even this relatively slight burden is often reduced by the fact that some participants bring their own water and tobacco to the party – as well as qat. He must also arrange a brazier (*mawgid*) of burning charcoal just inside or outside the door of the room for the replenishment of the tobacco pipes during the course of the party. If he has insufficient cushions or other essential articles, he may borrow them from friends. In general he is concerned to ensure the comfort and pleasure of the participants, but it is they who provide the expensive substance to be consumed. This contrasts with 'hosted' qat parties which involve the host in enormous expense since he buys the qat for all his guests.

People arrive at the daily qat party of their choice between about 2 and 3 pm, after lunch and midday prayers. Before or after lunch they will have bought their afternoon's supply of qat at the market, and that for their wives, or if they grow qat, they will have been to their terraces to pick it. Each person arrives at the party carrying his qat in a bundle under his arm, the leaves wrapped in plastic bags or sections of banana stem to keep them fresh. (If it is a 'hosted' party, qat is distributed by the host after they arrive.) Sandals and shoes are removed at the door, as is customary throughout Arabia, and on entering the room each person calls the standard greeting – *salam alaykum*, 'peace be upon you' – to which there is a mumbled response from those already present. It is unusual at qat parties to go round the room shaking hands and greeting people individually. The owner of the house might pour rosewater on the hands of the new arrival, who wipes it on his face, or he might waft sweet-smelling incense under his clothes.

The arrival is then ushered to a place on the mattresses, or finds his own. Before being seated he may hang his dagger, rifle, turban or shawl on one of the pegs above his place, or stuff them into a nearby cubby-hole. People always sit close together, but if the gathering grows larger than expected the armrests are moved closer and others are brought from elsewhere. Usually people line the four walls of the room in neat rows, but when a party is overcrowded some sit on the floor in front of those on the mattresses, or crowd

22 A qat party in Razih in May 1980. The room contains a number of imported articles which had become commonplace at qat parties throughout Yemen by 1980: insulated containers for keeping drinking-water cool, a radio-cassette recorder, a television set and a video recorder.

together near the door. Small boys and servants (in more affluent house-holds) sit by the door and the pile of shoes, and replenish the water flasks and recharge the pipes with charcoal and tobacco during the course of the party. The number of participants varies widely from three or four up to thirty or more.

The conventional way to sit when chewing qat is with one knee raised (usually the right) and the other leg outstretched, and with the body reclining on the left arm which is supported by the armrest. The top cushion on the armrest is called *matka,* and the whole qat party is often referred to as a *matka* after this comfortable way of sitting. When gawky foreigners take their seats, they are exhorted to lean properly against the *matka* and the back bolster, and often extra cushions are brought to alleviate their apparent discomfort. Apart from the furnishings, there is something about the orderly, structured nature of the seating arrangements at qat parties which itself induces a sense of relaxation and security. When you sink into the nest of cushions care and tension slip away.

Most participants arrive during the first half hour or so of the party, though there are sometimes a few latecomers. During the ensuing four or five hours until dusk people remain in the same places, conversing, smoking and slowly chewing their qat. The process of consuming qat and the accompany-ing activities are highly conventionalised. Each person puts his bundle of qat branches on the floor in front of him, or on his lap. (Occasionally qat leaves are sold loose in bags, but these are not normally taken to qat parties but are chewed while working.) He selects a branch from his bundle and turns it this way and that selecting the choice, chewable leaves. He shakes the branch and flicks the leaves to remove dust or insects, wipes them between his forefinger and thumb, plucks them off the branch and places them in his mouth. When he has picked all the good leaves, he flings the branch with its inedible leaves into the centre of the room. During the course of a qat party these discarded leaves and branches form a growing pile until the floor is completely carpeted with green foliage. Although most people bring and con-sume their personal supply of qat, during the party small exchanges of qat branches take place between certain participants; and if people are present with insufficient qat or none at all, others with plenty will magnanimously toss them some.

Qat leaves are not swallowed. They are chewed to extract their juices and the residue is discarded. The process of chewing qat involves placing the leaves in the cheek where they form a wad or cud which grows larger as more leaves are added to it. This causes the distention of the cheek which many foreigners have so disliked. Yemenis, however, draw attention to the con-sumers with the most swollen cheeks with amusement and admiration. It is actually difficult to keep the leaves in the cheek and not swallow them, and it takes time to master the technique. The cheeks of experienced consumers are said to become stretched and bulge more than those of new consumers. The Yemeni term for chewing qat, *yikhazzin,* means literally to 'store' and derives from this distinctive practice. It is possible that 'storing' the leaves in this way helps break down the vegetable matter or facilitates the absorption of the juices through the membranes of the cheek, but in my view the custom is more likely to be of symbolic than practical significance (see Chapter 9).

At the same time as this cheek store is being added to, the leaves are also being chewed. Once the wad is of a certain size or the cheek will hold no more, the consumer stops adding leaves and concentrates on chewing. The slow mastication of the qat is accompanied by frequent sips of cold water. Qat has astringent properties making the mouth dry and increasing thirst. It is also thought to make water taste especially delicious, and savouring cool or scented water is considered one of the principal pleasures associated with chewing qat. Partly for this reason some people take their own water to qat parties, sometimes flavoured with rosewater or incense. Nowadays it is increasingly common for people to bring cans of Pepsi Cola which they drink instead of or in addition to water. When someone wants water he signals for the person nearest a water jug or vacuum flask to fill the small cup for him, and he drinks from it with a loud slurping noise to indicate appreciation. At intervals people spit out excess juice or swill their mouths with water; they then reach for a spittoon and loudly expectorate a green jet of water and chewed leaves.

During the qat party the long hose of the tobacco pipe is passed from hand to hand, each man taking a few puffs before passing it on. This is also done in a conventional manner. The hand is curved round the mouthpiece so that the lips do not touch it; and when the stem is handed on, it is polite to bend it so that the mouthpiece points away from the receiver. When the tobacco is inhaled, the air passes through the water container at the base of the pipe, causing a distinctive gurgling noise. Many men also smoke cigarettes. The pleasure of tobacco is also said to be enhanced by the chewing of qat.

At some parties there may be a musician present who plays the lute and sings. Men may also get up and perform a traditional dance, flashing their steel daggers and stepping in unison down the centre of the room. During the 1970s, however, these forms of entertainment were increasingly superseded by television and video shows. At some qat parties, especially those which take place during Ramadhan or religious festivals, or when someone present is known for his beautiful rendering of religious texts, passages may be read or intoned from the Quran. During Ramadhan, male qat parties are held at night and often continue until morning when the hours of fasting recommence and most men sleep. Women, however, must sleep at night as their daytime responsibilities – cooking, caring for children, fetching water – cannot be avoided.

During the course of a qat party a distinctive atmosphere develops which includes the pattern of mood described in Chapter 3. As the afternoon draws to a close the sunlight fades and the room grows dark. By then it is hot and stuffy, the air cloudy and pungent from tobacco smoke. There is a distinctive aural component to this atmosphere. The rise and fall of conversation takes place against a background of noises – the slurping and spitting of the participants, and the gurgling of the 'hubble-bubbles'; as evening draws in, voices fade and these sounds come to the fore as people sit silent and deep in thought. At dusk the subdued participants quietly rise to go, pausing at the

23   A lute player at a qat party in Sanaa. December 1973.

24   Dancers at a qat party in Sanaa. December 1973.

door to find their shoes and mumble *ma' salamah*, 'farewell', to those remaining before striding off into the cool clear night air. After leaving the qat party most men go straight to the mosque for evening prayers, then home for a light supper and an evening with their families.

Hosted Qat Parties

Most Yemenis only host qat parties on prescribed ceremonial occasions, chiefly at marriage when qat parties are an essential component of wedding celebrations throughout Yemen. In Razih a male qat party draws the wedding day to a close. The wedding procession in which the bride is transferred from her father's home to that of her husband takes place soon after sunset, and upon arrival at the groom's house a large meal is served for friends and relatives of the groom and family, many of whom had earlier taken part in the procession. When the meal is over the women (who eat separately from the men) hold their own party at which they dance, sing and drink coffee and tea, and the men settle down to a qat party which lasts well into the night. (In other parts of Yemen women also consume qat.) The qat for this party is provided by the groom or his father.

Those present on this occasion are there by invitation; it would be a breach of etiquette to turn up for the meal or the qat party uninvited (though in parts of Yemen it is acceptable to attend the qat party uninvited if you bring your own qat). Also there is an expectation of reciprocity involved in the issuing or acceptance of invitations and in the bestowal of food and qat. The host is either reciprocating a similar invitation he has received in the past to the weddings of his guests or their sons, or he will expect to receive such an invitation in the future.

In Razih (and other parts of northern Yemen) qat parties are also held as part of the celebrations for another major life cycle event, circumcision. However, the host is not obliged to provide the qat on this occasion as he is at weddings, though he does for guests who have travelled long distances to attend. Qat is also provided by a host for guests when government or tribal officials visit communities on business of local importance. In Razih when tribal or religious notables are called in to mediate or adjudicate in intertribal disputes, it is essential to entertain them at qat parties and supply them with qat – in addition to providing them with all their meals and paying the appropriate fees for the work and time they expend.

These considerable expenses are met by gathering contributions from each male member of the corporate groups on whose behalf the notables are officiating. If they are representing one side in a dispute, it is hoped they will be spurred to more effective representation of that side's interests, and if they are acting as mediators, that they will be swayed to favour the more hospitable group. When government soldiers visit rural settlements on policing duties, they also have qat parties arranged for them and are supplied with qat in addition to their *per diem* fees. These expenses are paid by the offender, in whose home the qat party usually takes place, and it is expected that the present of qat and the conviviality of the qat party will act as a palliative – which no doubt it does. It would be hard to maintain a punitive stance

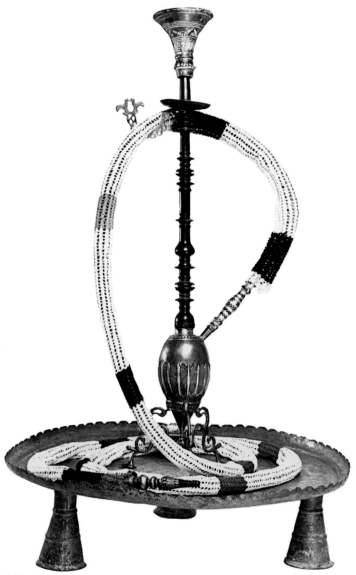

25 'Hubble-bubble' water pipe (*mada'ah*) for smoking leaf tobacco. Sanaa (except for the tobacco-holder). The bowl is of brass and fine pottery with a green glaze, the tripod stand for the bowl and the support for the hose in the shape of two cocks are of brass, the stem is of brass and turned wood, and the mouthpiece of the hose and the fitting which joins it to the bowl are of wood inlaid with white metal. The hose has a crochet cover in white cotton with variously coloured bands. The funnel-shaped bowl for holding the charcoal and tobacco is made of pottery decorated with powdered antimony (*kohl*), and comes from Shaykh Othman, Aden. The pipe is standing on a tinned copper tray with incised decoration and three legs.

    mada'ah H. 104cm. tray D.74cm. 1966 AS3 21 and 1979 AS1 244, 268–9, 273–5 and 280.

towards someone with whom you have spent an afternoon chewing qat (provided by him).

When a government delegation visited Razih from Sanaa to learn about local development problems, they were entertained at the expense of the local community and money was collected from each adult man to buy qat which was consumed at qat parties held in their honour. The people of Razih cherished hopes that their expensive hospitality would yield concrete benefits, such as water projects, hospitals or schools. These hopes were based on the local model of political relations. With local tribal officials such material gestures of hospitality and allegiance, combined with other pressures, can, over time, bear fruit. Unfortunately, this is less likely to occur with visiting government officials, however strenuously they are plied with delicious food and succulent qat, for relationships with state representatives are inevitably tenuous and temporary. Nevertheless, at the present embryonic stage in the development of a state bureaucracy, rural people place greater faith in the possibility of government officials helping them as a result of personal relationships that may develop during their visits – partly through the medium of qat parties – than as a consequence of formal position and responsibility.

A man can also decide to host a qat party just because he wants to hold one, not because there is an important ceremonial occasion which demands it. In such a case a day will be designated and invitations issued. Such parties are rare but when they take place they are an important means of winning friends and influencing people. Because of the expectation of reciprocity implicit in all hospitality, a large number of people are placed in the host's debt. But equally important is the prestige he acquires for having the financial resources to provide large numbers of people with qat – in 1980 a party for fifty people could cost well over US$500 – and for choosing to spend his money so generously. At all hosted qat parties the prestige of the host (be it an individual or community) is enhanced by high expenditure on qat, but the prestige value of lavish hospitality is all the greater when it is provided spontaneously rather than on a prescribed occasion.

Although there was no substantial increase in hosted qat parties during the 1970s, an apparent increase in early divorce and remarriage in some areas (such as Razih) may have resulted in an increase in wedding qat parties. There was no evidence of any significant increase in spontaneously hosted qat parties, but there was probably an increase in the quantity of qat consumed at such parties as they became larger and more lavish, although the effect on national consumption levels would have been relatively small because such parties were only a small proportion of those taking place.

Everyday Qat Parties
The recent increase in qat consumption is partly the result of more people chewing qat while they work, but above all it is a consequence of the enormous expansion and proliferation of 'everyday' qat parties. Qat consumption increased because more individual Yemenis decided to participate at qat parties – not because more hosts were bestowing hospitality in the form of qat.

A vitally important characteristic of ordinary, 'everyday' qat parties is that they are open to anyone who wants to take part. Men simply choose which party they want to attend, walk in and take a seat; no-one questions their presence for everyone has the right to take part. The all-embracing character of 'everyday' qat parties is intimately related to the fact that participants provide their own qat, and contrasts with the exclusive nature of 'hosted' qat parties where qat is provided and attendance is circumscribed and defined by the host's wishes and the constraints of the hospitality code. 'Everyday' qat parties also contrast in this, and other illuminating ways, with the only other everyday occasions when people gather formally for social reasons – lunch parties.

Lunches are arranged by a host in order to dispense hospitality to his invited guests and it would be a gross breach of etiquette to turn up for a lunch party uninvited. It is even bad manners to visit someone's home close to lunchtime lest it appear you are hoping for a lunch invitation. It would also be unthinkable to arrive at a lunch party with your own food, as you arrive at a qat party with your own qat. Lunches are a considerable expense for the host whereas qat parties are a minimal financial burden on the man in whose home they take place. At lunches it is known and expected that the host has spent a substantial amount of money; indeed he makes it obvious he has done so, for example, by ostentatiously pouring costly local (*baladi*) butter and honey over the dishes in front of the guests.

The guests at a lunch party are present primarily because of their relationship with the host, not with each other. They represent part of one man's personal network and do not necessarily have or want to develop relationships with each other, though they may do. Social interaction is rudimentary; in fact the way lunches are orchestrated restricts the possibility of socialising. They are brief occasions, the main business of which is to consume the food quickly then leave. There may be a few minutes to chat before the food is served, then the guests squat round the steaming bowls laid out on the floor, devour the food at great speed, rise to wash their hands and with little more ado make their farewells. Prolonged socialising belongs to qat parties. Lunch parties, like 'hosted' qat parties, are initiated by one man in order to cement relationships with his guests and to enhance his personal prestige. They are a form of gift exchange and carry an unavoidable expectation of reciprocity. Each guest is expected to return the invitation or repay the debt some other way.

By contrast 'everyday' qat parties do not create such specific reciprocal obligations. This is precisely because invitations are unnecessary and each participant supplies his own qat. No-one is dispensing hospitality or creating debts by bestowing a gift (food or qat) which must be reciprocated. The gatherings are thereby divorced from the demanding, binding elements of the hospitality code. The distinctive features of 'everyday' qat parties are therefore the absence of reciprocal obligation and the presence of choice. The vital point to stress is that they are *free associations of people who have chosen to attend,* not because they are invited, but for a variety of personal reasons.

Social Interaction

In every community qat parties are vital centres for the exchange of information; they are the hub of the local communication system, the focal point for the reception, digestion and discussion of news. Whenever men encounter each other in the fields, the street, on a mountain path, in the market-place or at the mosque, they exchange news. At qat parties such news is pooled and compared and passed on later in an enriched version ratified by consensus. Men tell their wives and more distant friends, and the information enters new and ever-widening circuits through other encounters and other qat parties. When rumours fly of some important event, men rush to qat parties to confirm the truth, hear more and discuss the implications. One often meets people who pass on some choice news, then add that they are going to the qat party at so-and-so's house to find out more. The importance of qat parties as a kind of institutionalised grapevine can be better appreciated when it is remembered that there is no telephone system in most parts of Yemen, and that the information provided in newspapers and on national radio and television programmes, is very limited, especially about local affairs.

Qat parties provide the opportunity to discuss the whole range of local and national affairs. Conversations reflect the interests and current preoccupations of those present, of their community and of the segments of society they belong to. Farmers may discuss their agricultural programme for the coming months, a group of elders and shaykhs may examine local political issues, merchants may exchange information on marketing problems and prices, religious experts may discuss theological problems and young men discuss problems which particularly concern their generation, such as the inflation in brideprices and the hazards of motoring on the newly built mountain tracks. (One young man told me that he was fed up with chewing qat with his peers because all they talked about was car crashes. At the same time he admitted that chewing qat with older men was less fun because they did not joke and lark about like younger men but conducted themselves with the gravity and dignity demanded of their age.) During the afternoon a wide range of issues can be aired, or any one issue can be explored in depth; everyone present has the chance to express his opinion and the diversity of existing views can be exposed. During such discussions important administrative, business and family decisions are taken.

In much of Yemen qat parties are also the major forum for more formal political activity, the main place where political leaders and legal experts received supplicants and pronounce judgements. Important officials take part in qat parties most afternoons and everyone knows or can easily discover where they can be found. It is a Yemeni custom that everyone has the right of access to officials, and although this custom has partly lapsed in the cities with the adoption of modern bureaucratic conventions, it still applies in most rural districts. A man with a problem or grievance enters the room where the official he wants to see is chewing qat, sits in front of him and explains his problem. The ensuing dialogue is witnessed by everyone present. Some may volunteer their opinions, others may have their views solicited by the official or the petitioner to corroborate facts or support decisions. It is perfectly acceptable for these social gatherings to be interrupted in this way; no line is drawn between a person's private, social persona and activities, and their 'official' position and duties, as in the West. Sometimes women even breach the preserve of male qat parties to plead a case on their own behalf.

Many political matters are hammered out in the context of qat parties. The day after one of the shaykhs of Razih made an unsuccessful attempt on the life of the governor of the province, the shaykhs of five other Razih tribes converged at the qat party of the judge (*hakim*) of the province to ascertain the circumstances of this threatening event, and to decide what action might be taken to prevent an escalation of the problem and retaliatory action by the government. People can of course meet privately for legal or political purposes at any time of day or night, and do so, but it is in the context of the qat party that the public expression of views, discussions of problems and decision-making takes place.

So many important matters are customarily settled in the context of qat parties that official meetings in stark modern offices can be considered less valid or effective. A Yemeni who wished to consult the President of Yemen was dissatisfied with the formal meeting in his office in the morning, but consoled by the invitation to attend his qat party in the afternoon. He felt more comfortable with the prospect of thrashing out his problem in the traditional mode and in a familiar setting. The President's invitation was also welcomed because it was recognised as an expression of his wish to form a more personal connection than was possible across a desk. To say 'I have chewed qat' with someone is to suggest the initiation or existence of personal relations of choice as opposed to official relations dictated by duty – or at least that an official or formal relationship has a positive personal dimension.

Forging Relationships

It will already be apparent that qat parties are an important medium for forging and maintaining relationships in a pleasant atmosphere, and this is frequently emphasised by Yemenis. Obermeyer (1973) notes that 'when asked about the function of the qat party in Yemeni society, it was striking how many informants described it as "a tool for gathering people and friends together". Serjeant (1983: 174–5) draws a comparison with a British consumption practice: 'In both the learned class from which the officials used mainly to be drawn and with the ordinary man in the street, qat chewing is associated with that good fellowship the Englishman finds in beer drinking.'

At qat parties individuals create and strengthen dyadic relationships, and are also assimilated into a group and have their group affiliation affirmed and publicised. This assimilative function of qat parties is best illustrated by specific cases which reveal the shift from outsider to insider taking place through the medium of a qat party.

Qat parties are an important means of welcoming and absorbing strangers into a community. A new arrival may be told where qat parties are being held at which he will find people with common interests, or he may ask around in the mosque or the market-place then decide where to go. An important visitor may, as mentioned, be invited more formally to attend a specific qat party of local notables – and perhaps be provided with qat. But a stranger can arrive in a village or town, buy his bunch of qat, strike up acquaintances and join in a qat party where superficial contacts can be consolidated and deepened. One of the first questions any foreigner is asked is whether they have chewed qat. This enquiry can appear to be soliciting an aesthetic opinion on the taste and effects of qat or approval of the central social activity of Yemeni life, but it has a deeper significance. If you have chewed qat you are assumed to have done so in company, and it is therefore a sign that you have achieved some degree of integration into Yemeni society, become acquainted with a particular community and some of its members, encountered some of its groups and networks and been exposed to their most pressing concerns.

Qat parties are also a means of welcoming home members of a community who have been away for long periods of time, for example, on pilgrimages, trading expeditions, working in Saudi Arabia or in government posts else-where in Yemen. Everyone who wishes to reaffirm his relationship with the returning traveller feels obliged to put in an appearance at the qat parties which he knows the returned man will be attending. Failure to do so is inter-preted as a sign that one no longer values the relationship and wishes it to be discontinued. Likewise, returning travellers spend days or even weeks doing the rounds of qat parties in their communities, re-establishing links which may have been weakened by their prolonged absence. The most intensive and frequent of such qat parties take place during Ramadhan when migrant labourers flood back to the villages and towns of Yemen.

The qat parties and lunches held during the rites of passage which mark major transitions in social status are a periodic reaffirmation of the existence and importance of a group defined by relations of kinship, marriage and friendship to the principals involved in the rites. They also provide a kind of updating of the current membership of the personal network of the host and his family which will be noted by everyone. For through time new members are acquired and old ones drop out, are dropped or die. Relations of blood or marriage lapse, as do relationships of choice, if the chain of reciprocal hospitality, invitations to ceremonies and exchange of gifts is broken – by giver or receiver. Such occasions therefore provide the host with an oppor-tunity to sever personal links, and publicise the severance, by failing to extend an invitation expected and 'prescribed' by the rules of kinship and friendship; or equally for a guest to opt out of his relationship with the host and his family by refusing a proffered invitation.

During my field work in Razih a political rite of passage took place at which a qat party marked the assimilation of an individual into a new tribe: a man decided to transfer his political allegiance from one tribe to another. This event began with a procession into the territory of the tribe the man was joining; it was then publicised by drumming and speeches, the latter emphasising the circumstances which had provoked the defection; and the change in political status was ratified by the slaughter of a sheep. These events culminated in a qat party at which the defector was the guest of honour. This was hosted by the shaykhs of the defector's new tribe and attended by its most prominent members.

Qat parties can also play a part in the restoration of normal relations between tribes after they have been suspended by political or legal disputes. Intertribal disputes in Razih involved many meetings between representatives of the tribes involved when each side put its case, damages were negotiated and judgements were pronounced by neutral mediators. Only after the dispute was resolved did the two sides join together in a qat party. In other areas such disputes are settled during qat parties.

'Everyday' qat parties, like those held at rites of passage, are also occasions when groups materialise 'on the ground', bonds are created or strengthened and members are assimilated. However, 'everyday' qat parties are created by the combined wishes of the participants. They are not orchestrated by a host from above; they emerge, so to speak, from the grass roots of society.

Although each individual is free to choose which party he attends, in practice he is attracted to some and constrained from attending others according to his personal interests and ambitions. Each man therefore makes it his business to find out who is chewing qat where each day, for the people he wants to mix with may assemble in different homes on different days. In the mornings in street and market-place, or at midday prayers at the mosque, men can be heard enquiring what qat parties are taking place that afternoon and asking their friends where they plan to chew. This selection process has been described by Stevenson for the town of Amran: 'Men harbor concerns about their final selection of a suitable place to spend the afternoon. For those who have no fixed chewing site or are merely seeing if there are better locations, the locus for such decisions is the teashops. Here men gather, discuss where they are going to chew, [and] inform their friends of any special events' (Stevenson, 1981: 36). So each intending qat party participant sifts his information and makes his choice. And after lunch and prayers each day, complex forces set men in motion towards this or that party.

Because participants choose which parties to attend or avoid, the constellation of people drawn to a particular party and the subjects they discuss reflect affiliations and issues of current importance in their community. The constitution of each qat party shows the present attachment of its participants to specific networks, kin groups, patron-client relationships, trading partnerships, political factions, professional relationships and so on. It also indicates their current preoccupations with regard to legal, political, agricultural, commercial, marital, professional, religious or any other imaginable matter.

Thus each qat party is a microcosm of some section of society and its consuming interests, and the aggregate of qat parties in each community mirrors and manifests its important groupings and concerns. Were it only possible to chart all the qat parties taking place in each community in Yemen over a period of years, and were it possible to plot each person's attendance patterns, we would see that some groups and concerns were ephemeral while others endured. And we would see that some individuals were constant in the parties they attended and the people with whom they associated, while others flitted here and there like social butterflies, eventually settling perhaps on a more limited range of parties. Others still we would find, attended none and stayed at home. Turner could have been describing qat parties when he said 'when one surveys large spans of social processes, one sees an almost endless variety of limited and provisional outcomes' (Turner, 1974: 14).

26 *left*. Brass spittoon, Sanaa. H. 11cm. *Centre*. Burnished water pot, Rahida south of Taizz. H. 24cm. *Right*. Green glazed tobacco holder for the 'hubble-bubble' pipe ornamented with birds, Hays. H. 21 cm. 1965 AS7 3; 1979 AS1 224 and 270.

8

The Ritual Significance of Qat Parties

Qat parties are not only a forum for social interaction and practical business, they are also rituals, a medium for symbolic statements about the social order. Rituals do not only reflect what is happening in another, more concrete realm which we call 'society', they also contribute to the creation of that realm by the power of their symbols over the minds and emotions of their participants. Rituals are thereby instrumental in the production of the distinctive structures and values of each society. To appreciate the ritual significance of qat parties it is therefore necessary to identify their symbolic elements and understand their meaning in relation to the social 'realities' they mirror and help produce.

The Spatial Representation of Status
A dominant characteristic of Yemeni culture is the profound extent to which social categories are defined, distinguished and ranked in a spatial idiom. The spatial representation of social status exists, of course, in all cultures, but in Yemen it is exceptionally pervasive, inescapable and charged with significance. As a consequence Yemenis are acutely sensitive to the spatial dispositions and relations of individuals and groups – much as an English ear is highly receptive to the fine nuances of accent which connote class. And they are correspondingly self-conscious about how, where and with whom they physically interact. From an early age they are culturally conditioned to the discipline of choreographing their personal physical comportment and behaviour in conformity with their station in life, and to aggregating in neat formations with others who share a common social identity or allegiance. In Razih it was striking how even small children were already imbued with a compelling sense that socially, and physically, there is 'a place for everyone and everyone in their place', and on public and social occasions would spontaneously sort themselves into orderly rows apart from the adults. Yemenis are so used to witnessing individuals dispose their bodies according to their social position, and to seeing social groups and categories 'on the ground', to having the social order physically displayed before their eyes, that their highly differentiated society and its spatial representations merge into one existentially powerful reality.

The spatial arrangement of people at qat parties is therefore highly significant to Yemenis and constitutes a potent statement of the social order.

Specifically, the seating order reflects and affirms, to a greater or lesser degree, the ranking of the participants. Other indications of identity and status usually evident at qat parties are the arrangement of furnishings and equipment within the room, the greetings, clothing and behaviour of the participants, and their manipulation and display of qat (described in the following chapter).[1]

The formality and scrupulousness with which the seating code and other symbolic elements are observed (in both senses of the word) depend on the social position of those present. Generally speaking the higher their status, and the greater the social mix, the more emphatically and effectively the ranking of the participants will be asserted. The qat parties held by the urban elite have therefore always been the most formal, and have also provided the model for those held among the lower classes in the towns and in the less sophisticated countryside.

The order in which the participants at a qat party sit round the walls of the room corresponds more or less to their relative social positions in that specific gathering. The most prestigious position is near the head of the room, at the far end of the wall in which the door is situated and facing the windows on the opposite wall. This is where the person of highest status sits, sometimes on a bed which also raises him above the rest of the gathering who are seated on mattresses on the floor. Other persons of high status sit along the adjacent walls near the head of the room (called *sidr al mafraj*). From there the prestige of the seating positions declines towards the wall at the lower end of the room. The most inferior position is close to the door where guests leave their shoes (see fig. 4).

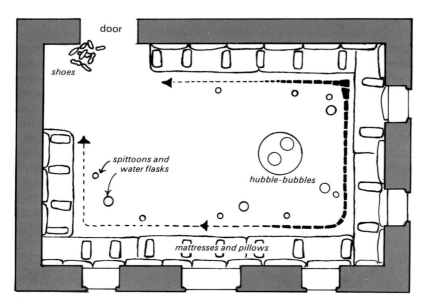

Fig. 4 Diagram showing the significance of the seating arrangement at qat parties.

Although the 'host' of the qat party may politely usher new arrivals towards the head of the room, the final seating arrangement is achieved by a kind of consensus. There is no master of protocol arranging place-cards as at a formal dinner in the West. The spatial ranking of the participants comes about by a dynamic interaction between each new arrival and those already present. Those confident of their unequivocally high status automatically take their places at the head of the room, and those who know and accept their positions at the bottom of the social pile shift further and further towards the lower end of the room to make way for their social superiors. Among those of intermediate rank a tussle may take place as each insists the other take a superior seating position while ostentatiously declining it himself. Eventually everyone settles down in the places they will occupy for the rest of the afternoon.

Status differences may also be emphasised in other ways. The furnishings at the head of the room may be more lavish and the space accorded each person greater than at the lower end of the room, where there may not even be mattresses or cushions and where the seating may be more cramped. The differences in status between the participants may also be accentuated by their behaviour and accoutrements, including qat:

> [The social hierarchy of Manakha] is inscribed in the general setting of the
> qat session also in another way. When the men arrived they were
> differently equipped. Some men came without bringing anything, but the
> overwhelming majority brought at least their own qat. In addition some
> of them had a small wooden box with their own tobacco. Others still
> brought not only qat and tobacco but also a thermos with their own
> water. Finally, there were two or three who brought also their own
> mada'a. In these cases a servant carried some of the belongings. When the
> men have been seated, the spatial distribution of these accessories forms a
> telling pattern. There are more and bigger bundles of qat at the upper end
> of the room than at the lower, more boxes of tobacco, more
> thermos-flasks and more gasabas [water-pipe hoses] in use. The men at
> the lower end of the room are dependent on those at the upper end for
> one or more of these accessories of a qat session: a striking illustration of
> their general dependence on the men of means and influence. (Gerholm,
> 1978: 180).

The social distinctions between the people seated in the different parts of the room may also be evident in contrasting modes of discourse – dignified, self-important and exclusive at the upper end; flamboyant, argumentative, jokey at the other. Those at the foot of the room may have their inferiority exploited and reinforced by those of intermediate status in the middle of the room, who may taunt them and make them the butt of sometimes risqué jokes while those of superior status at the head of the room look on with detached amusement. Qat leaves are also manipulated in a manner which accentuates inequalities in status. Small exchanges of choice branches take place between those of roughly equal status, and now and again someone at the head of the room will toss a small bunch of leaves to one of those near the door. This dramatises and activates a patron-client relationship; in return the recipient provides various services for the gathering – re-charging the water-pipes with tobacco and charcoal, and replenishing the water flasks (Gerholm, 1978: 182–3).

The formality with which the pecking order is represented spatially at qat parties, and the criteria foremost in men's minds as they take a seat and motion others to theirs, depend on the type and breadth of social mix. In the townships of Razih, as Gerholm describes for Manakha, the seating order and varieties of personal space at large, formal qat parties frequently reflect the traditional Yemeni model of social hierarchy whereby people are ranked in strata, or social categories, according to the nobility or baseness of their birth and the occupations associated with or monopolised by their social stratum. And it is at these parties that the seating protocol is most scrupulously and obviously observed.

At one such party in a small township in Razih a particularly high concentration of political figures was present. The shaykhs of several local tribes had congregated at the home of the judge (*hakim*) of the Governorate of Razih to discuss an important political event. The judge's status was unequivocally superior to that of all others present on account of his high government office and as the senior and most learned member of the most influential local *sayyid* family. The judge sat on a bed in the most prestigious position in the room (as he did at all the qat parties he attended). To his left seated on mattresses were, first, the senior shaykh of northern Razih, followed by his major ally, the shaykh of a neighbouring tribe, and thereafter the other shaykhs. Next in line came the younger brother of the judge, a prominant member of the Local Development Association, and next to him the head of the Association, a *gabili*. Further down the room were a number of other *gabili*s. There were no members of the 'butcher' (*jazr*) stratum present (the main low status category in Razih). At the door sat small boys who serviced the water pipes. On the *hakim*'s right, also seated on the bed, was the judge for the subdistrict – a *sayyid* from southern Yemen. This neatly avoided the possible awkwardness of allocating him an appropriate seat among the shaykhs to the *hakim*'s left while simultaneously recognising his important official position and his subordination to the senior judge.

During the qat party an interesting seating problem arose with the late arrival of an elderly *sayyid* revered throughout Razih for his religious knowledge and great piety. His arrival caused a great flurry. All present save the judges rose to kiss his knee and the hem of his gown in the traditional greeting of deference and respect, and attempts were made to drag him to the head of the room. But with a show of humility he refused to displace any of the shaykhs, and took a seat immediately after them while those lower down the room shifted positions to make room for him. As a senior *sayyid* of illustrious ancestry, his birth-ascribed status is equivalent to that of the senior judge. He is also his equal in religious learning and religious observance, and is quite as wealthy. However, he has no formal position in local political affairs and his influence within the community is mainly limited to the religious and moral sphere. The seat he took could therefore be interpreted as a reflection of his somewhat ambiguous status within that particular highly political gathering.

At less formal qat parties in Razih the relative social status of the participants was also reflected to some extent in the seating order within the room. During my fieldwork I lived in a neighbourhood inhabited by members of all three ranked social categories represented in that community: the 'noble' *sayyids,* the 'honourable' *gabilis* and the 'butcher' (*jazr*) category of base origins and despised occupation. The young men of this neighbourhood had grown up together, attended each other's weddings, and had close individual and family relations of friendship and mutual support. The disparities in their birth-ascribed status were not emphasised in casual daily encounters and transactions (though they were manifested in terms of address and the way they referred to each other in private). When they gathered for qat parties, however, they became more evident. There was always a lot of the horseplay and joking common among young men, but in contrast to this apparently egalitarian and familiar interaction was a seating pattern which reflected the differences in their birth and status. The *sayyids* usually sat at the head of the room, the seats next to them were usually occupied by the wealthiest, most influential *gabilis* from the 'best' families, and below them sat *gabilis* of lesser status followed by members of the butcher stratum.

The fact that the seating order at qat parties in Razih mirrors the traditional model of social hierarchy based on pedigree and occupation is directly related to the fact that there the traditional elite still retains its social exclusivity and a monopoly of power and influence, despite the establishment of a republican government officially dedicated to eradicating the privileges and powers of 'noble' birth. Members of the butcher stratum are still disadvantaged socially and politically by strict marriage prohibitions and exclusion from political office. However, if there is a mixture of *sayyids,* tribesmen and butchers at a qat party, it does not follow that they will automatically be seated in that order round the room. A poor, ill-educated *sayyid,* or one whose acquisition of property and station has been blocked by the longevity of his father, would not occupy a position superior to a rich and influential tribesman. High social status is not an *automatic consequence* of birth, although birth and 'good' family connections may be vital components in attaining it, combined with education, strategic marriage alliances and inherited or acquired wealth. However, in Razih a butcher is still limited in the social level to which he can elevate himself – however rich, learned or pious he becomes – and this is reflected and affirmed in the inferior position he normally takes at qat parties which contain a mixture of people from all three social strata. At gatherings of butchers alone, other ranking principles prevail.

At qat parties attended by members of only one of the ranked social strata, or by members of one family, the seating arrangements reflect and reinforce, at least to some extent, internal hierarchies based on seniority, the control of property, wealth and political position. At small gatherings of household members in Razih, the head of the household normally occupied the head of the room – a reflection (and assertion) of his authority and control of family property. The seating arrangements of other participants were not obviously of great significance, but children, and sometimes an old neighbour bereft of family and property, would huddle near the door. In one family where an elderly household head had already divided his property among his sons (property division is more usually post-mortem), his senior son, while not actually usurping his father's position at qat parties, assumed a prominent position at his side and behaved in an assertive manner unusual in those whose fathers retain control of the household. In another case where two brothers held the land of their deceased father in joint ownership, the elder brother consistently took precedence over the younger when they chewed qat with a few friends. This was less a reflection of the age difference than the recognition of inequality in their political status, for while the younger brother worked their joint landholdings, the older brother held a political position and had considerable influence in community affairs.

An individual may therefore occupy different positions in different qat parties according to who else is present, and this determines the ranking criterion which predominates on each occasion. Gerholm points out that at qat parties of non-*sayyid* townsmen in Manakha 'the most destitute of the *sada* are treated like ordinary servants ... [and] ... invariably given seats indicating humble status, no different from that of other members of the servant category. In a session at a fellow *sayyid*'s house, however, the relative rank is differently assessed, and the old distinction between an ordinary *sayyid* and an ordinary servant is again strenuously upheld' (Gerholm, 1978: 129). He might have added that while such a destitute member of the *sayyid* stratum would be seated in a more prestigious position than a non-*sayyid* servant, his richer and more powerful fellow-*sayyid*s would also ensure that he sat in an inferior position to them.

From the evidence available the principle of rank appears to inform the seating arrangements at qat parties throughout Yemen. Even in the Tihamah, for example, where qat parties are held in the open and the partici-pants recline on beds for coolness, despite the seemingly greater potential for a haphazard egalitarian arrangement of seating than in the confines of a room, the beds are so arranged that the best and highest are allocated to the most prominent men (Mary Hebert, personal communication). Further-more, the hierarchical arrangement of qat party participants does not appear to be restricted to the more 'traditional' parts of rural or tribal society, but is also evident at gatherings of members of the new professions which are emerging and expanding in the towns. A doctor told how at qat parties which he attended with medical colleagues, the senior surgeon of their hospital invariably sat at the head of the room, and the doctor stressed that no-one would have dreamed of usurping his position. Similarly, a senior member of the University of Sanaa takes pride of place in gatherings of graduate students and lecturers.

Qat parties therefore promote hierarchy, but not necessarily the tradi-tional heirarchy based on birth and hereditary occupation. It may be failure to realise this that has led some anthropologists to suggest that qat parties are tending towards greater egalitarianism (for example, Kennedy *et al*, 1980 and Varisco, forthcoming). Just because in some areas *sayyid*s, *gabili*s and butchers (or others of low status) are no longer seated in that order at qat parties does not signify that qat parties have become more egalitarian, but that a new social order is emerging in those areas in which different (and possibly conflicting) hierarchical principles are becoming predominant.

This is evident from Varisco's own description of qat parties in al-Ahjur. He claims that 'social interaction is relatively egalitarian in al-Ahjur ... [and] there is seldom a hierarchy of seating at qat chews. A butcher may indeed share the waterpipe with a *Sayyid*'. But then he adds: 'The host invariably sits against the inside wall with an unobstructed view out of the window. The seat of honour is to his immediate right or left, but status is not the determining factor for the seat of honour.' What he means is status derived from the traditional hierarchy, but the seating is clearly not egalitarian. He also concedes that 'specific individuals may attempt to use the occasion [the qat party] for personal or group advantage', and that 'more attention is paid to seating when it is a formal occasion, especially a tribal meeting or when dignitaries arrive'. Of course it is precisely at such formal occasions that one would expect rank to be most forcibly and obviously asserted.[2]

The Representation of Status in Other Contexts

The ritual significance of qat parties can be seen in sharper perspective when they are compared with other public gatherings at which aspects of the social order are expressed in a spatial idiom. On most of these occasions the spatial configuration of participants defines important segments of society and expresses their dominant ideologies. First, however, we should glance at the main 'portable' symbols of individual social status – costume, greetings rituals and modes of address.

Obviously costume distinguishes men from women, and within each sex styles of dress also indicate social status. Here we are concerned with the public display of status among men (for women do not have public gatherings). Traditionally men's position in the hierarchy was indicated by several items of dress, in particular by their turbans and by the kinds of daggers (*jambiyyah*) they wore and how they wore them. Differences in status were also accentuated by greetings rituals. A high-low distinction was observed in greetings between members of different social categories and age groups. Those of inferior birth or age status stooped to kiss the hand or knee or the hem of the gown of their social superiors. Equals kissed hands in a studiously level and symmetrical routine. Those of lower rank would also acknowledge the superiority of *sayyid*s by addressing them by the honorific *sidi*.

In much of Yemen these symbols have become devalued since the civil war as indicators of hereditary rank and have acquired new significance. It is now impossible to tell most men's traditional social stratum from their dress. Instead costume has become more a vehicle for displaying modernity and wealth, especially among the young. Only a small minority of *sayyid*s now wear the smooth white turban that formerly distinguished them from the rest of the population. Similarly, the dagger no longer connotes one's position in the traditional hierarchy based on birth and occupation. But it still has considerable significance. Depending on the context, its absence from a man's person may now represent, for example, Western-style modernity, and its presence political traditionalism. In communities where the dagger is still worn by the majority of men there has been a levelling of its symbolism. In Razih, the lowest social category (the 'butchers') formerly wore their daggers in a slanting position on the left of their bodies, but since the civil war have worn them like *gabili*s in an upright position on the front of their bodies. In Manakha the lowest social categories have also adopted the *gabili*-style dagger, whereas before they were forbidden to wear one at all (Gerholm, 1980). Most *sayyid*s have also adopted the central, upright *gabili* dagger. During the 1970s only senior *sayyid*s and religious specialists from other strata continued to wear the narrow *sayyid*-style dagger, beautifully decorated in silver, which is worn in a slanting position on the right of the body. This symbol has therefore ceased to be so redolent of high birth and privilege, and has come to signify religious learning and piety, which are still revered. Although the dagger has lost its precise connotations of rank, it continues to symbolise two vital components of male status: power (individual and collective) and wealth (for daggers are very expensive).

In much of the country there has been a similar toning down of greetings rituals, though the traditional forms still persisted in Manakha in 1974–75 (Gerholm, 1978: 129, 170), and in Razih in 1980. There, greetings indicating unequal status were still performed, and the honorific *sidi* was invariably used, even by young men to their *sayyid* peers. However, in southern areas of the country such self-effacing behaviour, and such a deferential and politically loaded term of address, had become anathema.

In addition to the qat party, there are two other frequent events when men gather in relatively large numbers and where the potential exists for symbolic statements about the social order. These are the weekly market day in the rural areas (or any day in the busy town markets) and prayer-times at the mosque. Gerholm, who was concerned with how the traditional model of social inequality based on birth and occupation was perpetuated in Manakha, highlighted the various ways in which 'hierarchy is affirmed and maintained in the market and the *mafraj* . . . [and] . . . denied but not in practice contravened in the mosque' (Gerholm, 1978: ix). Here we are more concerned with elucidating the contrasts as well as the similarities between the ritualisation of the social order in the *mafraj* and elsewhere in order to arrive at a better understanding of the particular significance of the qat party.

The market place (*suq*) thronged with people is a place where 'society' is inevitably displayed as a highly differentiated mass of individuals. There is a wide social mix and, as Gerholm describes (1978: 166–173), status is much in evidence in the diverse occupational activities, styles of dress, personal comportment and greetings rituals. There is also an intensification of self-awareness and awareness of others, a sense of being on show. On market day each man is asserting his identity, presenting his 'best face' to the other members of his community and visiting strangers. In Razih men who were casual about wearing their daggers and turbans on other occasions would be sure to wear them for their foray into the crowded *suq*. But although the market is full of symbolic representations, the cacophany of symbols is not melded into a coherent semantic whole. The crowd of marketeers mill about in haphazard fashion intent on shopping and chatting, and encounters are mainly fortuitous and relatively casual. People do not form groups or arrange themselves in any ordered, meaningful way. There is no over-arching, integrating symbolic structure into which everyone fits and by means of which they are unavoidably compared and ranked. Also with the changes in the significance of costume and with the modifications of greetings rituals, the market has become less a display of the traditional hierarchy and increasingly an expression of a new social order based on greater individualism, wealth and the implicit rejection of birth-ascribed rank.

Aspects of the social order are more forcefully represented when men gather for daily prayers at the mosque. The mosque that a man attends indicates his community membership. Small local mosques serve hamlets and villages; larger mosques are attended daily by the inhabitants of the 'urban' settlements in which they are situated, and on Fridays by people from the surrounding smaller settlements for the main weekly prayers. The congre-gations of each mosque therefore manifest social membership of the local neighbourhood and of the wider community, as well as spiritual membership of the entire Muslim community.

Within the mosque men align themselves for communal prayers – as in much of the Muslim world – in rows, shoulder to shoulder, facing in the direction of Mecca. This spatial arrangement is an overt expression of the religious ideology of the equality of men in their submission and devotion to God and to the divine law handed down through the Prophet Muhammad. The elite take no priority over those of inferior status, nor do people sort themselves into socially significant groupings within the mosque. In Razih there are occasions when prayers are conducted in the open, and it was possible to confirm that practice conformed with ideal. Gerholm (1978: 176) suggests that in Manakha, although 'there is no *organized* maintenance of social hierarchy within the mosque . . . the status groups tend to be repro-duced' because 'men arrive with their peers . . . carrying the outside order with them'. But men are as likely to arrive singly or with their social superiors or inferiors. The line order and who stands with whom depends on when you arrive and who you meet on the way and is therefore arbitrary. Any reflection of hierarchy in the mosque is therefore accidental. Individual status is de-emphasised; and the egalitarian ethos of Islam and the concept of community (spiritual and temporal) predominate.

There are other less frequent public gatherings which provide a further illuminating contrast to qat parties. Here we will draw mainly on ethno-graphic data from Razih which can be taken as broadly representative of the northern Highlands. In Razih political meetings are held to settle occasional disputes between tribes at which the spatial arrangement of participants is significant. Those taking part in the negotiations sit on the ground in a circular formation, the main protagonists and their supporters facing each other from opposite sides of the circle and the mediator mid-way between them. Although there may be disparities in the status and power of those present, and of the tribal groups they represent, this is not emphasised. It is their equality – or better still equivalence – which is symbolically stressed. The circular formation is a levelling device which precludes anyone appearing to take precedence. The seating arrangements reflect the ideal, if not the reality, that settlements are negotiated by the impartial and even-handed application of tribal customary law. In this context it would clearly not do to suggest that might is right by elevating the mighty to superior positions.

Other occasions in Razih when men gather in public are more ceremonial – the two major rites of passage, weddings and circumcisions. At these events the identities of the groups involved are accentuated, but there is little symbolic differentiation between the individuals taking part in the ceremonies – with the exception of those whose transition from one stage in life to the next is being celebrated and effected.

At weddings the main social distinction emphasised is between the wife-givers and the wife-takers, and there is a clear spatial separation of the two groups during the public part of the wedding celebrations. The bride is conveyed in procession from her home to the groom's by her relatives, and the procession is received at the house of the groom by a corresponding group of his kin. The dominant theme is the transference of a woman from one group to another equivalent group.

Circumcision ceremonies involve a wider spectrum of the local community. The ceremonies consist of singing and dancing by young men and boys, including those to be circumcised, and draw a large audience from the local tribe and neighbouring tribes. The onlookers cluster in groups according to sex and age. Women watch from the rooftops, and girls, boys and older men form discrete groups on the ground. Two types of dance are performed. In one, similar to that performed formerly at qat parties, men dance shoulder to shoulder in threes and fours, waving their daggers and stepping in unison. In the other, a large rotating circle is formed by thirty or more men dancing in step and singing. The circumcisions are performed inside this circle to the noisy accompaniment of gunshots and firecrackers.

This ritual is the occasion for a dramatic demonstration of the strength and solidarity of the tribe and its constituent groups. Their strength is symbolised by their arms and numbers, their solidarity by the symmetrical dance formations and songs emphasising tribal cohesion. In this ceremony, therefore, an undifferentiated, egalitarian view of the social order predominates, and no symbolic attention is paid to the differences which oppose individuals and groups in recurrent disputes. Emphasis on this conflicting reality would undermine the powerful ritual expression of power and unity.

The Distinctive Features of Qat Parties as Rituals

The distinctive characteristics of qat parties can now be defined more precisely in contrast to other group rituals. At the latter the dominant emphasis is on the identity of groups which are relatively permanent, and membership of which is ascribed and imposes a variety of ritual and social obligations. You attend a certain mosque, circumcision ceremony or wedding, and

27 *above*. The circular
formation of a tribal meeting.
Razih, late 1979.

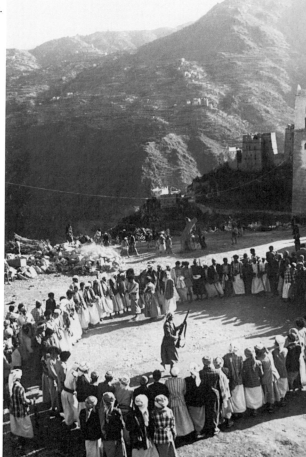

28 *right*. Men dancing in
circular formation at a
circumcision celebration.
Razih, late 1979.

29 Men praying in lines. Razih, early 1980.

30 Men seated along the walls of the room as is customary at qat parties throughout Yemen, Razih, mid-1977.

support a certain political group, because you live in a certain hamlet, town or urban neighbourhood and were born into a particular political unit or kinship group. Even the market you attend reflects your community membership and though you are not obliged to attend it you have little choice. All these affiliations can, however, be altered – by moving to another area and failing to maintain ties, or by legal means, as in the case of the man who changed his tribal allegiance described above. Persistent, deliberate abstention from the ritual activities which express and affirm one's loyalty to various corporate groups will also place membership in jeopardy. If you constantly renege on the ritual, customary or legal obligations of group membership, you eventually disqualify yourself from their benefits – the co-operation and support of your fellow members. There are two points to stress here. First, these groups are the enduring structures of society; they have a permanent existence which transcends the life spans of their constituent members and any shuffling of individuals between them. Second, group membership and therefore important aspects of your personal identity are imposed upon you by fate. You are opted into these structures and obligations by birth, and only by action of a deliberately rejectionist nature can you opt out of them.

The social importance of residential groups, kin groups and political, tribal units varies throughout Yemen, but in every community there are ascriptive groups which have vital and well-defined corporate functions and whose members depend on one another for support and help in various spheres of life, including when their interests are threatened by outsiders. In many areas, such as Razih, the effectiveness of these groups depends largely on their size and demonstrable unity in relation to others. It follows that on the major occasions when the identity and importance of these groups are ritualised, there should be no symbolic recognition of the individuality, inequality or competitiveness of their constituent members. Emphasis on those other realities would conflict with and detract from the dominant themes and purposes of the occasion: the expression of an egalitarian and co-operative group ethos, and the display of group strength and cohesion. Individual identities and status differences are therefore subordinated to and merged in the identity of the group.

The essential features of qat parties contrast sharply with those described above. The groups of people who assemble at qat parties do not form or represent any enduring social-structural entity which extends reliably into the future, even if they can be seen to have achieved a certain longevity retrospectively. They are essentially ephemeral; they have no names. They are also free associations of people assembled by choice. There is no obligation to attend as a consequence of some ascribed affiliation; however, you do not belong unless you have such an affiliation. And qat parties are individualistic, hierarchical and competitive, not egalitarian and co-operative.

The contrasts between qat parties and other group rituals can be summarised in table form:

qat parties	*other group rituals*
ephemeral groups	permanent groups

voluntary attendance	obligatory attendance
out till opt in	in till opt out
create relations of choice	maintain ascribed relations
hierarchical	egalitarian
individualistic/competitive	co-operative

Some of these contrasts are highlighted by Adra's description of male dances in the Highland community of al-Ahjur, where there are two categories of formal male dance: *bar'a* and *li'ba*. *Bar'a* is similar to the larger circumcision dance performed in Razih except that the men dance in a horseshoe formation. The dance is performed by members of one tribe, and Adra interprets it as an expression of the 'tribal concept' of co-operation (*gabyalah*). She contrasts *bar'a* with *li'ba*, at which 'attendance is *entirely up to individual whim*. There are no individuals, within or outside the village or kin group, who are required by etiquette to attend . . . . Any adult present . . . may dance, yet dancing is *not compulsory* for anyone.' Later she adds that spectators watch the dance carefully: 'Emotional bonds that are independent of kin ties and contractual obligations are important components of the personal realm. One finds a similar emphasis on ties of friendship in *li'ba* . . . . If strangers dance together the dancing is said to *form a bond of friendship* between them' (Adra, 1982: 257, 260, 283; my emphases).

Participation in *bar'a* is therefore an expression of ascriptive group (tribal) membership and by implication obligatory; and *li'ba* is a medium for forging relationships of choice (friendships), and participation is voluntary. There is therefore a striking similarity between *li'ba* and features which I have stressed as distinctive of qat parties. This similarity assumes greater significance in view of the fact that *li'ba* dancing is being increasingly replaced by qat parties. The *li'ba* dance is customarily performed in the afternoons when the day's work is done, but with the increase and spread of qat parties, which are a recent phenomenon in al-Ahjur, *li'ba* dancing has greatly declined and qat parties now largely fill the period in the day formerly devoted to *li'ba* dancing.

By contrasting qat parties with ritual aspects of other public gatherings, we have defined some of their essential features. To complete the picture we should contrast the institution of the qat party with what it has replaced, for, as indicated in Adra's data, the expansion of institutionalised qat consumption has meant a transformation in modes and patterns of socialising. Obviously there was 'social life' before qat; qat parties have not occupied a vacuum. People got together for a similar variety of purposes before qat penetrated their lives to the profound extent of the past decade; socialising, and all it entails, does not depend on the communal consumption of qat or any other substance, although in Yemen, as in most societies, social gatherings were usually accompanied by some form of communal consumption.

Before the qat boom the majority of the population socialised in a simple, informal manner with a limited range of associates – kin, neighbours and work colleagues – with whom they had close ties of mutual dependence, reciprocity and obligation. When men (and women) were not preoccupied with work, they would call on each other at home, or meet in the market-place, at the mosque or in the shade of a tree to chat about mutual concerns, and in al-Ahjur and elsewhere they might also dance. In the home, coffee or tea or the tobacco pipe would be offered as tokens of hospitality. These were part of a network of economically undemanding exchanges of gifts and services which took place continually between members of each small and relatively self-contained community. This informal, materially modest and narrowly circumscribed socialising of the majority was in marked con-trast to the formal, lavish gatherings of the wealthy minority who could afford to host and attend qat parties and maintain a wide range of influential contacts.

The proliferation of institutionalised qat consumption throughout Yemeni society has obliterated the former sharp differentiation between these modes of socialising. The elitist, exclusive qat party, vehicle of privilege and power, and medium of patronage, has virtually disappeared, and the less formal gatherings which constituted most people's social life, though they still take place, have diminished in importance. As the qat party has become the main focus of social life in Yemen for most men, and a large minority of women, other forms of socialising have become peripheral. At the same time a greater degree of formality has been imposed on socialising. It has become more heavily institutionalised; the qat party is an event with a name, and has a structural identity which the informal, casual gatherings it has largely replaced did not possess to anything like the same degree.

Asserting Affiliations

Men go to qat parties in their capacity as independent individuals and of their own volition. They do not go to fulfil an obligation associated with membership of a corporate group but in response to two distinct forces: the push of personal ambition and the pull of social pressure. The combined effect of these forces is to impel men to attend qat parties and to propel them to one rather than another. People go to qat parties to be in the swim of local affairs, but the pools they choose depend on what kind of fish they are or aspire to be. The ritual aspects of qat parties are as much a consideration in making this choice as the practical business described in the last chapter.

When you step from your house and head for a particular qat party you make a self-conscious public statement of your interests, affiliations and aspirations – to those you join and to those, so to speak, looking on. This statement does not go unnoticed; everyone knows, or makes it their business to find out, where people chew qat – precisely because it is so significant. If you chew qat with the same people repeatedly, the stronger the message becomes, to them and to others. You then create facts about your social identity; eventually your status will start being defined with reference to the people you habitually choose to mix with at qat parties (whether equals or superiors), and the multitude of everyday encounters and transactions will inevitably be affected. If the people are of much higher status you may not become their equal, but some of their social essence will rub off on you.

This was explicitly formulated to me in Razih when I enquired about the possibility of upward mobility from the lowest social category of 'butcher' (*jazzar*) to the more 'respectable', 'honourable' category of 'tribesman' (*gabili*). I knew that category status could be changed by faking origins, but was a more overt change of status possible? The answer was, in short, that you could never change the circumstances of your birth; you would always be a *jazzar* by blood. And no *gabili* would ever let you marry their daughter. But what you could do was 'behave like a *gabili*'. This included mixing with *gabili*s and trying to be accepted socially as though you were their equal. There is a specific verb for this process, *yigabyil,* which can be translated as 'to try to be like a *gabili*'. There is also a verb for 'trying to be like a *sayyid*', *yisayyid,* which was applied to certain *gabili*s who consistently chewed qat with prominent local *sayyid*s and were regarded as social climbers. They could not acquire a noble *sayyid* genealogy, nor develop equal affinal relationships, because *sayyid*s in Razih still prohibit intermarriage between their women and men of lower social categories, but they could achieve a degree of identification with a socially superior group through the institution of the qat party.

For people of relatively low status, a major constraint in selecting what qat parties to attend is the ritual emphasis on social inequality. Once you cross the threshold of the room, you are unavoidably submitting yourself to being ranked in relation to the other participants. You may be subjected to remarks and behaviour which put you firmly 'in your place', and your social place will be defined by your seating position. As Gerholm notes for Manakha, men of the lowest social stratum (*akhdam*) who aspired to social advancement avoided the large formal qat parties attended by people of high status where they would be likely to have their inferior positions reinforced. Others, however, were content to trade the ignominy of being treated in a condescending or humiliating manner, and being seated at the bottom of the room, for the advantages of a relationship of clientship with a socially superior and powerful patron. They were resigned to their low social positions, and making the best of it. At the same time they were of course colluding in the maintenance of a system of hierarchy which disadvantaged them.

In Razih members of the lowest social category (the 'butchers') generally kept to themselves for qat parties except for the young men who chewed qat with their age mates. In this situation they could mix with people of superior social strata without being 'put down' too much by, and in front of, influential members of the community. As described, inequality was marked by the seating pattern, but at least it was among friends. Otherwise the only 'butchers' who regularly attended the qat parties of *sayyid*s and prominent *gabili*s were a few men who had acquired a religious education, cultivated reputations for piety and become jurists (*fuqaha*). They dressed in the flowing robes and white turbans of religious specialists and were sometimes asked at qat parties to recite from the Quran. Their learning had gone some way towards redressing the stigma of their birth, and they were treated with respect at qat parties.

A man of low status may also gain the confidence and ability to launch himself into 'higher society' by acquiring wealth. Stevenson describes how in Amran the social aspirations of a trader (*baya'*), a low status category there as in much of Yemen, were transformed by his acquisition of wealth and manifested in his qat consumption habits. His new social career was initiated after a pilgrimage to Mecca and a side trip to Cairo for medical treatment (the latter being an increasingly popular way of acquiring prestige in Yemen).

> Before this trip he was known for his generosity. Daily his second wife prepared food for some poor neighbours . . . . Upon his return he dramatically changed his patterns. Instead of chewing qat alone or with some friends in the *suq*, he began to chew in the house of a *gabili* family of former importance and now gathering place for some influential men. Unlike some guests, he was scrupulous in bringing the necessary provisions for the water pipe and was always the first to leave to pray. (Stevenson, 1981: 267).

An anecdote by Adra implies that a women of the lowest social category in al-Ahjur (market traders known as *Bani Khums*) had succeeded in achieving close social identification with the elite *sayyid*s through wealth. It is note-worthy that Adra chooses to illustrate this identification with reference to the seating arrangements at qat parties:

> At large social gatherings of women, *Bani Khums* and *sada* [*sayyid*s] tend to sit near each other, sharing a water pipe and the thermos of cold water that accompanies the chewing of qat, because they are the only women in Ahjur who smoke the water pipe and chew *qat*. Because of their access to cash and urban markets, *Bani Khums* are sometimes better dressed than many *gaba'il* [*gabilis*]. (Adra 1982: 75).

So if you have low social status and are unwilling to gamble the possibility of having your position reinforced against the chance of moving up the social hierarchy, several alternatives are open to you: do not go to qat parties at all, which as they are so pervasive means virtually 'dropping out' socially; stick to qat parties of equals (and inferiors); or chew qat and socialise in a setting which does not accentuate social inequality. The first alternative is the only option available to the poor (from all social categories). The second is in fact the one most commonly taken by people from all the lower social levels, for the maintenance and improvement of position must primarily be effected among those close to you socially: social competition takes place mainly in the shallows of peer-group interaction, with some forays into deeper waters by the intrepid, confident and ambitious. The third option means transposing the activity from the house, for a living room is so charged with spatial significance it is difficult to imagine how it could be neutralised (in theory Yemenis could mingle uncomfortably like Westerners at a cocktail party, qat in one hand and other props balanced awkwardly in the other, but this would be culturally quite alien).

In Razih a number of men did in fact chew qat together in an alternative context: in the numerous small, galvanised-iron shops which burgeoned around the market-place during the boom in small-scale trade and commerce of the 1970s. If you peered into these small huts in the afternoons you would see perhaps three or four or five men huddled behind the counter, or even sitting on it, chewing qat and sharing a hubble-bubble pipe. The true significance of these 'fringe' gatherings can only be properly assessed in the long term. However, their effect is largely to divorce socialising and qat consumption from notions of heirarchy. Most of the men who chewed qat in this way were youths and therefore of relatively low rank, and they appeared to be creating and asserting an alternative social milieu apart from, and in opposition to, that dominated by the paternal generation. If so, it is appropriate that this should have been taking place in the market for it is there that many young returning migrants were investing their savings in small shops and attempting through trade to establish their economic independence.

These 'alternative' qat parties may therefore represent an assertion of identity and cohesion by the rapidly expanding commercial sector, or a rejection of the 'traditional' status system. Probably both elements are present. Perhaps they are best seen as a stage through which men pass, a phase of chummy, relatively uncompetitive consolidation of friendships with age-mates and trading associates on the brink of fuller engagement in community affairs, and a launching pad into wider and more competitive social involvement, as was apparently the case with Stevenson's trader.

Those of high status are also constrained and influenced by the symbolic significance of where and with whom they chew qat, though their concern is to maintain their superior position and prestige, and prevent any erosion of their structural and ideological supremacy. Any top-ranking individual who persistently attended the qat parties of his social inferiors would undoubtedly undermine his personal social position. Such individuals certainly mix with their social inferiors, but the latter must usually come to them. Those at the apex of different hierarchies also avoid each other's qat parties: if one deigned to attend the party of another, how could he be certain the visit would be reciprocated? Better to play safe and not risk losing face. And better not to risk the danger of failing to be awarded pride of place in the room. In Razih the leading members of the main *sayyid* family and of the shaykhly family did not attend each other's qat parties, presumably for this reason. Even on the occasion of the important political meeting described above, the local shaykh was conspicuous by his absence.

The Pressure to Consume Qat

Men often speak of the social pressure to attend qat parties whether or not they like qat. One of the advantages of working abroad is said to be the escape from this pressure and from the constant drain on financial resources which qat consumption entails. But even those who resolve not to go to qat parties when they return invariably end up doing so. They have no choice if they want to be fully participating social beings and if they want to maintain, assert and improve their social positions. But it is not only in their own interests to do so; it is also in other people's.

By choosing to chew qat with certain individuals and groups you are unavoidably indicating your willingness to maintain or create social distance with others. By frequenting certain gatherings you are expressing their importance to you and in local society generally, but simultaneously, if only by default, you are rejecting and devaluing others. This may be unacceptable to people who think you belong in their ranks and not elsewhere. If you have no standing, they might not care, but if you do they will pressure you to join them. Everyone's status is enhanced if the qat parties in which they participate are popular and well-attended.

A young influential *gabili* in Razih preferred to work and save money than spend it attending qat parties and on the infrequent occasions when he did participate he usually joined gatherings of prominent, senior *sayyids*. There he established a client relationship with several important patrons and as he was not competing for status, managed to get away with chewing a token amount of qat. However, he came under constant pressure from his *gabili* and *sayyid* age-mates to chew qat with them, which he resisted. Then he extended his home and acquired a room large enough to hold a qat party. Immediately his friends announced that now they would be able to chew qat at his house too. Whether or not he was ready to participate more fully in the local round of qat parties – the aquisition of an extra room may have indicated that he was – he had no choice. Hurriedly he bought mattresses, cushions and rugs and unearthed the family water pipes, and his friends duly descended on him. They specified a day and invited themselves.

A young doctor raised and educated abroad, and with influential family connections, had no intention of attending qat parties when he returned to work in Sanaa, but his medical colleagues persuaded him to join them and he felt compelled to do so or he would have damaged his relationship with them. Before long he was a regular participant, even though he disliked qat and just went through the motions of chewing it and stuffing his cheek with a respectably sized wad of leaves.

Qat parties are therefore also instruments of social conformity. They are not only a medium where you make something of yourself, but also where something is made of you. People not only want to find and define their social place, but others want to put them in it.

9

The Role of Qat

The first step towards understanding the importance of qat is paradoxically to remove it from its hitherto starring role as a substance which dominates social life in Yemen and relegate it to a supporting role as a passive agent appropriated by culture and manipulated by social forces. We should not think of qat as a powerful substance holding Yemen in its thrall, but as a relatively weak, bland substance which has had power and importance, so to speak, thrust upon it. The second step is to realise that people do not go to qat parties primarily to chew qat; since they usually buy it themselves they could just as easily chew it at home. People go to qat parties to participate in important business and communications, to cultivate relationships, to demonstrate affiliations, and to compete for social status. The only way to understand the phenomenon of qat consumption in Yemen is to understand the role of qat in these vitally important activities and processes, and to recognise the various intrinsic properties which qualify qat for the part it plays.

Qat as an Emblem of Social Interaction

In much of Yemen a qat party is called a *takhzin,* which can be translated as a 'chew', though, as mentioned, it literally means 'store' after the distinctive practice of accumulating qat leaves in the cheek. The verb 'to attend a qat party' (*yikhazzin*) is from the same root, and there are a variety of other usages referring to the qat party which stress the consumption of qat rather than the broader social aspects of parties. For example, when you ask someone what party they plan to attend, you would say 'where are you chewing (storing) today?'[1] Yemenis also show great excitement and enthusiasm when setting off for qat parties, and this can appear to be generated more by the anticipation of chewing qat than of socialising. For these reasons many foreigners have mistakenly assumed that the primary motive for attending qat parties is to experience the physiological effects of qat.

However, the way Yemenis talk and behave in relation to qat should not be taken as evidence that they go to qat parties mainly to satisfy their desire for qat – any more than the desire for a cup of coffee or tea or a beer is necessarily the main reason an English person goes to a 'coffee morning', a tea party or a pub. Coffee, tea, beer and qat stand for much more significant activities than simply the communal consumption of a pleasant substance. It is the significance of those activities which largely generates any excited anticipation, and this excitement is transferred onto the substances which are the focus of the gatherings. Qat, like most substances consumed socially, is an emblem of social interaction, a simple shorthand way of talking and thinking about something of greater complexity and social importance than bodily satisfaction.

Communion

It would be a poor social gathering in most societies at which no 'refreshments' were consumed, but almost anything will do provided it is enjoyable because it is the psychological effect of the communal consumption which is of paramount importance. The simple fact that everyone is doing the same thing and getting pleasure from it helps generate bonhomie. If the 'refreshment' also banishes the pangs of hunger, quenches thirst, or stimulates the emotions, then the more effectively it will perform as a social lubricant. However, it is difficult to distinguish between physical and psychological effects. If you always experience satisfaction and elation when attending a tea party, and especially if you rarely otherwise drink tea, you may believe tea can cause those effects. And of course if you believe it, it can. From the social-psychological point of view it is therefore immaterial how effective the stimulant chemicals in qat may be for different consumers, as the placebo effect of expecting and wanting qat to make you feel and behave a certain way may be equally important.

As described in Chapter 3, soon after the participants have taken their places, settled down and begun to chew qat, a phase of euphoric intercommunication and close communion takes place. This is followed by a quieter phase when people feel elevated to a plane of philosophical contemplation; after this they 'come down to earth' and return to normal awareness of everyday reality. Again we should be cautious in assuming that this sensual pattern can be attributed entirely to qat. Similar patterns of mood and atmosphere could be observed, for example, during women's parties in Razih where only tea, coffee and popcorn were consumed. Like the anticipatory excitement before the qat party, they could also be primarily generated by the social significance of the event. However, from what we know of its stimulant properties qat can and does facilitate and accentuate these effects, though the placebo effect should also be taken into account. Some participants may not be affected by qat in the strict physiological sense, but in the context of the qat party they are probably caught and carried along by the mood of those who are. The important sociological consideration is that these distinctive sensual effects are among the main reasons Yemenis consume qat communally, for they are believed to mediate the process of human bonding, to generate the bonhomie and communication which forges closer connections between individuals, and which all human beings value in their social encounters.

The value Yemenis place on the social effects of qat has often been expressed poetically, as in the following poem translated into French by

Chelhod. The poem extols the sensual, aesthetic virtues of qat, and concludes by praising its role in gathering people together and uniting them:

Il y a dans kat une consolation
Pour qui est accablé de soucis et de chagrin.
Du vin, il a la délicatesse,
Mais il n'est point prohibé.
Il en posséde la pureté, pour l'oeil,
Et le même goût agréable, pour la bouche.
En lui le lettré trouve le réconfort,
Et on y découvre aussi une protection contre l'affliction.
C'est le messager de la fraternité:
Il groupe les gens et les unit. (Chelhod, 1972).

As the qat party comes to an end, the sky grows dark and a heavier mood descends on the gathering which some writers have interpreted as melancholic withdrawal from the stimulation of qat. However, it is a common feature of the conclusion of both secular and religious rituals in all societies. It is when people become aware of having taken part in an event of 'sacred' significance essentially different from the mundane transactions of everyday existence.

The dual aspects of qat parties – the close communion of the participants and the emphasis on their inequality – are both evident in the following description of women's qat parties (called *tafrita*) in Sanaa:

The social conditions of *tafrita* are such that they seem to stress nearness and community rather than discordance. Since it is common for over fifty women to be sitting on the floor in a room of three by six metres, perspiring and smoking together, one obvious result is that status differences *will appear to be less relevant*. In other words, the absence of physical distance seems to prevent the building of social distance . . . . What this crowdedness emphasises is, *if not the equality, at least the sense of community* of the participants. And actually, status differences are not great, because they are only marked by subtle variations in types of cloth, brocades, velvets or jewelry. In other words *tafrita* provides a daily drama which pretends to ignore dissonance and conflict, and hence may serve to reinforce existing social conditions . . . . In the traditional *tafrita* [women engage in conversation on family topics which] . . . tend to reinforce female identity and community. But conversation is not only verbal exchange; it has also a silent language. Equally important is the implicit part of the conversation, the fact that it takes for granted, *or perhaps pretends*, that participants belong to the same social world. (Makhlouf, 1979: 26–7; my emphases).

The spatial representation of status at women's qat parties in Yemen is less evident than at men's, though there is usually some meaning in the crowded chaos of bodies. However, economic differences are more obviously displayed in the costume and jewellery. 'Subtle variations' in fabrics and ornaments have greater significance than Makhlouf implies. At the *tafrita,* therefore, as at male qat parties, the participants are unified in recognition of their diversity and inequality.

Qat thus binds people more closely in recognition of their different positions. Relationships are strengthened, but so are their inherent inequalities. As one Yemeni cogently explained: 'Qat parties encourage intimacy between unequals; but at the same time they increase sensitivity to others' pride in position. You wouldn't dream of usurping someone else's rightful seat lest he feel uncomfortable and cease to contribute to the sociability of the gathering.'

Commitment and Conformity

Qat also demonstrates each participant's attachment to the ephemeral groups which manifest their existence at qat parties. This is formally registered by his physical presence, but a sign of his commitment to the group and its members is his bunch of qat. Even though he consumes most of it himself, nevertheless because qat is expensive, his purchase is a sign to others of the value he places on socialising with them.

This interpretation is suggested by a dominant feature of Yemeni culture: the profound extent to which relationships are mediated and their importance expressed by material gifts. In Western society it is usually enough to 'spend time' with other people (plus perhaps the price of a box of chocolates or other nominal gift) to show how much they mean to you. In Yemen it is absolutely essential to spend money. Presentations of money, or of goods with precisely known monetary values, are essential for the initiation, maintenance and restoration of the full spectrum of human relations. At marriage a huge brideprice is paid to the bride's guardian and lavish presents are given to the bride; presents are due to relatives on prescribed occasions such as Muslim festivals or when a man returns from travelling abroad; friendships are initiated and maintained by lunches or loans; relationships between individuals and groups, ruptured by disputes, are restored by money payments or slaughtering animals; and political relations are established or strengthened by tribute in money or kind.

The maintenance of relationships is so dependent on gifts that default on a prescribed gift to a relative, for example, may be interpreted as a withdrawal from that relationship and seriously threaten its continuation. One man told me, 'If I failed to give my sister the customary payment of money at the festival after Ramadhan I could no longer visit her house. I would even have to make a detour to avoid it.' In the case of the many presentations which carry an expectation of reciprocity, refusal to accept the initiating gift also amounts to a severance of relations (see Mauss, 1969: 11).

The presentation and exchange of money, food or goods are such a fundamental, integral part of every important relationship that the offering or withholding of such gifts, and by a kind of transference the gifts themselves, can arouse deep emotion. I have seen men deeply downcast when others have refused offers of gifts. A bride was driven to tears when told her paternal uncle had refused his portion of her brideprice and bitterly retorted 'he is no longer my friend' (for she could hardly deny the blood relationship). A newly engaged girl who quivered with excitement over her expensive engagement gifts – emblems of her transition to womanhood – had shown nothing but indifference on learning the identity of her prospective husband. It did of course matter to her, but the trousseau represented that relationship and her newly acquired status, and it became the focus of her turbulent emotions. It is also commonplace for a husband's gifts of gold jewellery to be regarded as proof that he loves his wife, and his failure to make such gifts on prescribed occasions is taken as evidence that 'he no longer loves her'. Given the vital importance of material presentations in relationships, it certainly indicates a careless attitude to his marital bond.

It is integral to the meaning and efficacy of such gifts that they have substantial monetary worth, for their value indicates how important certain ties are to the giver. Qat has a similar import because of the high proportion of income a man must sacrifice to buy it – and he more or less has to buy it to attend qat parties. This is one reason why qat, like gold, food and other customary gifts, carries such an intense emotional charge. It is ultimately generated by the importance of the relationships it mediates. When a man joins a qat party his bunch of qat shows that the company of the other participants is worth spending a lot of money to enjoy. And the more often he joins them, the more highly he obviously rates their company and the importance of strengthening his relationships with them rather than others. We might say that in choosing certain parties he is 'putting his money where his mouth is', and in the case of qat it is literally so.

Because qat has this significance, a person who chooses not to attend qat parties when he can afford to buy qat is considered anti-social. In Jabal Hufash an expression for an anti-social person is 'he doesn't chew qat with people' (*ma yarbukh 'and al-nas*) (Morris, 1984). Friends may be offended if you do not join them at qat parties and your relationship with them can be damaged. There is almost a sense in which you stand accused of thinking they are not worth the necessary bunch of qat.

In certain circumstances offence may also stem from resentment at what is seen as, and may be, a rejection of traditional values and customs and evidence that certain individuals regard themselves as more modern and superior. As mentioned, returning migrants who announce their intention to give up qat parties – while away they perhaps forget the essential part qat plays in Yemeni life – are invariably pressured back into the fold by their friends. An upper class woman who was raised in Egypt and only settled in Yemen as an adult told me of the hostility she received from other women when she refused to join their qat parties, and how she was made to feel a social outcast. A minister in Sanaa was approached by one of his employees who wanted promotion. This man avoided qat parties and pursued other interests instead, which was taken by many to indicate a 'superior attitude', and the minister responded that he would not consider the request until the man started to attend qat parties. As also mentioned, many people feel that they can only get decisions from ministers after chewing qat with them. Qat is therefore also an instrument of social conformity, and to buy qat is literally and metaphorically to be a subscribing member of Yemeni culture.

Qat as a Gift

Qat takes on the emotional significance of a gift even when it is not literally given but is simply bought as an entrée into the group. It can, however, also be a gift in the full sense of being presented by one person to another. The precise significance of such gifts of qat depends on the circumstances, the relative status of giver and receiver, and the intention implicit in the presentation.

An important feature of 'hosted' parties is the element of reciprocity. The host provides the guests with qat on the understanding that they will reciprocate with similar invitations in the future, or he is reciprocating a similar invitation which he has received from them in the past. Such hospitality is a vital means of maintaining and strengthening ties with relatives and friends, and is part of a network of reciprocal acts of hospitality and generosity which mediate social relations in everyday life. The main difference from everyday hospitality is that because of its obligatory nature and the intrinsic importance of the ceremony, the 'hosted' qat party is an especially opportune occasion to show special friends how much you value them, and conversely to downgrade other relationships by failing to issue invitations.

'Hosted' qat parties also provide the opportunity to display wealth (as does the meal which precedes the qat party.) In Razih great publicity is given to the money spent on qat for wedding guests (and indeed to all wedding expenditures). This information is eagerly sought by those who do not attend and it becomes one of the salient facts when the events of the wedding are recounted later. There is not, however, any special procession to convey the qat to the house where the wedding party is held, as was the case in Aden, and perhaps therefore in Yemen, in the last century. The following is a vivid description of such a nineteenth-century procession, showing how decorations and music drew attention to the lavish supplies of qat the host was providing.

> The same morning fifty to a hundred men proceed to . . . the Barrier Gate, and bring into Aden with pomp and ceremony a camel-load or more of kat, which has arrived for the bridegroom's father. The camels bearing the kat are adorned with silver ornaments, and the kat itself is covered with an embroidered cloth; the men accompanying the cavalcade sing, beat drums, and burn incense up to the bridegroom's house, where the camel-drivers receive a present of rich apparel. The camels are unloaded, and the kat taken into the shed . . . with great ceremony. As soon as the kat is fairly installed in the marriage shed, the guests begin to arrive, each bearing kat (to the value of from one to two dollars), tobacco, and water-vessels, for his own use. This kat, etc., is in addition to what is provided by the bridegroom's father. The day is passed eating kat, singing hymns, smoking, and burning incense; in the evening supper is served, after which all retire to their houses. (Hunter, 1877).

The elements of reciprocity and display are also integral to other 'hosted' parties, such as those held by community representatives for visiting government officials. There is a dual aim: to create indebtedness by generous gifts of qat, and thereby sway decisions in their favour; and to show that the community and its leaders are people of material substance worth reckoning with.

It is not common for 'hosted' qat parties to be held except on prescribed ceremonial occasions. However, Morris (1984) provides an example from Jabal Hufash of the use of such parties in the competition for social status between the local shaykh, who failed to live up to expected standards of generosity, and a rich and ambitious low status butcher. The shaykh had a reputation for stinginess because he dealt with disputes in the morning in the neutral space of the local health centre instead of opening his *diwan* to plaintiffs in the afternoons – that is, during qat-chewing hours. This was understood to be in order to avoid giving qat to the poor men who would inevitably turn up. The butcher had set himself up as a rival to the shaykh, and part of his strategy for upward mobility and the acquisition of power was to hold regular qat parties at which he provided all the qat at great personal expense.

Although at 'everyday' qat parties each participant normally provides his own qat, people may give each other small amounts of qat during the course of the party, and the significance of such gifts is similar to the more grandiose presentations of 'hosted' parties. Such gifts strengthen relationships both of equality and inequality. In the first case, choice sprigs of qat are exchanged reciprocally between those of roughly equivalent social status, usually those seated at the head of the room. This demonstrates their social cohesion, and creates social distance between them and those who are excluded from the exchanges. According to Schopen (1978: 138), this circulation of qat branches is thought to symbolise the binding together of the participants and is called *gabyalah* – a term which he construes as 'behaving like relatives', and which can equally well be translated as 'creating close relationships'.

In the second case a one-way traffic in qat takes place between social superiors and their inferiors. Gerholm describes how this interaction dramatises and affirms patron-client relationships in Manakha:

> While examining his qat bundles, the man at the upper end of the room
> selects a few branches of second-rate quality, ties them loosely together,
> and throws them in a wide curve down the room so that they land in the
> lap of one of the servants or right in front of him. In exchange the latter
> will be ready to serve his patron in various ways. He may help in
> re-arranging the cushions if need be, he will make sure that the *mada'a*
> [tobacco pipe] is functioning properly, and he will refill the *buri* [tobacco
> holder]. (Gerholm, 1977: 182)

These services cause the recipient to move around the room, and he becomes the butt of physical teasing and sometimes lewd joking. This is an extreme example of how a gift of qat can reinforce a relationship of domination and subordination, and affirm the high status of some participants by the humiliation of others. But at any socially mixed qat party, the patronising bestowal of qat by a superior on an inferior is an affirmation of their unequal social positions – precisely because of the shared cultural value which attributes such significance to gift-giving. Such gifts of qat cannot be refused. Nor can they be reciprocated in kind – only in services. Morris (1984) notes what a breach of custom it is for an ordinary person to offer qat to a big man, and describes the shocked silence which descended on a qat party in Jabel Hufash when a prosperous butcher ostentatiously flung some qat onto the lap of a high official. Such gestures against the establishment by the socially disadvantaged must be occurring increasingly all over Yemen. Otherwise, as Gerholm points out for Manakha, the main recourse for low status social climbers is to avoid the large mixed parties where the improved social identities they are trying to establish might be severely tested.[2]

An interesting illustration both of the power of a gift of qat to create a relationship and of the coercive aspect of gift-giving concerns the rare occurrence of a two-forked branch of qat known as a 'branch of peace' (*ghusn al-salam*). According to one account, if a man finds such a branch among his qat during a party, he gains the right to throw it at a shaykh and demand his daughter in marriage. This demand must be granted if the man escapes from the room before the shaykh can kill him (Abd al-Malik al-Maqrami, personal communication). This cruel penalty is undoubtedly a myth and there is no evidence of it ever being carried out. In another version of the custom recorded in Jabal Hufash, a man who finds a two-forked branch throws it at anyone in the room crying 'I take you with the branch of peace' (*ana jabak bi ghusn al-salam*). If he can then escape before qat or anything else is thrown back at him, the man at whom he threw the qat is obliged to supply him with a lavish lunch and supplies of qat on a later occasion. According to Morris (1984), 'This custom was said to be a way of cementing friendship among men who are not related and to be distinct from the other form of establishing fictive kinship by naming one's son after one's friend or patron.'

Conspicuous Consumption
Probably the most important role qat plays is as an article of conspicuous consumption – a means of displaying wealth and acquiring prestige. This was undoubtedly the case in the past as well as today. The following description of Adeni practices early this century clearly reveals the desire to draw attention to one's qat purchase:

> In Aden the mabrazes [qat party rooms] of the rich are private and often furnished with oriental luxury. Among the Somalis and the commoner Arabs the mabraz is a well-ventilated room hired and furnished for their favourite diversion. The habitué of the public mabraz leaves his house at the appointed hour with his khat tied up in a bright shawl and conspicuously displayed; he wishes all the world to know that he goes to enjoy himself.

The same author quotes verbatim his Arab servant's description of 'hosted' qat parties held at weddings. Like Rihani's description of Lahej (quoted earlier), this shows that, in addition to qat, people took various other paraphernalia to parties to display their wealth. This also sometimes happens in Yemen today. It also shows the importance of people being seated according to their status:

> Rich people will be seen nicely dressed, umbrella in hand, fine shawl on shoulder, a boy after him with the [hubble] bubble . . . on their way to [the qat party]. Reason why rich people like to get everything from home is that all things they use for khat eating are specially made and very amusing, so they like to be proud of them in large assemblies. Well when the [room] is full up, khat distribution will go on and khat chewing begins. The way how they distribute it is that as soon as a man has come in the marriage makers will politely come to ask him whether that man is rich or poor and take him to a seat where they will make him sit and put a bunch of qat in his hand. (Moser, 1917).

We have seen that a host enhances his reputation by the munificent provision of qat for his guests, but 'hosted' qat parties are comparatively infrequent and the social credit from such ostentatious generosity is diluted by the fact that they are mainly prescribed and involve a considerable element of social debt repayment. It is at 'everyday' qat parties that qat gives its most interesting performance as an article of conspicuous consumption. The individualistic consumption of qat at these parties is largely sustained by the desire to acquire prestige through the display and disposal of wealth. Wealth is indicated in two ways: by the quality and quantity of qat you chew on each occasion, and by the frequency with which you attend qat parties. This is a competitive situation. Each person is endeavouring to enhance his esteem and standing in relation to everyone else. This dynamic causes each consumer to pay as much as he can afford and attend qat parties as often as he can. This is why, as we saw in Chapter 6, levels of qat consumption are so closely correlated with income, and why qat is available in such a variety of qualities and prices.

It is social and economic forces which sustain qat consumption, as noted by Obermeyer after his visit to Yemen in 1972:

> The richer a person is the more qat he uses and, also, the richer a person becomes the more he spends on qat. These, of course, are now truisms related to common facts of 'economic man' that the more one has the more one spends. In the Yemen, the direction of spending is usually in the daily purchase of qat. This applies to a full range of professions from ministers to street cleaners. It is common knowledge that the rich and more affluent chew the small, tender shoots from the top of the fresh qat branch (kafla) for which they pay up to ten rials per day while the poor chew the larger and less succulent leaves from the bottom of the branch which may be two days old and for which they pay three to four rials per

day. The qat branch is an indicator of class and social mobility in Yemen. (Obermeyer, 1973)[3]

Why then has qat become an increasingly important vehicle for displaying wealth in Yemen, and precisely how does it perform as an article of conspicuous consumption?

Wealth has always been a vital component of high status in Yemen and was always conspicuously displayed by those who possessed it. Now that it has become more attainable across the full spectrum of the population, it has generated a surge of consumerism and a transformation in social aspirations – a heady sense of the potential for upward mobility based on material achievement. However, identifying qat consumption with the wider phenomenon of increased consumerism does not explain the efflorescence of this highly 'traditional' way of acquiring prestige. Why was qat not rendered obsolete as a means of displaying wealth by the influx of luxury goods with more 'modern' connotations? For it was mainly the manufactured products of the industrial world which people were eager to acquire and display; materially speaking, modernism was as important as consumerism. The answer lies in examining the characteristics of qat which make it a reliable and suitable repository of cultural and monetary value, and in understanding the particular way it functions as an article of prestige consumption and a vehicle for displaying variable expenditures.

When natural objects are appropriated by cultures to serve as symbols of status, to reflect prestige on those who own or consume them, they normally possess some intrinsic qualities which render them appropriate for the task. They at least conform with the aesthetic values of the culture concerned and should certainly not flout them. Of course, as Veblen noted, when objects are elevated to positions of prestige and invested with high monetary value, the appreciation of their innate characteristics is heightened and sustained by their 'pecuniary' worth. There is a 'blending and confusion of the elements of expensiveness and beauty' (1970: 97). Nevertheless, the raw material usually holds some initial promise.

Qat is well-qualified for cultural esteem. It is a lush, leafy product of the earth in a country which has always depended on agriculture, where drought and famine were frequent, and where greenery means prosperity. Qat also flourishes in the most fertile parts of Yemen, verdant mountains blessed with high rainfall or plentiful streams and envied by farmers who toil for their harvests in the dry Tihamah and on the bleak, wind-swept plateaux. It is therefore easy to understand why qat arouses admiration and aesthetic appreciation. The people of the qat-growing area of Razih would point to the terraced slopes clothed in dense foliage and enquire rhetorically whether anywhere could be as green and beautiful. After qat is picked its fresh, crisp leaves still gladden the eye. Merchants select and trim the branches like florists arranging a bouquet, and men proudly unwrap their newly purchased bunches to display them to friends. Qat also gives physical pleasure in a culture where the sensual pleasures permitted by religion are enjoyed with uninhibited enthusiasm. So in its appearance, associations and effects, qat is a suitable candidiate for high cultural and monetary valuation. In addition it is a luxury. It is not necessary for physical survival like food or clothing, nor has it any practical use. Uncluttered by other uses and meanings it can reflect more clearly the values attributed to it.

Two further qualifications for an article to become prestigious and its consumption institutionalised are scarcity and availability. Were supplies unlimited it would inevitably be devalued. This is why the flow of diamonds onto the world market is so carefully regulated. The supply of qat is largely regulated by nature, for it only flourishes in limited areas and, so far at least, production has never swamped demand. However, the supply must also be constant and reliable, especially if, as with qat, the article is both continually and literally consumed. Were there, for example, a blight on qat lasting many years, unless a comparable substitute were found, the whole ritual edifice surrounding qat consumption could crumble. But qat is a hardy crop and despite many droughts has never been wiped out. Supplies wax and wane, but in Yemeni experience it never entirely disappears. Without this confidence people would perhaps not still be building ornate and expensive *mafraj*s.

Qat also derives prestige from its intrinsic value as a product of the earth in a country with limited agricultural resources. The diversion of prime agricultural land to the cultivation of a luxury product automatically imbues it with prestige and, as argued in Chapter 5, the commercialisation of coffee originally translated this prestige value into monetary worth. An article can simply be awarded prestige or monetary value in any culture – as with shell valuables in New Guinea – but in the case of qat this value is literally rooted in the land and could only disappear were the whole agricultural economy of Yemen destroyed, unless land retained its value as real estate.

If it is further required that an object differentiate between individuals according to a scale of values, it must be correspondingly susceptible to internal differentiation and evaluation. And the distinctions it makes must be easily perceived. These criteria are adequately fulfilled by qat. It comes in large, rustling bunches of leaves which naturally lend themselves to flamboyant consumption. The visual and aural impact of, say, tobacco powder or coffee – to name two other substances consumed socially in Yemen – is obviously appreciably less. And one cup of coffee or one bag of tobacco powder looks much like another. Qat, however, varies in the size, shape and colour of its leaves, the length of the branches, the style of packaging and the size of the bunch. These features, together with alleged differences in flavour and effects, are the basis for an indigenous botanical and geographical classification of qat into hundreds of types, and make qat an ideal commodity for discussing and displaying variable expenditures.

Though the differences between them are often slight, Yemenis are expert at identifying the varieties of qat in the markets they frequent. The virtues of different types of qat are also much discussed. There is in fact a connoisseurship surrounding qat comparable to that surroundng wine in the West (see United Nations, 1956, and Kennedy *et al*, 1983). This is not an automatic consequence of the innate characteristics of qat. The actual differences in the properties and appearance of qat could as easily be glossed over as emphasised. The raw material has intrinsic potential for differentiation, but it has just as much potential for being regarded as a homogeneous whole. The differences are elaborated and emphasised because they provide an idiom for the expression of variable expenditures. The alleged qualities of qat provide a rationale for price gradations, and the high visibility of qat means that the price paid is evident to any other connoisseur. (The desire for maximum visibility may be why long qat branches have higher market value than short shoots, though there is no difference in the quantity of chewable leaves) (Tutwiler and Carapico, 1981: 53.) Qat is just an undifferentiated bunch of leaves to a foreigner, to whom qat means nothing, but the perceptions of Yemenis are finely tuned to all its distinctive features precisely because they are of such social significance.

The evaluation of other people's qat begins even before the qat party. Men stop each other in the street to assess the quality of qat they have bought, and admonish friends if their qat is not consistent with their status. Stevenson describes how men gather in the teashops of Amran before going on to qat parties and 'inspect with a trained eye the quantity or type of qat which their friends have purchased, and perhaps, if the supply of qat is good, buy an additional bunch of leaves' (Stevenson, 1981: 36). Such extra last-minute purchases might perhaps be made to avoid being outshone in the qat party. It should be stressed that *Yemenis can tell even from across the room what kind of qat a man is chewing and estimate how much he paid for it.*

The different types of qat are equivalent in significance to those features of manufactured commodities which are deliberately developed to mark social categories. The differentiation of a consumer product into a variety of types (and prices), and the necessary development of expertise and connoisseurship in identifying and appreciating them, is often associated with the increased consumption of a luxury item which was originally restricted to a rich elite. While the item is confined to a small, relatively undifferentiated minority, it mainly serves to distinguish between the 'haves' and the 'have-nots', and at that stage a relatively uniform and indivisible commodity may serve the purpose. But it will no longer do so when its use spreads across a wide spectrum of the population. Hence the familiar increase in decorative accretions and the proliferation of brands when this happens. For example, the increased diversification in brands and vintages of wine in the United Kingdom – or the emphasis placed upon their differences in the centres of wine consumption and especially among the better-off – was related to the rise in incomes and social aspirations within the population as a whole during the 1960s. When the majority could only afford beer, wine indicated superior financial and social status. When the majority could afford wine of some sort, the rich resorted to Château Rothschild. Similarly, tea was originally a luxury item but once it spread to the masses, elite brands such as Earl Grey (note the aristocratic name) developed, and a paraphernalia of fine china and silverware maintained tea-drinking as a symbol of high status among the rich.

What these and countless other commodities have in common with qat is that they are vehicles for expressing and achieving economic and social status and are indicators of social aspirations in stratified societies. It appears that in such societies manufactured products become increasingly differentiated, the innate differences in natural objects become more highly accentuated, and these differences are subject to a greater degree of financial grading the more widely consumed the product becomes. A hierarchy of brands develops which roughly corresponds to the social hierarchy. The prices rise as you ascend the hierarchy of brands, though their monetary evaluation may frequently be discussed in an aesthetic idiom – especially in cultures such as the English where discretion in money matters is good manners, but also in Yemen where it is not. (If a product which was initially cheap and widely available becomes rare and expensive, a kind of reversal of the above process can take place. For example oysters were ordinary plain English fare, along with other shellfish, until the pollution of the Kent oysterbeds made them rare and expensive. They then became an elite food with the exquisite flavour only a rich gourmet has the palate – or wallet – to appreciate.)

The diversification in qat types and prices which appears to have taken place in the nineteenth century, and certainly took place during the 1970s, is therefore a consequence of the spread and increase in qat consumption throughout Yemeni society. As each person's income rose, so they bought qat according to their means and in order to display their (differential) capacity for 'luxury' expenditure in the context of the qat party.

Qat has two further interrelated characteristics which are important for the particular way it functions as a mode of conspicuous consumption. The first is that it can be chewed fresh and does not need to be cooked, infused or subjected to any other cultural transformation before it is consumed. Were it necessary to process qat, the present meaning of qat consumption would be reduced or lost. Most obviously the distinctive, visual features of qat would be physically destroyed. Also, whoever processed it would probably assume the role of host in providing fuel and labour, if not the commodity itself. Qat would then inevitably be assimilated to food in its social and symbolic significance. But precisely because each man usually provides and chews his own fresh qat, everyday qat consumption is dissociated from the strict hospitality codes which surround food. This is obviously vital for the preservation of the voluntary, individualistic character of qat parties, and the exhibition of personal economic position.

This suggests the possibility that the way qat is consumed in Yemen, by chewing the fresh leaves, is culturally determined – for qat can be consumed in other ways. The historical sources refer to qat being drunk as an infusion (*kaftah*) by the early *sufi* mystics (see also Serjeant, 1983: 173), and in present-day South Africa dried qat leaves are used to make tea (*Bull. Narcotics*, 1956).[4] Burton (1966: 196–7) records that in Harar, Ethiopia, qat leaves were 'pounded with a little water in a wooden mortar: of this paste, called 'al-Madkuk', a bit was handed to each person, who, rolling it into a ball, dropped it into his mouth'. Schopen (1978: 85) also mentions that a paste of qat is sometimes consumed by travellers in Yemen, and refers to pulverised qat (*qat madgug*), which is made from leaves that have been left to dry seven days in a dark room and are then ground with a mortar and pestle.

Perhaps the custom of 'storing' qat leaves in the cheek also stems more from the desire to consume it conspicuously than from an essential digestive process – for those with very bulging cheeks attract admiration. And there is theoretically no reason why small mouthfuls of qat should not be chewed and expectorated in succession; chewing and 'storing' the leaves without swallowing them is in fact a difficult technique to master. It is even questionable whether it is necessary to spit out the used leaves, for in Ethiopia the residue is swallowed (*Bull. Narcotics*, 1956). The expectoration of qat may therefore also be an aspect of the ostentation of qat consumption, for noisy hawking and spitting is customary in Yemen, and is often an expression of the cultural ideal of male assertiveness.

Were qat processed, or pooled then shared out, the meaning of qat consumption would be very different. For the essential feature of 'everyday' qat parties is that they do *not* involve the communal consumption of a substance provided by a host, nor the sharing out of a pooled supply to which everyone has contributed, like bottle parties in the West. Each member of the gathering independently consumes his personal supply.

The second important characteristic of qat, related to the above, is that it is physically consumed in the sense of being 'used up' or destroyed. In this respect it resembles the conspicuous consumption of food, as when a man's high domestic expenditure on 'luxury' foods is broadcast, or when he gives lavish lunch parties. But food is also essential to life and its consumption cannot so easily be dissociated from the practical connotations of bodily sustenance (although Europeans do their best by swallowing oysters without chewing them, and the ancient Romans managed it by disgorging their food at intervals during gluttonous feasts). Food in Yemen is also inextricably entangled with the hospitality code and with the obligation to share. It would be as unthinkable for a Yemeni to tuck into this personal snack without pressing it on others as it would be to attend a lunch party uninvited.

Perhaps this is why qat is not classified as 'food'. After all it does have some nutritional value, and Yemenis eat plenty of other raw vegetables. It is interesting to note here a comment by a Yemeni expert on qat: 'It is considered bad manners to mention food at qat parties. It would spoil the enjoyment of qat and make people uneasy because it evokes the idea of something very different from what they are consuming' (Abd al-Malik al-Maqrami, personal communication). Precisely because qat is not 'food', it is acceptable for everyone to bring their own and consume it publicly with no obligation to share.

As articles of conspicuous consumption qat and food do however share one important feature: as material evidence of financial position they both have a short life span. In a manner of speaking a man is only as good as his last lunch party or his last bunch of qat. This feature of qat consumption helps explain why it has persisted and increased as a means of displaying wealth despite the competition from imported consumer durables. Before the prosperous 1970s there were a limited number of portable possessions which demonstrated economic and social status – mainly daggers, guns, costumes and jewellery. However, these have now been greatly augmented by foreign clothing and fabrics, watches, radios, tape-recorders, televisions, video-recorders, furnishings and motor vehicles. This influx of foreign goods, the acceleration of consumerism, and the powerful new ideology of modernism might well have caused the 'traditional' practice of qat chewing to decline, for there were now many alternative ways of demonstrating financial position and many other pulls on the purse strings. But qat chewing flourished as never before. This is partly, perhaps mainly, because qat conveys significant information about a consumer's economic position which is not supplied by his other possessions and expenditures – precisely because qat is not a consumer durable but a consumer ephemeral.

The ephemerality of qat fits it for a unique role as a medium of financial information. Expensive material possessions may indicate many things about their owner – that he is prepared to defend himself, moving with the times, identifies with a certain generation, profession or class, and so on – but whatever the rich and complex connotations of a Kalashnikov rifle, Toyota jeep or digital watch, the financial information they convey is limited and dated. It shows how much money the owner could gather at the time of the purchase, but he may thereby have exhausted his supplies, and he may have borrowed the item, or be paying for it in instalments. Such possessions give little idea of a man's cash-flow position. Neither any longer does land; as a source of information about disposable income it has been devalued by present economic conditions. Unless it is planted with lucrative cash crops, it may actually be draining a man's resources because of high labour costs. In any case changeable weather conditions and competition from imported foodstuffs make profits and yields unpredictable. Also, with so many men tapping new sources of income, the old equation of wealth with land-owning is being undermined.

Recent economic changes have created great uncertainty about economic status. In these conditions qat remains a clear indicator of the production of disposable income, precisely because of its 'built-in obsolescence'. It is consumed continuously and repetitively, and therefore provides a regular 'print-out' on current financial position. In Chapter 6 we saw that an individual's expenditure on qat correlates with the amount of income he has surplus to essential economic and social obligations. It is this which is demonstrated by his pattern of qat consumption – by the amount and quality of qat he buys, and the regularity and frequency of his attendance at qat parties. Qat consumption is a far better barometer of disposable income than the intermittent purchase of consumer durables or the ownership of immovable property.

To acquire maximum prestige from high expenditure on qat, the constant drain on financial resources must appear effortless. If others discern a struggle to maintain consumption levels, and that other necessary or luxury expenditures are being adversely affected, the effort to enhance status can rebound in negative ways. Messick provides interesting examples from Ibb of large expenditures on qat being used to condemn and praise, respectively, people of low and high economic and social status:

The *akhdam*, the poorest and most oppressed segment of the townspeople, are also subject to a critical appraisal of their supposed conduct. It is typically said that the *akhdam* spend all their income on qat, and do not restrict their consumption to the standard afternoon session.

Qat consumption is used as a metaphor for excess behaviour in general. A negative formulation that may be applied to individuals of all statuses is that the male sells food grain and otherwise deprives his family of living necessities so that he may buy and consume excessive amounts of qat. Extraordinary expenditures for qat may, however, be connected in public gossip with ideas of power and prestige. When the President of the Republic came to visit Ibb, the comments that circulated concerned how much he had spent for the afternoon's qat session. Similarly the fine qualities or large quantities of qat posed before a shaykh or other important individuals in an afternoon session are later the subject of remarks . . . . Formulations about the handling of wealth are, instead of factual statements, vehicles for expressions of status differences, and for critical or approving glosses on the behaviour of categories of individuals. Concepts about wealth are a means of summarizing negative or positive evaluations and for expressing differences. (Messick, 1978: 416–7).

High expenditure on qat is therefore evaluated in relation to general spending patterns, and only builds up social credit to the extent that it can be sustained without undue deprivation in other areas of life. The ideal would be to keep a wife and family dressed in the latest fashions, supply them with the best food, hold frequent lavish lunch parties, have a splendidly furnished house, own the full array of consumer durables – and be a frequent consumer of the most expensive qat. Every Yemeni is faced with the choice between these alternative ways of acquiring prestige unless his means are unlimited. And most give qat consumption high priority because it yields such great social benefits.

Social Competition
It is essential to attend qat parties to be a fully participating member of society. Those who do not are cut off from a vital forum of social interaction, outsiders to the 'smoke-filled rooms' of Yemeni society. Those who attend frequently are privy to the significant discussions and transactions in the community, up to date on current news, well-informed on the economic and social positions of their fellows, and able to strive for social advancement and public recognition of improvements in their social position. The key to this important milieu is qat. If qat parties are the 'men's clubs' of Yemeni society, then qat is the admission fee for every attendance.

But access depends on financial position. Qat parties do not comprise men assembled solely on the basis of interests and relationships; they are also selected according to the criterion of wealth. A means test is applied through the discriminatory medium of qat. The institution therefore favours the well-off, and disadvantages those of limited resources. The rich can afford to attend qat parties as frequently as they want, and to reinforce their superior positions by buying large quantities of expensive qat. Men of medium income must limit their attendance and ration the quality and quantity of qat they consume. And the poor are disqualified from attending at all, unless they are prepared to accept a servile, client role in exchange for gifts of qat. 'Poverty' here is relative and socially defined. The 'poor' man may live in physical comfort, have a roof over his head, and keep self and family adequately clothed and fed. His is not the poverty of malnutrition or exposure to the elements, but of exclusion from the central social activity of Yemeni life and the consequent reduction of his chances for upward mobility. In this context 'the rightful measure of poverty ... is not possessions, but social involvement' (Douglas and Isherwood, 1980: 11). Once this is grasped, it is easier to understand why men at the lower end of the economic scale spend such a high proportion of their income on qat. Far from being profligate, they are making a rational attempt to enter into the networks and relationships which might advance them out of their lowly social position. They are gambling short-term economic 'deprivation' against long-term social advantage.

The competitive aspect of institutionalised qat consumption is all the greater because qat is physically consumed. There is no circulation or redistribution of the money spent on qat among the participants of qat parties. The money circulates within the national economy, but unless they are also qat producers, the wealth of most consumers is diminished. Each individual is engaged, as it were, in a personal 'destruction potlatch', systematically and publicly destroying money (for here qat = money) in the endeavour to maintain or improve his social position. Obviously this also favours the rich and discriminates against those of limited means, for the rich can sustain the continual destruction of wealth without seriously affecting their other activities, whereas those with smaller financial resources cannot.

Money is not only important in conducting 'social' relationships but is also vital for effective participation in the spheres of law and politics. In both tribal customary law ('urf) and shari'ah law, every offence is precisely evaluated in financial terms and attracts an appropriate fine. Litigation involves buying expensive food (when food = money),[5] or paying large fees for the services of arbitrators; and many legal and administrative officials can be swayed by the payment of money.[6] Relatively small amounts can speed up bureaucratic processes; large amounts can purchase jobs, reduce tax demands and buy political loyalty.

Closely related to the importance of disposable cash in Yemeni society is what Veblen might have called an acute 'pecuniary consciousness'. People's minds are sharply focussed on financial matters; they are intensely and overtly curious about prices, wages, incomes and savings. This information is acquired by incessant questioning and is long remembered. When discussing others they frequently allude to some aspect of their financial resources as a primary way of defining their social position, and there is unease about those whose means are uncertain which is manifested in efforts at detection and rampant rumour. One of the first things a stranger is asked is how much he earns, followed by enquiries about the value of all his visible possessions.

(Yemenis often volunteer such information without being asked.) As people feel around in ignorance for a way of placing someone socially, questions of a financial nature usually take priority.

Such overt, unashamed curiosity about other people's financial affairs is normally considered indelicate in Western society. To ask what someone earns is the height of indiscretion, and we would not think of asking a new acquaintance for a cost inventory of everything they were wearing, as happens in Yemen. But in our society the financial position of our fellows has far less direct influence on most of our lives than it has in Yemen – though when such knowledge can affect our personal welfare (in litigation, divorce proceedings, business deals) we strenuously try to acquire it and discretion falls by the wayside.

In Yemen the greater your cash resources, the greater your potential for being effective and powerful. You can extend your network of relationships beyond the narrow confines to which a poor man is restricted, obligations to close kin can be fulfilled without undue strain, and a wider range of kinship relationships can be activated which would otherwise lie dormant. Strategic relationships of 'friendship' can also be supported and 'friendship' can be reciprocated when it is solicited by others. In the political and legal spheres you can protect yourself more effectively, and better influence people and events. A poor man is therefore of little account in social affairs; however well-born you carry little clout unless you are also a man of means. For this reason the epithet *dha'if,* meaning literally 'weak', is applied equally to a man who is poor and to one who is without influence or power. *Dha'if* connotes specific types of powerlessness in different contexts. In the commercial sphere it may refer to a man without trading capital or with large debts; legally it indicates vulnerability to litigation or the abuse of rights; politically it implies a lack of supporters (who often have to be 'bought'); socially it may refer to a man's financial inability to proffer lunch invitations, to marry off a son – or to attend qat parties. The inevitable corollary of material poverty is social impotence.

As Messick puts it: 'The poor are never capable of operating in the systems of power and influence controlled by the rich . . . because they do not have the money to buy influence, nor the influence to be paid money.' He provides a vivid illustration of the Yemeni view of this fact of life. In a play written and performed in Ibb at the time of the 1962 revolution there were two main characters: the rich man's son (*ibn al-ghani*) and the poor man's son (*ibn al-faqir*). The former spoke uneducated Arabic, the latter erudite classical Arabic, but despite this the school education prize was awarded to the rich man's son 'according to his wealthy background rather than by merit' (Messick, 1978: 411–12). One of Messick's informants remarked that under the loose control of the new republican government, 'a person with money these days can do anything he wants' (ibid: 214). Allowing for hyperbole, however, that was probably always the case; the difference is that now a far greater proportion of the population has money to wield. Money still talks, and in the same language, but more people are, as it were, engaged in the conversation.

Because of the importance of money in all aspects of Yemeni life the social effectiveness of the man who spends all his surplus income on qat will be severely diminished. Though the cash resources of the rich man are also reduced, and by a greater amount as his expenditure on qat is higher, he is better able to sustain the loss. And the remaining surplus may be employed legally, politically or socially to better effect with the reduction or elimination of the cash surpluses of others. The rich therefore have a vested interest in maintaining the high price and prestige of qat, for both symbolically and instrumentally it helps support their high social position.

The symbolic and instrumental aspects of institutionalised qat consumption are closely related and interdependent. By attending qat parties frequently, and chewing a good quantity and quality of qat, a man can establish impressive financial credentials, and may eventually improve his social position in concrete ways. Conversely, a man who rarely or never attends qat parties is held of little or no account. A *sayyid* in Razih who never appeared at qat parties was dismissed contemptuously as an 'unsociable' person who 'dislikes his fellow men'. However, the truth was more probably that he owned no qat terraces and was too poor to buy qat, and declined to place himself in a dependent, subordinate, client relationship to his rich cousins who would have provided him with it.

Conclusion

The recent efflorescence of qat consumption took place because the social and ritual importance of qat in Yemeni life was enormously enhanced by the economic and social changes of the 1970s. Greater social, economic and geographical mobility created uncertainty about social position and intensified the desire and necessity to define personal identity, assert affiliations, forge relationships and strive for advancement. At the same time the widespread rise in financial prosperity greatly increased the importance of money in social relations and in the competition for prestige and status. The increase in individualistic qat parties is therefore to be understood as the expansion and transformation of a traditional social ritual to embrace these new realities. An institution which was formerly a bastion of exclusivity and superiority for a rich and powerful elite became an arena in which most Yemenis were jostling for social position.

Those whose birth placed them at the summit of the traditional social hierarchy obviously had no vested interest in the establishment of a social order based on achieved status or new wealth. For them qat parties continued to be an instrument in the attempt to maintain the 'traditional' categories and structures. For those beneath them on this social scale, however, qat parties became a medium for trying to improve social standing through the intensive building of personal networks and the deployment and display of qat. At qat parties attended by people of varied social status, these opposing interests came into open confrontation. Otherwise social and ideological competition between the old elite and its principles of hierarchy and the *nouveaux riches* and theirs was implicit in the overall pattern of qat party attendance and avoidances.

To the extent that most people can now afford to attend qat parties, qat consumption has been democratised and the qat branch is, as it were, being brandished by the majority at the traditional system of rank and privilege which it once helped support. But the notion that society is unequal and hierarchical, that there are winners and losers, is not apparently in question. What is being challenged is who is qualified to enter the race.

The proliferation of qat parties is not merely an incidental effect of recent social change but an integral part of it. The adjustments and transformations which are taking place in Yemeni society under the impact of oil wealth are doing so in part through the medium of the qat party, the central social ritual of everyday life. The social order is in flux and under continual negotiation, and whatever new structures and categories are emerging, and these undoubtedly differ from one community to another, the increase in qat consumption reflects the greatly increased importance of disposable wealth in Yemeni life.

Notes

169

Preface

1 This figure can be approximated by calculating either consumption expenditure or the production value of qat. If we assume that the average weekly expenditure on qat per consumer in 1979–80 was about US$55, and therefore about $2750 for the year, and that three-quarters of a million Yemenis were average consumers (see Chapter 6), we arrive at national expenditure for the year of about $2000 million. If on the other hand we assume that about 40,000 ha of land was under qat cultivation in 1980 (USAID, 1982: 81), and that the market value of one harvest of qat was $45,000 per ha, then the market value of national qat production was about $1800 million. However, this is a conservative estimate as many plantations yielded two or three harvests. The estimate of qat value/ha is based on my research in Razih (see Weir, 1985).

In World Bank, 1979, Tables 15, 16 and 39 the gross return per ha on qat is estimated at YR79,500 (US$17,666), and in USAID, 1982: 233 the net return per ha is estimated at between YR60,000 and YR300,000 (US$13,333–66,666), though it is not stated what precisely is meant by 'net return'.

1 The Yemen Arab Republic

1 See Steffen *et al*, 1978: I/8–11 for the climatic characteristics of the main regions of Yemen.
2 See Steffen and Blanc, 1982 for an analysis of population distribution and settlement size in Yemen. The population figures I have given for the three main towns of Yemen are their estimates for 1980 based on the national census of 1975.
3 See Wenner, 1967, Halliday, 1974, Stookey, 1978, Peterson, 1982 and Pridham, 1984, for accounts of the history, religion and politics of Yemen.
4 It is beyond the scope of this book to elaborate the enormous economic changes which took place in Yemen during the 1970s. For information on the economy generally, and on the agricultural sector in particular, see World Bank, 1979, Tutwiler and Carapico, 1981, Kopp, 1981, USAID, 1982, and Pridham, 1985.
5 By World Bank standards Yemen is considered one of the twenty-five least developed countries in the world (Socknat and Sinclair, 1978: 1). According to USAID (1982: 71), the World Bank rates Yemen as a middle-income economy with an estimated GNP per capita in 1980 of $430, which places it in the same category as Indonesia, Mauritania and Senegal, and below Angola and Liberia. However, as the writers of the report point out, cursory observation shows consumption and investment to be much higher.

6 These figures are based on Steffen *et al,* 1978: I/73 and Steffen, 1979: I/100 ff. The *de facto* population on census day, February 1975, was 4,705,336 persons, and short-term migrants numbered 331,649. To these figures were added 20,000 to allow for underestimation of short-term migrants, and 250,000 for estimated long-term emigrants with whom their families had lost touch, and who were therefore not accounted for in the census. Added together, this gives a *de jure* population of Yemen in February 1975 of 5,306,985. Steffen (1979: I/171) calculated that by 1980 the number of short-term emigrants would have risen to 575,000. (In 1982: 100 Steffen and Blanc give a higher estimate of 385,000 short-term, temporary migrants in February 1975.) The figures are contested by the Government of the Yemen Arab Republic which conducted a second national census in 1981 and reported a population of 8,540,119 (including emigrants).

7 These figures were provided by informants in Razih.

8 All remittance estimates are based on the amounts of Saudi riyals and other foreign currencies which are converted into Yemeni riyals in transfers through the Yemeni banking system. They therefore fail to take into account the Saudi riyals which are imported and never banked. These probably represent a considerable sum, as Saudi riyals are the main currency of daily use in much of north-west Yemen, and only a small proportion need to be converted to Yemeni riyals for use elsewhere in the country. The bank figures also fail to take into account the high value of goods imported into Yemen by returning migrants, such as transistor radios, clothing and particularly gold jewellery. They also exclude foreign earnings invested abroad. In USAID, 1982: 43 it is estimated that the value of cash and goods which are officially unrecorded could amount to between one-third and one hundred per cent of the officially recorded figures based on bank deposits and currency conversions.

9 The remittance figures I have quoted are from Serageldin *et al,* 1981: 207. The figures they give for 1974–78 are (in US$ million): (1974) 135.5; (1975) 279; (1976) 676.5; (1977) 914.3; (1978) 899.6. These estimates are lower than those quoted elsewhere (for example in World Bank, 1979: 65 and USAID, 1981: 42) because the compiler (G. Swamy) corrected bank figures to include only individual transfers and to exclude corporate business transfers. The latter are included in the higher figures provided in other sources (Stace Birks, personal communication). Steffen and Blanc (1982: 103) estimate the annual remittances per individual migrant to have risen from an average of YR1378 (US$275) in 1970–71 (when there were an estimated 172,000 temporary migrants working abroad) to YR12,575 (US$2800) in 1977–78 when there were an estimated 505,000 migrants.

2 Qat

1 I am grateful to Nigel Hepper for this information. For detailed botanical information on *Catha edulis* see United Nations, 1956; Getahun and Krikorian, 1973; and Wood, forthcoming.

2 Cuttings are taken from the small shoots which grow around the base of the stem or trunk of the qat plant. In Razih, where these shoots are called *'agib/a'gab,* they are laid horizontally a few centimetres below the surface of the soil and after a few weeks, depending on rainfall, a new shoot grows from the cutting. It is also possible to transplant qat bushes.

3 For the history of qat importation to Aden from north Yemen and Ethiopia, see Brooke, 1960. There was already a considerable trade in qat from north Yemen to Aden in the early days of British rule (which was established in 1839). In 1844 '... the sale of qat ... was restricted to one and later to a small number of sellers licensed by the Government ... sales were heavy and the qat contractor, being

able to dictate prices to producer and consumer alike, made profits of up to 1000 per cent'. Haines, the Political Agent at Aden (1939–54), proposed to break up the qat monopoly by auctioning it and dividing it. In the late 1860s qat imports represented 6 per cent of the total value of landward imports to Aden; coffee represented 29.5 per cent, grain 16.6 per cent and livestock 15.6 per cent (Gavin, 1975; 58,121 and fn.103). Qat consumption in Aden soared with the economic recovery and improvement in transportation facilities after World War II. The rise is also attributable to the great increase in the population of the Colony with massive immigration of Yemenis from the south of Yemen and the Aden Protectorate. Large quantities of qat were exported to Aden from Yemen and Ethiopia during the decade after the War. Imports of qat to Aden doubled from nearly 2 million lb in 1947 to nearly 4 million lb in 1956. During the same period the cash value of qat increased ninefold – from £6 a cwt in 1947 to £56 a cwt in 1956 (Brooke, 1960).

4 For areas in which qat was cultivated in Yemen in the 1930s, see Heyworthe-Dunne, 1952: Appendix E. For the names of areas and mountains where it was being cultivated in the mid-1970s, see Steffen, 1978: I/25 and Schopen, 1978: 61–5. Schopen also specified the various altitudes, climatic conditions and soil types where qat is grown.

5 For average rainfall estimates for the different climatic zones of Yemen, see Steffen, 1978: I/10.

6 In Razih farmers formerly allowed friends and neighbours to take qat cuttings for nothing, but the recent expansion in qat cultivation has given them a new commercial value outside the area. In 1981 the farmers of Razih were exporting cuttings to the new qat producers of eastern Razih and the central Plateau for SR30–70 (US$8–20) a sack.

7 Schopen (1978: 71) says the distance between the plants varies according to region. In Wadi Dhahr qat was planted up to 2.5 and 3.5 metres apart. Schopen (1978: 66–74) provides further detailed information on the cultivation and harvesting of qat in Yemen.

8 Gerholm (1977: 55) has suggested that the coffee trade generated a 'big merchant' structure because of the desirability of transporting the beans rapidly through the Tihamah to the ports, as the beans could quickly deteriorate in the heat and humidity of the coast. This was best done, he argues, in large consignments and therefore the trade favoured those with the capital to accumulate beans in the cool Highlands. However, beans could surely have been transported rapidly and just as easily in small consignments, and sometimes were. It therefore seems that other factors must have operated, such as the greater security of travelling in large caravans of camels through hostile tribal territories, the preference of coffee exporters at the ports for buying in bulk, and favourable conditions for speculation in coffee, i.e. if coffee prices were stable, those with capital would be more likely to buy crops in advance and thus monopolise the market.

9 Various estimates have been made of the relative returns on qat, coffee, sorghum and other crops, but obviously precise comparisons depend on variable market prices and input costs in any year. According to the figures of the Yemen Ministry of Agriculture (quoted in Yacoub and Akil, 1971: 28), between 1965 and 1969 the net return (presumably to the farmer) on coffee was seven times, and on qat twenty-four times, that on sorghum and millet. However, there is no indication of how these figures were arrived at. Ruthenberg and Nagel (1970: 116, quoted in Kopp, 1981: 152) published comparative financial yields on different crops cultivated on irrigated land near Sanaa. According to these figures the annual yield from sorghum (including an estimate of its fodder value) was 1000–1800 DM/ha, and from qat 10,000–100,000 DM/ha, i.e. between ten and fifty times as much. However, it is not clear whether or not these figures are net of

inputs. Other figures quoted by Kopp (1981: 171) show that in 1973 qat had a market value five times that of coffee. In the Report by the Japan International Cooperation Agency, on *The Master Plan Study for Hajja Province Integrated Rural Development in the Yemen Arab Republic,* 1979 Vol II p. ix–34, (quoted by Varisco, forthcoming), it also states that qat is at least five times as profitable as coffee. These latter two estimates correspond to what I was told by Razih farmers.

10 See for example Scott (1942: 95), El-Attar (1964: 125), UNDP (1971: 144), Chelhod (1972), and Kopp (1981: 237).

11 Although coffee is not as profitable as qat, it remains a lucrative crop in Yemen. In fact in 1981–82, the price coffee fetched on the domestic market – YR30 (US$6) per kg of unhusked coffee – was far above the world price of YR15 ($3) for husked Arabica berries (USAID, 1982: 281).

12 I am grateful to John Wood for bringing these ecological aspects of qat and coffee cultivation to my attention, and for passing on his observations on the altitudes at which each crop is to be found in Yemen.

13 'Compared with other perishable [cash] crops . . . qat has the highest market value, the lowest water requirements, and demands the least input of heavy labour.' (Tutwiler and Carapico, 1981: 52).

14 Obermeyer (1973) also notes that as qat is a domestic crop, no complicated infrastructure is needed for the marketing and administration of the qat trade, whereas coffee 'calls for much more complex organisation to deal with taxation, export and international relations and therefore development of the total economic structure'. It should be added that some effective and reliable mechanism for grading and quality control would also be needed were Yemeni coffee to compete on the international market.

3 The Physiological Effects of Qat

1 In a survey of 108 qat consumers conducted in 1970, half gave as their principal reason for chewing qat that it 'gives a person more strength and activity to work', and a third gave social reasons. Sixty per cent of the sample felt they could not stop chewing qat if they tried to do so, while forty per cent thought they could. The reasons given by the first group for their perceived inability to stop chewing qat were that they felt sick and lazy without it, that it was a part of daily life, that it gave strength and energy for work, that there was nothing else to do in the afternoon, that it was available, and because friends and relatives chewed it (Yacoub and Akil, 1971: 32). None of this suggests serious physiological dependence, at least nothing more serious than that experienced by regular tea or coffee drinkers, but points rather to an economic and social basis for qat consumption.

2 Serjeant (1983: 172) says the 'pleasant musings' of the participants at this stage of the party are described by them as 'waking dreams' (*hulm al-yaqdhah*), and as 'swimming in thought' (*yisbah fi'l-fikr*).

3 When I asked a Razihi how he would use the verb *kayyaf* (to experience *kayf*) in relation to things other than qat, he replied that you could use it with regard to a beautiful garden or a pretty girl or a television programme which you had seen. Perhaps the best translation of *kayyaf* would be the slang expression 'to be sent'.

4 This doctrine does not necessarily survive in its classical form in present-day folklore or practice, although it is available in books which are used by specialist practitioners of 'native' medicine.

5 Obermeyer (1973) notes that it is considered good to eat the following 'hot' foods before chewing 'cold' qat – *hilbah,* lamb, honey or grapes – and to avoid 'cool' foods such as a barley and sour milk dish, fish without ginger, and apples. Ansell (1979) notes that *hilbah* (the most important component, next to meat, of the main

Yemeni meal, lunch) 'is considered to be particularly essential before chewing qat and might be considered very important [i.e. as a food] simply for this fact'. Kennedy *et al* (1980) note: 'Custom dictates that for best results a large meal be eaten before chewing. . . .' Chelhod (1972) is mistaken when he says that a good meal is not considered necessary before chewing qat.

The Yemeni classification of foodstuffs is much more complex than my brief account suggests. Other categories into which foods are divided are light/heavy and soft/hard (see Ansell, 1979 and Myntti, 1983: 180–91). Ansell points out that food classification in Yemen is not rigid, and people may contradict each other on how they define certain foods. However qat seems to be universally regarded as cooling and drying.

6 Schopen (1978: 97–9) says that qat which does not reduce potency is called qat *rijali*, literally 'manly qat', and that which does is called qat *nashwani*. He does not translate the latter term, but were it pronounced *niswani* it could mean 'womanly qat', so possibly Schopen has erred in his transliteration. Obermeyer (1973) says: 'Qat . . . is said to be an aphrodisiac. This is generally discounted by the more sophisticated informant and even the opposite effect is claimed by some. It was stated a number of times that males see qat as increasing sexual prowess, while the females argue otherwise.' And Stevenson (1981: 37) says: 'Despite their passion for qat, many, if not all, men realise that qat is an expensive pastime. Many like to cite the apparent evils of qat, most notably its effects on sexual performance and the fact that they may spend twice as much money on qat as they do on food. Still, although they complain, they chew.'

7 In the article devoted to qat in the 1956 *Bulletin on Narcotics* (see United Nations, 1956) it is stated that 'experience in the case of other alkaloid plants shows that the effects vary with the soil and climatic conditions in which the plant grows . . . that the alkaloid content changes and that under certain conditions some effects may disappear entirely'.

8 A number of writers have noted this distressing tendency, for example Messick (1978: 44) and Kennedy *et al* (1980).

9 It is interesting to note that similar effects to those described in this chapter have been attributed to qat, within and outside Yemen, for over five hundred years. For example, in the Masalik al-Absar written between 1342 and 1349, Ibn Fadl Allah describes the effects of consuming qat (as observed in Ethiopia) as follows: 'Il excite l'intelligence et donne la joie; il permet de se priver en partie de manger, de boire et d'avoir des rapports sexuels. Tous en mangent, en sont très friands et desirent en manger, particulièrement les gens qui recherchent le savoir, qui ont une grave occupation, qui cherchent à prolonger leurs veilles pour faire un voyage ou pour executer un travail.' Later in the same work the inhabitants of the Amhara area in Ethiopia are described as having qat 'qu'ils emploient pour exciter l'intelligence et pour affirmer la memoire' (Gaudefroy-Demombynes, 1927: 12, 25–6).

10 The fact that qat leaves contain vitamin C may be of significance here. In Harar, Ethiopia, people also believe that qat can effect medical cures. It has been suggested by Getahun and Krikorian (1973) that qat may represent a major portion of daily food intake in Ethiopia where the residue remaining after the wad is chewed is swallowed. They also provide a chart indicating the food value of qat. Serjeant (1983: 174) quotes a Yemeni source in which a variety of medicinal effects are attributed to qat.

11 The health problems which Western doctors have attributed to qat consumption include stomatitis, esophagitis, gastritis, constipation, malnutrition, cirrhosis of the liver, anorexia, anaemia, spermatorrhea and schizophrenia (Mancioli and Parrinello, 1967; Halbach, 1972; Luqman and Danowski, 1977). The following are the main findings of the Kennedy team. Gastro-intestinal problems were very

common among their sample population of both non-qat users and qat users; they were slightly higher among male qat users, and were more strongly associated with high qat use among the females in their sample. (These problems may be exacerbated by the tannins present in qat leaves.) But these complaints were not severe and were such that they could be easily alleviated by various appropriate measures. They also found a correlation between insomnia and qat use in both males and females. Psychosomatic problems in men also correlated with high qat use, but the incidence in their sample was low. There were also indications that heavy qat users among women had a higher incidence of liver problems than non-qat users, although the prevalence of liver disease in their sample was low. They found no positive association between heavy qat use and oral cavity problems, including stomatitis. The article does not deal with the possible sexual effects of qat, nor with its allegedly adverse effect on lactation. There is a low incidence of cardiovascular disease in Yemen, and it has been suggested that this could be related to qat use. No evidence to disprove this hypothesis was discovered by the Kennedy team.

12 See Halbach, 1972, Krikorian and Getahun, 1973, Szendrai, 1983, and Krikorian, 1983, for the history of investigations into the chemistry and pharmacology of qat. The first report on the chemistry of qat was published by Fluckinger and Gerock in 1887.

13 The subjects of Nencini *et al*'s study were Somalis in Mogadishu. Elmi does not explicitly state the nationality of his subjects, but it can be inferred from the text that they were also Somalis in Mogadishu. Nencini *et al* do not mention how many subjects they had in their sample. Elmi tested the effect of qat on physical performance and endurance of fatigue on eighteen resting subjects and fourteen fatigued subjects.

14 With regard to addiction, the Kennedy *et al* article (1980) states: 'Present evidence supports the hypothesis that a mild form of physiological dependence does result from *extremely heavy* use. . . .' The same can of course be said for tea, coffee and numerous other stimulating and non-stimulating substances or habits. They add that 'since the percentage of people using [qat] at the very high level is small, true physiological dependence appears to be relatively unimportant in the overall Yemeni picture'.

4 Attitudes and Explanations

1 A number of experts contributed to the handbook, including Scott, but the sections for which they were responsible are not identified. However, Serjeant (1983: 171) identifies Scott as the author of this piece, and quotes the same passage as an example of the prejudice and distaste with which most foreigners have regarded qat parties.

2 For accounts of the preventative measures taken by various governments, see *Bulletin on Narcotics,* 1956; Hjort, 1974; Bach, 1980; 121–24; Baasher, 1980: 92 and Shahandeh *et al,* 1983.

3 For more detailed accounts of the religious debate on qat, see Hess, 1973–78, Rodinson, 1977, Schopen, 1978: 174–80, Centre for Yemeni Studies 1983 and Serjeant, 1983: 172–5.

4 For example, UNDP (1971: 69) refers to qat as a 'social evil' and World Bank (1979: 13) to 'notorious qat'.

5 Historical Aspects of Qat Consumption

1 This is not intended to be an exhaustive account of the history of qat, but an attempt to point out certain sociologically illuminating features of qat

consumption in the past. I have drawn chiefly on the historical summaries of Hess (1976), Rodinson (1977), Schopen (1978: 45–52, 174–84) and Krikorian (1983) on qat, and Van Arendonk and Chaudhari (1974) and Ukers (1936) on coffee.

2 Marʿade is the Arabic name for Taguelat, the Ethiopian name of Amda Seyon's capital (Huntingford, 1965: 55–6). The fact that Sabr al-Din is here represented as using the Arabic term is of course another slight to the Christians, presumably calculated to provoke the reader's sense of outrage still further.

3 There are other translations of this text by Perruchon and Dillman; the references are cited in Rodinson (1977).

4 It would be interesting to know why qat consumption was not adopted by the Christians in Ethiopia in the past, and why, according to Krikorian (1983), they are beginning to adopt it now. There is nothing intrinsically Islamic about qat chewing and in Yemen, unlike in Ethiopia, it never became a symbol of religious identity. Yemeni Jews consumed qat as much as Yemeni Muslims, and Jews who emigrated to Israel continue to do so today.

5 The French word I have translated as 'leaves' is *moelle,* which normally means 'pith'.

6 *Al-Muʿtamad fi mufradat al-tibb* by the Rasulid Sultan Umar II, b. Yusuf al-Malik al-Ashraf, who reigned 1295–96 (Rodinson, 1977).

7 *Bughyat al-Fallahin* by the Rasulid Sultan al-Malik al-Afdal al-Abbas, b. Ali, discussed and translated by Serjeant (1974).

8 *Mulakhkhas al-fitan* (Serjeant, personal communication). Qat is also not mentioned in the Arabic geographies of the tenth century, including the geography of the famous Yemeni scholar al-Hamdani (d. 945/6) who names the main plants of the country (Schopen, 1978: 48).

9 An early fifteenth-century Arabic reference to qat in Ethiopia, including a description of its physiological effects, is provided by al-Maqrizi (d. 1442), *al-Ilmam bi-akhbar man bi-ardh al-Habash min muluk al-Islam* (*The History of the Muslim Kings of Ethiopia*), ed. T. Rinck, Leiden, 1790 (cited in Hess, 1973–78 and Serjeant, 1983: 173). According to Krikorian (1983: 27), al-Maqrizi's work draws heavily on al-Umari's earlier account (see Gaudefroy-Demombynes, 1927).

10 Schopen's sources for the poetry of Ibn Alwan and Miswari are Abdallah Baraduni, 'al-Qat . . . min zuhurihi ila istiʿmalihi' in *al-Yaman al-Jadid,* 3, 1972, and Qasim Ghalib, 'al-Qat fi ardh al-qat' in *Tatawur al-khidmat al-sahhiya bil-Yemen 1962–67,* Cairo, 1971.

11 Ibn Alwan's tomb was destroyed by Imam Ahmed (1948–62), who as a Zaydi disapproved of sufism and considered the pilgrimages politically threatening, and it was rebuilt after the revolution of 1962 (Schopen, 1978: 50; Messick, 1978: 58).

12 Harold Jacob (*Perfumes of Araby,* 1915: 22) says: 'Before kat is taken at a gathering, the Fatiha, or opening chapter of the Koran is recited, after invoking a blessing on the "Sheikh of Kat", one Ibn Zarbain.' Serjeant, who quotes this reference (1983: 173 n. 189), thinks this 'probably applies only to the Lower Yemen'. The tomb of Shaykh Ibrahim Abu Zerbin is at Zayla on the Red Sea coast of Somalia near Jibouti.

13 A linguistic observation of Rodinson (1977) is relevant here. He says that the Arabic term *qat* would appear to antecede the Ethiopian term *chat* since in other cases of Arabic loan words in Ethiopian languages, the Arabic sound *q* becomes *ch,* whereas the reverse does not occur.

14 Yemen shares a substantial flora with Africa, and some botanists claim Yemen should be classified with Africa as one botanical area. (I am grateful to Nigel Hepper for this information.)

15 This poem has recently been published in Arabic in Centre for Yemeni Studies, 1983: 197 ff. Serjeant (1983: 172) refers to a similar composition by a

nineteenth-century author named Ahmad al-Mu'allimi. He translates the title as 'A boasting match between coffee and qat'.

16 Shaykh Abd al-Qadir al-Jaziri.

17 This is of course a legendary account and has little basis in history. Al-Shadhili is only one of several men credited with introducing coffee to Yemen (see Van Arendonk, 1974). Mokha was the main port from which Yemeni coffee was exported until the development of Aden by the British in the nineteenth century. The term 'Mocha', applied originally to Yemeni 'Arabica' coffee, derives from the name of the port; nowadays it is also widely used to refer to coffee of non-Yemeni origin.

18 In Yemen the term *sufi* has rather different connotations from elsewhere in the Middle East. In the Shafi'i south of the country it can be synonymous with *sayyid* (Myntti, 1983: 152). And in at least parts of the Zaydi north of the country the term *sufi* is applied to experts in traditional medicine and 'magical' practices such as amulet writing. None of those I knew in Razih were *sayyids,* but all had acquired great wealth, and usually high social position, through these activities. They did not, so far as I am aware, engage in 'mystical' practices.

19 Serjeant does however say earlier (1983: 164) that in the Statute of Sanaa 'the gist of the argument of the Preamble supports price-fixing, which if not adopted leads to injustice and fraud. The author seems to imply that price-fixing had fallen into abeyance before the ... early nineteenth century.' Serjeant's translation of the Preamble (ibid: 182).

20 The Turkish author of this document was Ahmed Rashid, and it was translated and published by the French orientalist A. C. Barbier de Meynard as 'Notice sur l'Arabie meridionale d'après un document turc', in *Mélanges Orientaux*. Texte et Traductions publiés par Les Professeurs de l'École Spéciale des Langues Orientales Vivantes, 2nd series: IX: 87–123, Paris: Leroux. The comment quoted is on p. 109.

21 According to Krikorian (1983: 9), who provides an excellent summary of the references to qat in early Western sources, the first European mention of qat appears to be by a French orientalist named Barthelemy d'Herbelot de Molainville (1625–95) in a work called *Bibliothèque Orientale* published after his death in 1697.

22 The reference to qat use by labourers and artisans is on p. 58 in the earlier German version of Niebuhr, 1774 (published in 1772) (Schopen, 1978: 53).

6 The Economics of Qat Consumption

1 There were ninety-five qat shops (presumably this includes stalls) in the Sanaa market at the time of Dostal's research in March 1971 (1983: 257–8). This represented 18 per cent of the shops selling foodstuffs and oral commodities such as tobacco, and 5.6 per cent of total market businesses (handicrafts, hardware, commercial and services). Food provisions shops accounted for 43.5 per cent of the total shops in the market. Schopen, who did his research in 1974, says there were about a hundred qat dealers in Sanaa at that time (1978: 82). It would be of interest to know how many there were by 1980.

2 The World Bank Country report on the Yemen Arab Republic notes that there is 'ample evidence that qat growing has increased rapidly in recent years' (1979: 93); and in USAID, 1982 (p. 10) it is estimated that qat production increased 'two to three fold' during the period of the Yemen government's first Five Year Plan (1976/77–1980/81).

3 According to Varisco (forthcoming), the Yemen Ministry of Agriculture and Fisheries estimated the annual value (presumably market value) of qat produced

in Yemen around 1980 to be US$800 million. My own estimate for 1980 is closer to double that figure (see Preface, note 1). Such figures alarm development economists, but it should be remembered that this money is circulating within the Yemeni economy and not leaving the country as is the case ultimately with money spent on imported goods – though the high national expenditure on consumer durables seems to cause far less official anxiety. It is often said that the money spent on qat would be better invested in more economically productive ways, but Yemeni individuals and communities already spend a great deal of money on local development projects and small-scale capitalist ventures, and if more investment opportunities were available, would doubtless spend more. However, Yemenis also give a high priority to investing in social relations, which is in essence what expenditure on qat represents – as this book sets out to demonstrate.

4 It is impossible to give exact figures in the absence of a detailed survey of a representative sample of the population. Schopen (1978: 60) estimates that ninety to ninety-five per cent of the [adult] population were qat consumers in the mid-1970s (he presumably includes women). Kopp (1978: 236), quoting Christiansen–Weniger, estimates that eighty per cent of the adult population including women chew qat regularly according to their financial status. Baasher (1980) states that in 1976 it was estimated, on the basis of health workers' information, that fifty per cent of adult males in Aden chewed qat, and that 'in cities in the Yemen Arab Republic, such as Sanaa and Ta'izz, where qat is more easily available and the social milieu is more conducive to its use, the proportion of adult males who chew khat may be as much as eighty per cent'. It often has to be assumed by the reader that such estimates refer to regular qat consumers, since what is precisely meant by people who 'chew qat' is rarely defined. Without the vital information about consumption levels and rates, such estimates are sociologically of limited usefulness.

5 As Gerholm (1977: 63), Varisco (1982: 39) and Myntti (1983) have pointed out for different parts of Highland Yemen, there is no rigid or permanent class distinction between owner-cultivators and sharecroppers. Many households are both simultaneously, or shift from one category to the other with changes in household composition.

6 'Through exporting their labour and almost fully appropriating the consequent flow of remittances or off-farm income, farm families have increased their disposable incomes enormously. This has freed the rural sector from total dependence on low-level subsistence agriculture, and accelerated its shift to commercialization. Rising incomes in towns and villages have further expanded demand and prices for local foods and other crops' (USAID, 1982: 223).

7 These figures are based on information from people in Razih.

8 Tutwiler and Carapico (1981: 173) give the following daily wage rates for unskilled labourers during the 1970s: under YR3 (early 1970s), YR3–4 (1974), YR4–6 (1975), YR30 (1977), YR50 (1978–79), YR60–70 (1980). In USAID 1982 (p.219) the average daily wages during the 1970s for agricultural labourers are given as YR2 (1972), YR3–4 (1973), YR5–6 (1974), YR10 (1975), YR20 (1976), YR37 (1977), YR45 (1978), YR50 (1979). There is of course considerable regional and seasonal variation in wages.

In USAID, 1982 (p. 85) it states: 'Since the 1960s agricultural wages [in Yemen] have increased 20 to 25 fold.' A 1981 study of household incomes conducted by Sanaa University in the Taizz and Ibb areas revealed a median household income of YR2000–3000 ($440–660) per month, or a per capita income of $810–1220 assuming 6.5 persons in each household (USAID, 1982: 221, 253).

9 In USAID, 1982 (p. 10), referring to the period 1976–81, it says: 'Qat prices . . . have substantially exceeded the inflation rate.'

10 Information on qat prices at different periods and for different regions is

extremely sparse and not directly comparable. Sources quote average prices only for a particular time of year and some quote the price of a bunch (*rubtah*) of qat while others quote the average individual daily expenditure on qat. The following chart summarises the information on *rubtah* prices or daily expenditure which I have gleaned from the literature and from personal observation.

Date	Rubtah price/average individual expenditure per day	Area	Source
1972	YR3–4 (poor man) YR7–10 (rich man)/day		Obermeyer (1973)
1973	YR3–5/rubtah	near Sanaa	Mundy (1981: 240)
1974	YR2–60/day	south YAR	Swanson (1979: 41)
1977	YR18–20/rubtah	near Sanaa	Mundy (1981: 240)
1977–80	YR100/day (moderate earner)	Khamr	Dresch (1982: 12)
1978	YR80/day/bunch	al-Ahjur	Adra (1982: 87)
	YR125/day/bunch	Sanaa	Ibid
1978–9	YR40–50/day	Amran	Stevenson (1981: vi)
1979 summer	YR50/rubtah	Jabal Sabr	Hebert (personal communication)
1979 winter	YR60/day/rubtah	Sanaa	Personal observation
1979/80 Dec/Jan	YR45/rubtah	Razih, Saadah, Hodeidah	Personal observation
1980 winter	YR20–40	Hajjah	Swanson (1982: 57)
1980 June	YR30–60/rubtah	Ibb area	Tutwiler and Carapico (1981: 95)
1980 June/July	YR60–80/rubtah	Amran area	Ibid

11 Older Yemenis in Razih perceive the past as a time when they worked harder than today, and this was probably indeed the case on the days when work was necessary or available. But the demand for labour was only sufficient to absorb all or much of the workforce for part of the year. Stevenson (1981: 67) also notes that the people of Amran claim to have worked much harder in the past, and from dawn to dusk.

12 The situation with regard to women's work is of course more complex than this generalisation suggests, as female responsibilities and tasks depend on the specific economic conditions in each area.

13 *Rubtah* means literally 'something tied', ie. a bunch or bundle. This is the most common term found in Yemen, but other local terms are used for the corresponding unit, and for larger and smaller ones (see Schopen, 1978: 77).

14 According to Schopen (1978: 82) the qat dealers in Sanaa normally add ten per cent to the price of each bunch for themselves, and twenty per cent on Fridays and feast days when demand for qat is greatest. He notes that forty per cent was added to the qat from Wadi Dhahr near Sanaa which is alleged to have a superior flavour and effects. This account of the retail process implies either that the retailer buys the qat from the trader in bulk then sells it to the customer, or that there is a fixed market price for qat which the retailers raise by a certain percentage to give themselves a share in the profits. However, neither is the case in the major qat markets of Saadah and Hodeidah. There no money is exchanged between the qat trader and the retailer until after the qat is sold – for the highest

price it will fetch on the day. Then the retailer subtracts an agreed percentage – usually ten per cent – as his share of the profits, and the trader takes the rest. There are no price-fixing mechanisms in Yemeni markets.

15 Schopen (1978: 82) mentions that customers in Sanaa shake the bundles of qat to see how fresh it sounds.

16 The Arabic terms given in this section are those used in Razih, and are not necessarily used elsewhere in Yemen. Additional Razihi terms are given in the Glossary.

17 It is interesting to note that in a laboratory experiment conducted in Somalia, each subject consumed about 150 g of leaves and tender twigs in a period of five hours (Elmi, 1983: 154).

18 I have used the term *rubtah* here for convenience, but it is not generally used in Razih.

19 For detailed information on the major categories of qat differentiated by Yemenis, the criteria employed for differentiating them and their various alleged sensual and physical effects, see Schopen (1978: 97–102).

20 Schopen (1978: 104) notes (with reference to the mid-1970s) that the upper classes chew one or two bunches per qat party, and more at important social events.

21 In addition to regular consumers there is a category of poor people who only chew qat when prices drop way below normal levels because of oversupply of markets or wilting leaves, or who chew leaves discarded as inedible by regular consumers.

22 These wage levels are very high for a developing country because they are directly affected by those obtainable in Saudi Arabia. Actual incomes are also often even higher because of profits from trade, landowning, etc.

23 These estimates are based on personal observation, the comments of other researchers and Yemeni views as to what constituted 'normal' or 'average' consumption in 1979–80, and on the relation between consumption and income.

24 When the full results of the research of the Kennedy team are published we will have more detailed information on qat consumption patterns, since the consumer survey included the following questions: '(1) The number of chewing days per week; (2) The number of times [qat is] chewed per day; (3) The number of hours per chewing session; (4) The number of *robdas* [*rubtahs*] per chewing session, and (5) The amounts paid for qat per session and per day. Another set of questions attempted to get at the length of time the respondent had used qat. All of these questions were asked for every season during the past year, as well as for the prior month' (Kennedy *et al*, 1980: fn. 4).

25 Baasher (1980) estimates that a consumer spends about twenty-five per cent of his daily earnings on qat. Kopp (1978: 238) also assumes that at least twenty-five per cent of family income goes towards qat.

7 The Social Importance of Qat Parties

1 For a detailed description of the architectural and decorative features of the typical Sanaani *mafraj,* see Lewcock and Serjeant (1983: 455–63). A life-size reconstruction of a particularly fine *mafraj* described and illustrated by Lewcock was displayed in the 'Nomad and City' exhibition held at the Museum of Mankind in London between 1976 and 1978 (see also Kirkman, 1976).

8 The Ritual Significance of Qat Parties

1 All these symbolic elements are noted in Amin Rihani's typically colourful description of an extremely formal 'hosted' qat party he attended at the Palace of

the Sultan of Lahej (now in PDRY) around 1922. In this he refers to 'Royal cousins in a row on the diwan, according to their rank and age' (Rihani, 1930a: 346–8).

2 Kennedy *et al* say: 'Considerable mingling of social classes takes place, particularly in the villages, but the forces of status and interest increasingly militate against such openness. The trend is more and more toward general group uniformities in chewing patterns. For example, at sessions held at homes of wealthy merchants or important political figures, some poorer men from the immediate neighbourhood still may be found clustered near the door, but most of the guests tend to be of nearly equal status.' The authors seem to imply a reduction in emphasis on ranking within qat parties, but where the participants are of similar social positions, one would expect that to be reflected symbolically too.

9 The Role of Qat

1 In Razihi dialect they would ask each other *wayn ba-tikhazzin al-yom?* (where are you chewing today?). Stevenson (1981: 46) says that in 'Amran *khazin* can mean both 'to store' and 'to buy' qat, and *'khazant?'* could therefore mean 'have you bought your qat?' at midday as well as 'did you chew qat today' when asked in the evening. In Jabal Hufash the unusual verb *rabakh/yarbukh* is used for chewing qat or attending a qat party (Morris, 1984).

2 The dynamics of qat exchange and other behaviour of qat parties have been vividly described by Gerholm (1977:176–85).

3 The status connotations of high expenditure on qat and attendance at long and frequent qat sessions were also appreciated by Schopen (1978:84, 103) when he points out that different qualities of qat correspond to status, that only the upper classes dedicate whole afternoons to parties, most of the lower classes are restricted to a shorter session then return to work, and the lowest groups only gather to chew qat on feast days, Fridays and important social occasions when they 'copy the style of the upper classes'.

4 There are a number of references to the consumption of qat as an infusion in Krikorian (1983:32).

5 In Yemen food is frequently equated with money and its various social functions. For example, in the tribal customary law of Razih, the daily living expenses paid by the tribe to a tribesman who did frontier guard duty during tribal hostilities were called *marag* – literally 'soup'. The best English translation would be 'subsistence'. There are also many expressions similar to that quoted by Dresch (1982:75) for the Hashid area of Yemen: 'If a man is deliberately killed by an outsider then his kinsmen are said to have a choice *bayn ghada wa naqa;* that is between "lunch" (in other words, cash compensation) and "good name" (in other words wiping out the stain by killing in revenge).' The common expression for 'corruption' throughout Yemen is to 'eat' money.

6 Messick has described how money is employed in the town of Ibb to manipulate situations in one's own favour and how such payments are viewed: 'Such payments are routine and ubiquitous, and, for the most part, petty. They can be considered transaction costs, one of the array of expenses everyone knows about and expects in the conduct of business with the government. . . . There is an important local distinction between corruption or bribery, which is called *rashwa,* and facilitation payments, referred to as *tashilat.* While the former can result in the loss of clear rights and brings unjustified enrichment to the participant, the latter simply expedites matters and assures reasonable outcomes.' (Messick, 1978:212).

Bibliography

The following works are those cited in the text of this book. There are good bibliographies on all aspects of qat in: United Nations (1956), Radt (1969), Getahun and Krikorian (1973), Schopen (1978), and Shahandeh *et al* (1983), especially the chapter by Krikorian.

Abdullahi, M.A., M.C. Anania and P. Nencini. 1983. 'Long lasting analgesic effects of cathinone', in Shahandeh *et al*, 1983

Aden Colony. 1958. *Report of the Qat Commission of Inquiry*, Aden: Government printer

Admiralty: see British Admiralty

Adra, Najwa. 1982. *Qabyala: The Tribal Concept in the Central Highlands of the Yemen Arab Republic*, unpublished PhD thesis, Temple University

Agence France Presse. 1982. 'Yemenis hooked on chewing the qat', London: *The Times*, 11 May 1982

Al-Attar: see El-Attar

Al-Maqrami, Abd al-Malik. 1982. *Qat and Development: an Empirical Study in Yemeni Society*, unpublished MA thesis (in Arabic), University of Cairo

Al-Thani, Ibrahim. 1983. 'Development: the Saudi solution for the problem of khat', in Shahandeh *et al*, 1983

Ansell, Christine. 1979. 'Notes on food classification in Yemen', unpublished manuscript

Arendonk, C. Van. 1974. 'Kahwa' in the *Encyclopaedia of Islam*, new edition, pp. 449–53

Attar: see El-Attar

Baasher, T.A. 1980. 'The use of khat: a stimulant with regional distribution', in *Drug Problems in the Sociocultural Context: a Basis for Policies and Programme Planning*, pp. 86–93, ed. G. Edwards and A. Arif, Geneva: World Health Organization

Bach, François. 1980. *Le Qat (Catha edulis) en République Arabe du Yemen: Aspects Medicaux et Socio-économiques de la Consommation d'une Plante Stimulante*, unpublished thesis (Docteur en Médecine), Université Scientifique et Médicale de Grenoble

Becker, Hans, Volker Höhfeld and Horst Kopp. 1979. *Kaffee aus Arabien: der Bedeutungswandel eines Weltwirtschaftsgutes und seine Siedlungsgeographische Konsequenz an der Trockengrenze der Ökumene*, Wiesbaden: Franz Steiner

Bornstein, Annika. 1974. *Food and Society in the Yemen Arab Republic*, Food and Agriculture Organization of the United Nations

Botta, Paul Emile. 1841(a). *Relation d'un Voyage dans l'Yémen entrepris en 1837*, Paris: Duprat

1841(b). 'Notice sur un voyage dans l'Arabie Heureuse', *Archives du Musée d'Histoire Naturelle*, no 2:63–88

British Admiralty (Naval Intelligence Division). 1946. *Western Arabia and the Red Sea*, London

Brooke, Clarke. 1960. 'Khat (*Catha edulis*): its production and trade in the Middle East', *The Geographical Journal*, Vol CXXVI, pt 1

Bulletin on Narcotics: see United Nations

Burton, Richard. 1966. *First Footsteps in East Africa*, London: Routledge and Kegan Paul

Bury, G. Wyman. 1915. *Arabia Infelix or the Turks in Yemen*, London: Macmillan

Centre for Yemeni Studies. 1981. *Al-qāt fī hayāt al-Yaman wa al-Yamāniyīn* (Qat in Yemeni Life), Sanaa

Chaudhari, K.N. 1974. 'Kahwa: Trade with Europe' in the *Encyclopaedia of Islam*, new edition, pp. 453–5

Chelhod, Joseph. 1972. 'La société Yéménite et le kat', *Objets et Mondes*, 12 (1): 3–22

Cruttenden, Charles. 1838. 'Narrative of a journey from Mokha to Sanaa by the Tarik-esh-Sham, or northern route, in July and August 1836', *Journal of the Royal Geographical Society*, Vol. 8

Dixey, R. and M. Talbot. 1982. *Women, Leisure and Bingo*, Leeds

Dostal, Walter, revised by R. B. Serjeant and Robert Wilson, 1983. 'Analysis of the San'ā' market today', in Serjeant and Lewcock, 1983: 241–75

Douglas, Mary and Baron Isherwood. 1980. *The World of Goods: Towards an Anthropology of Consumption*, Harmondsworth: Penguin Books

Dresch, Paul. 1982. *The Northern Tribes of Yemen: their Organisation and their Place in the Yemen Arab Republic*, unpublished D.Phil. thesis, University of Oxford

El-Attar, Mohamed Said. 1964. *Le Sous-Développement Economique et Social du Yémen: Perspectives de la Révolution Yémenite*, Algeria: Editions Tiers-Monde

Elmi, Abdullahi. 1983. 'Effect of khat on resting and fatigued subjects', in Shahandeh *et al*, 1983

Forsskål, Petrus (Per). 1775. *Flora-Aegyptiaco-Arabica*, ed. Carsten Neibuhr, Copenhagen

Gaudefroy-Demombynes, M. 1927. Translation of *Masālik al-abṣār fī mamālik al-amsar* by Ibn Faḍl Allāh al-'Umarī, Paris: Geuthner

Gavin, R.J. 1975. *Aden under British Rule, 1839–1967*, London: Hurst

Gerholm, Tomas, 1977. *Market, Mosque and Mafraj: Social Inequality in a Yemeni Town*, Stockholm

1979. 'Provincial cosmopolitans: the impact of world events on a small Yemeni town', *Mediterranean Peoples*, 9, Oct–Dec

1980. 'Knives and sheaths: notes on a sexual idiom of social inequality in north Yemen', *Ethnos*, Vol 45: I–II: 82–91

Getahun, A. and A.D. Krikorian. 1973. 'Chat: coffee's rival from Harar, Ethiopia. I. Botany, cultivation and use. II. Chemical composition', *Economic Botany*, 27: 353–89

Greenway, P.J. 1947. 'Khat', *East African Agricultural Journal*, 13: 98–102

Halliday, Fred. 1974. *Arabia Without Sultans*, London: Pelican Books

Hansen, Thorkild. 1964. *Arabia Felix: the Danish Expedition of 1761–1767*. Trans. James and Kathleen Mcfarlane. New York: Harper and Row

Harris, Walter B. 1893. *A Journey Through the Yemen and Some General Remarks Upon that Country*, Edinburgh and London: Blackwood

Hess, J. 1927 and 1976. 'Kat' in the *Encyclopaedia of Islam*

Heyworth-Dunne, Gamal-Eddine. 1952. *Al-Yemen: a General Social, Political and Economic Survey*, Cairo: the Rennaissance Bookshop

Hjort, Anders. 1974. 'Trading miraa: from school-leaver to shop-owner in Kenya', *Ethnos*, 1–4

Hunter, F.M. 1877. *Account of the British Settlement of Aden in Arabia*, London

Huntingford, G.W.B. 1965. *The Glorious Victories of 'Amda Seyon, King of Ethiopia*, Oxford: Clarendon Press

Ingrams, Harold. 1966. *Arabia and the Isles*, London: John Murray

Ingrams, Doreen. 1970. *A Time in Arabia*, London: John Murray

Kalix, P. 1983. 'The pharmacology of khat and of the khat alkaloid cathinone', in Shahandeh *et al*, 1983

Kennedy, J.G., J. Teague and L. Fairbanks. 1980. 'Qat use in North Yemen and the problem of addiction: a study in medical anthropology', *Cult. Med. Psychiat*, 4: 311–44

Kennedy, John G., James Teague, William Rokaw and Elizabeth Cooney. 1983. 'A medical evaluation of the use of qat in north Yemen', *Soc. Sci. Med.*, Vol 17, no 12: 783–94

Kirkman, James (ed). 1976. *City of San'ā'*, London: World of Islam Publishing Company

Kopp, Horst. 1981. *Agrargeographie der Arabischen Republik Jemen: Landnutzung und Agrarsoziale Verhaltnisse in einem Islamisch-Orientalischen Entwicklungsland mit Alter Bauerlicher Kultur*, Erlangen

Krikorian, A.D. 1983. 'Khat and its use: an historical perspective', in Shahandeh *et al*, 1983

Krikorian and Getahun: see Getahun and Krikorian

Lewcock, Ronald and R.B. Serjeant. 1983. 'The houses of San'ā', in Serjeant and Lewcock, 1983:436–500

Luqman, W. and T.S. Danowski. 1976. 'The use of khat (*Catha edulis*) in Yemen: social and medical observations', *Annals of Internal Medicine*, (85): 246–49

Makhlouf, Carla. 1979. *Changing Veils: Women and Modernisation in North Yemen*, London: Croom Helm

Mancioli, M. and Parrinello. 1967. 'Il qat (*Catha edulis*)', *La Clinica Terapeutica*, 43, no 2: 102–72

Maqrami: see Al-Maqrami

Mauss, Marcel. 1966. *The Gift: Forms and Functions of Exchange in Archaic Societies*. Trans. Ian Cunnison. London: Routledge and Kegan Paul

Messick, Brinkley Morris. 1978. *Transactions in Ibb: Economy and Society in a Yemeni Highland Town*, unpublished PhD thesis, Princeton University

Morghem, M.M. and M.I. Rufat. 1983. 'Cultivation and chewing of khat in the Yemen Arab Republic', in Shahandeh *et al*, 1983

Morris, Tim. 1984. 'Qat in Jabal Hufash', unpublished manuscript

Moser, Charles. 1917. 'The flower of Paradise', *National Geographic Magazine*, Vol 32

Mundy, Martha. 1981. *Land and Family in a Yemeni Community*, unpublished PhD Thesis, University of Cambridge

Myntti, Cynthia. 1983. *Medicine in its Social Context: Observations from Rural North Yemen*, unpublished PhD thesis, University of London

Nencini, P., M.C. Anania, M.A. Abdullahi, G. Amiconi and A.S. Elmi. 1983. 'Physiological and neuroendocrine effects of khat in man', in Shahandeh *et al*, 1983

Niebuhr, Carsten. 1774. *Description de l'Arabie*, Amsterdam and Utrecht
1776. *Voyage en Arabie et en d'autres Pays Circonvoisins*, Amsterdam and Utrecht

Obermeyer, Gerald. 1973. 'Anthropological aspects of qat and the use of qat in the Yemen Arab Republic', unpublished report for the World Health Organization of the United Nations

Peterson, J.E. 1982. *Yemen: the Search for a Modern State*, London: Croom Helm

Pridham, Brian (ed.) 1984. *Contemporary Yemen: Politics and Historical Background,* London: Croom Helm
(ed.) 1985. *Economy, Society and Culture in Contemporary Yemen,* London: Croom Helm
Radt, Charlotte. 1969. 'Contribution à l'histoire ethnobotanique d'une plante stimulante: le kat. Le kat au Yémen. (Note préliminaire)', *Journal d'Agriculture Tropicale at de Botanique Appliquée,* Paris: Muséum National d'Histoire Naturelle
Rihani, Amin. 1930(a). *Around the Coasts of Arabia,* London: Constable
1930(b). *Arabian Peak and Desert: Travels in al-Yemen,* London: Constable
Rodinson, Maxime. 1977. 'Esquisse d'une monographie du *qat', Journal Asiatique,* 265
Schopen, Armin. 1978. *Das Qat: Geschichte und Gebrauch des Genusmittels* Catha edulis *Forsk. in der Arabischen Republic Jemen,* Wiesbaden: Franz Steiner
Scott, Hugh. 1942. *In the High Yemen,* London: John Murray
Serageldin, Ismail, James Socknat, Stace Birks, Bob Li and Clive Sinclair. 1981. *Manpower and International Labor Migration in the Middle East and North Africa,* Washington DC: World Bank
Serjeant, R.B. 1974. 'The cultivation of cereals in Mediaeval Yemen. (A translation of the *Bughyat al-Fallāḥīn* of the Rasulid Sultan, al-Malik al-Afḍal al-'Abbās b. 'Ali, composed circa 1370 AD)', *Arabian Studies* 1, London
1979, 'The Yemeni poet al-Zubayri and his polemic against the Zaydī Imāms', *Arabian Studies* 5, London
1983. 'The market, business life, occupations, the legality and sale of stimulants', in Serjeant and Lewcock, 1983:161–78
1983. '(1) The Statute of San'ā' (*Qānūn San'ā'*) (2) Additional documents', in Serjeant and Lewcock, 1983: 179–240
Serjeant, R.B. and Ronald Lewcock (eds). 1983. *San'ā': an Arabian Islamic City,* London: World of Islam Festival Trust
Shahandeh, B., R. Geadah, A. Tongue, E. Tongue and J. Rolli (eds). 1983. *The Health and Socio-Economic Effects of Khat Use,* Proceedings of an International Conference on Khat, Antananarivo, 17–21 January 1983. Lausanne: International Council on Alcohol and Addictions
Socknat, James and Clive Sinclair. 1978. *Migration for Employment Abroad and its Impact on Development in the Yemen Arab Republic,* University of Durham: International Migration Project
Steffen, Hans. 1979. *Population Geography of the Yemen Arab Republic: the Major Findings of the Population and Housing Census of 1975 and of Supplementary Demographic and Cartographic Surveys,* Wiesbaden
Steffen, Hans and Olivier Blanc. 1982. 'La démographie de la République Arabe du Yémen', in *La Péninsule Arabique d'Aujourd'hui,* Tome II, ed. Paul Bonnenfant, Aix en Provence: Centre d'Études et de Recherches sur l'Orient Arabe Contemporain
Steffen, Hans, Urs Geiser, Werner Dubach *et al.* 1978. *Final Report of the Airphoto Interpretation Project of the Swiss Technical Cooperation Service,* Berne
Stevenson, Thomas. 1981. *Kinship, Stratification and Mobility: Social Change in a Yemeni Highlands Town,* unpublished PhD thesis, Wayne State University
Stookey, Robert. 1978. *Yemen: the Politics of the Yemen Arab Republic,* Boulder: Westview
Swanson, Jon and Mary Hebert. 1982. *Rural Society and Participatory Development: Case Studies of Two Villages in the Yemen Arab Republic,* Cornell University, USAID/Y Project 220–0045
Szendrai, K. 1983. 'Recent Progress in khat chemistry', in Shahandeh *et al* (1983)
Thani: see Al-Thani
The Times: see Agence France Presse

Trimingham, J. Spencer. 1952. *Islam in Ethiopia*, London: Oxford University Press

Turner, Victor. 1969. *The Ritual Process: Structure and Anti-Structure*, Chicago: Aldine

Tutwiler, Richard and Sheila Carapico. 1981. *Yemeni Agriculture and Economic Change: Case Studies of Two Highland Regions*, Sanaa: American Institute for Yemeni Studies

Ukers, William. 1935. *All About Coffee*, New York: The Tea and Coffee Trade Journal

UNDP: see United Nations Development Programme

United Nations. 1956. 'Khat', *Bulletin on Narcotics*, Oct–Dec
1978. 'The botany and chemistry of khat: report of an expert group', Antananarivo, 27 Nov–1 Dec 1978
1981. *Bulletin on Narcotics*, Vol 32, no 3, 1980. Special issue devoted to *Catha edulis* (khat)

United Nations Development Programme (UNDP). 1971. *Bilateral and Multilateral Aid in the Economic Development of the Yemen Arab Republic with Particular Reference to the United Nations Special Fund Projects in Agricultural Development*, Yemen Arab Republic, Information Paper no 9

United States Agency for International Development (USAID) in co-operation with the Ministry of Agriculture, Sanaa. 1982. *Yemen Arab Republic: Agricultural Sector Assessment*

USAID: see United States

Van Arendonk: see Arendonk

Varisco, Daniel. Forthcoming. 'On the meaning of chewing: the significance of *qat* (Catha edulis) in the Yemen Arab Republic', *International Journal of Middle Eastern Studies*

Veblen, Thorstein. 1970. *The Theory of the Leisure Class: an Economic Study of Institutions*, London: Unwin Books

Weir, Shelagh. 1985. 'Economic aspects of the qat industry in north west Yemen', in Pridham, 1985

Wenner, Manfred. 1967. *Modern Yemen: 1918–1966*, Baltimore: Johns Hopkins

Wood, John. Forthcoming. *The Flora of Yemen* (provisional title), London: Kegan Paul International

World Bank. 1979. *Yemen Arab Republic: Development of a Traditional Economy*, Washington DC

Yacoub, Salah and A. Akil. 1971. *A Socio-economic Study of Hojjuriyah District, Yemen Arab Republic*, American University of Beirut: Journal no 371, Faculty of Agricultural Sciences

Glossary and Index
of Arabic Terms

The system of transliteration used below will be easily interpreted by those familiar with Arabic. The only departures from conventional systems are the use of *g* instead of *q*, and *ḍh* for both *ḍ* and *z*, in colloquial words. This is in order to represent more accurately how these sounds are pronounced in Highland Yemen.

The glossary includes words relating to the cultivation and trade in qat in Razih which are not necessarily used elsewhere in Yemen. These are marked (R). Not all are mentioned in the main text of the book. I am grateful to Bonnie Glover for correcting my transliterations of these words, and indeed for her invaluable help in understanding the Razih dialect which she studied intensively in the field. I am also grateful to Owen Wright for help with transliteration.

akhdām, 23, 145, 164   social and occupational category of lowest social status
'āgib/a'gāb (R), 170n2   shoots which grow at the base of the trunk of a qat bush or tree, and which are transplanted to make new qat plants
'arab, 22   farmers and landowners
'āraḍh/'awāraḍh (R)   secondary branches which grow from the primary branches (*rida'*) of a qat tree
'araqi, 66   alcoholic beverage made from grapes
ashrāf (see *sharīf*)

bāghah, 93   plastic sheets
baladi, 108, 124   local, i.e. locally produced crops or foods
Bani Khums, 146   market traders of low social status
bar'ah, 143   male dance
barkas/barākis (R)   packages of qat wrapped in banana stem (alternative name for *guruf*)
barkas (yibarkis) (R), 95   to package qat in banana stem
barrah (yibarriḥ), 93   to strip off old inedible leaves from a qat branch
baya', 146   market trader
bukūr (pl) (R)   young qat plants which have never been harvested
buqshah/buqash, 79, 80   coin, subdivision of a *qirsh*
būri, 155   implement for holding tobacco at the top of the hubble-bubble (*madā'ah*) *also:* mid-morning break (R), 33

dha'īf, 166   weak, poor
dīwān, 111, 114, 155   relatively large reception or family room

faqīh/fuqahā', 145   jurist
fatwā, 72, 74   legal ruling

gabīlah/gubul, 15, 23   political unit, tribe
gabīli/gabā'il (*see* tribe in Index)   male member of a tribe, man of 'tribesman' social status
gabyal (yigabyil), 145   to try to be like a *gabili*
gabyalah, 143, 155   'tribal' ideal of co-operation and mutual help; creation of close ties
garraf (yigarrif) (R), 95   to split the layers of banana stem for packaging qat (see *guruf*)
gaṣabah, 132   water-pipe hose
gataf (yugtuf) (R), 93   to pick, e.g. qat leaves (see *magtaf*)
gātfah/gātfāt (R)   harvest or picking of qat
gawwāt/gawwātīn (R)   qat trader

gayyad (yigayyid) (R), 93   to tie small bunches of qat (*zurbah*) in larger bundles (see *tagyūd*)

gharas/yughrus (R)   to lay qat shoots (*a'gāb*) under the earth (see *gharīsah* and *maghras*)

gharīsah/gharāyis (R)   shoots (*a'gāb*) laid horizontally beneath the earth to propagate a new qat plant

ghāt   wrong transliteration of qat

ghuṣn al-salām, 156   'branch of peace', two-forked branch of qat

gurfah/guraf (R)   brown outside skin of banana stem, split to make ties (*marbūṭ*) for qat packages (*guruf*)

guruf/agrāf (R), 93, 95, 98   package of qat in banana stem sections, the basic trading unit in Razih

guṣri/giṣār (R)   small bunches of short qat shoots, chewed locally in Razih not traded

hadhāwi (R), 93   qat branches which have no chewable leaves on them

ḥākim, 126, 133   judge, legal representative of government

ḥarām, 42, 66, 75   forbidden to Muslims

Hāshimi, 23   synonymous with *sayyid*

ḥilbah, 43, 172n5   fenugreek broth

ijaw/ijū' (R), 93, 95, 96   cowhide bag for qat (also for fodder)

Imām (*see* Index)   religious and temporal leader of the Zaydis; title of the kings of Yemen

izzah/izaz (R), 93, 95   banana stem

jafri/jafar (R), 93   waste qat branches stripped off and discarded during *tabrīḥ* or used in packing qat; also waste branches discarded during the qat party

jambiyyah, 136–7   dagger

jazzār/jazr, 133, 134, 145   butcher, member of the 'butcher' social category

kaflah, 157   tender shoots from the tip of the qat branch

kaftah, 161   an infusion of qat

kās/akwās   small aluminium cup for water

kāt   alternative correct transliteration of qat

kayf, 41, 42, 52   pleasurable feeling engendered by qat chewing

kayyaf/yikayyif (R), 172n3   to experience *kayf*

khādim/akhdām   see *akhdām*

khamr   intoxicating liquor

khāt   wrong transliteration of qat

khazzan (yikhazzin), 44, 118, 149, 180n1   'to store', term used for chewing qat

li'bah, 143   male dance

mabkharah, 116   incense burner

mabraz, 111, 156   public room for qat chewing (Aden)

mabzag/mabāzig (R)   spittoon

madā'ah/midī', 57, 116, 122, 132, 155   'hubble-bubble', water-pipe for tobacco smoking

madfal (also *matfal*), 116   spittoon (see *mabzag*)

madgūg   pulverised, e.g. *qāt madgūg*

mafraj/mafārij (*see* Index)   reception room where qat parties are held (also written as *mufraj* and *mifraj* in some publications)

maghras/maghāris (R)   the occasion or activity of planting qat

magtaf/magātif (R)   new qat shoots which grow from the stumps of the previous picking (see *gataf*)

majmar/majāmir (R)   brazier (see *mawgid*)

malgaṭ/malāgiṭ   tongs

marbūṭ/marābiṭ (R)   ties made from split banana-stem skins (*gurfah*); used to tie packages (*guruf*) of qat

mardūf (R)   'doubled', large packages of qat containing two *agrāf* (see *guruf*)

ma'sharah/ma'āshir   tray on which hubble-bubble pipes and other equipment are placed during a qat party

mathāni (R)   branches which have paired, a secondary *rida'ah* having grown beside another after a good rainy season

matka', 118   cushion used as armrest; also qat party
mawgid, 116   brazier (see *majmar*)
mowlā'i, 38   qat connoisseur or gourmet
mugawwit/mugawwitīn, 24   qat-seller or trader (see *qawwāt*)
mukhaddir, 38   drug
mudman, 39   addicted

nadhal/yundhul (R)   to empty qat branches out of the *ijaw*
nadhalah   qat branches from which the tips (*urūs*) of good leaves have been broken off (i.e.
   during transportation)
nāqis/nuqqās, 23, 105   'deficient', term for a number of social categories of low social status

qādhi/qudhāh, 22, 23   hereditary legal specialist and administrator
Qahtāni, 23   people of south Arabian origin, non-*sayyids*
qānūn, 79–80, 176n19   statute
qāt   Arabic term for *Catha edulis* Forssk.
qāti/qātiyyāt (R)   qat plant or tree
qirsh, 79, 80   silver coin
qishr, 44, 54   husk coffee

ra'āyā, 22, 23, 105   farmers and landowners
rabakh (yarbukh), 153, 180n1   to chew qat (Jabal Hufash)
Ramadhān   the Muslim month of fasting
rās/urūs, 93, 95   tips of qat branches with new leaves
rid'ah/rida' (R)   primary branches of the qat tree
rubtah/rubat (*see* Index)   bunch of qat, principal retail and consumption unit in most of Yemen
   (also written *ribtah/ribat* in some publications)

sāgah (R)   main stem or trunk of the qat bush or tree
sayyad (yisayyid), 145   to try to be like a *sayyid*
sayyid/sādah (*see* Index)   descendant of the Prophet Muhammad
Shāfi'i (*see* Index)   school of orthodox Sunni Islam
shāgi, 79   manual labourer
sharī'ah, 22, 165   Islamic law
sharbah/sharabāt (R)   pottery water bottle
sharīf/ashrāf, 15, 75   synonymous with *sayyid*
shaykh/shuyūkh, 15, 105   political leader of a tribe
sidr al-mafraj, 131   the head (literally 'heart') of the *mafraj*
sūfi, 66, 73, 78, 161, 175n11, 176n18   religious mystic
Sunni   orthodox Islam
sūq, 137–8   market place
sūqi, 24   derogatory term for market trader

tabrīh (R)   process or occasion of stripping unwanted leaves off qat branches
tafritā, 151, 152   women's qat party (in Sanaa)
tagyūd (R), 93, 95   bundles of (usually three) *zurbah/zurab* of qat
takhzīn, 149   a qat party, literally a 'chew'
tazrīb (R)   activity of bunching qat together
thallājah/thallājāt   vacuum flask

'urf, 165   tribal customary law

wādi, 30   water course, valley
wala'ah, 38   choicest qat
wali, 73   Muslim 'saint' often with a commemorative tomb

zakāh or zakāt, 16, 19   Islamic tax, agricultural tithe
zarrab (yizarrib) (R), 93   to bunch qat together (see *zurbah* and *tazrīb*)
Zaydi/Ziyūd (*see* Index)   adherant of a sub-sect of *Shī'ah* Islam
zurbah/zurab (R), 93, 95, 98   bunch of qat, subdivision of *guruf*

Index